T0064248

THE ENFORCEMENT OF OUR WILL

As it was in the beginning . . .

SALADIN SHABAZZ-ALLAH

authorHOUSE®

AuthorHouse™
1663 Liberty Drive
Bloomington, IN 47403
www.authorhouse.com
Phone: 833-262-8899

Published by AuthorHouse 03/03/2021

ISBN: 978-1-6655-1901-4 (sc)
ISBN: 978-1-6655-1900-7 (e)

Library of Congress Control Number: 2021904623

Print information available on the last page.

Any people depicted in stock imagery provided by Getty Images are models, and such images are being used for illustrative purposes only. Certain stock imagery © Getty Images.

This book is printed on acid-free paper.

Because of the dynamic nature of the Internet, any web addresses or links contained in this book may have changed since publication and may no longer be valid. The views expressed in this work are solely those of the author and do not necessarily reflect the views of the publisher, and the publisher hereby disclaims any responsibility for them.

CONTENTS

DEDICATION

I DEDICATE THESE WRITINGS TO MY QUEEN, CHILDREN, GRAND CHRILDEN AND GREAT GRAND CHILDREN

All of you are exceptionally beautiful children and I am proud of you all it does not matter what mistakes you might have made, your father does and always will love every one of you. I am grateful for the wonderful six grandsons, the three beautiful granddaughters, and the four wonderful great-grandchildren, two great-grandson and two beautiful great-grand daughters. It is extremely important that you all understand that your father, your grandfather, your great grandfather loves all of you. All of you are my inspiration for my writings and I will leave this legacy after I am gone, for all of you to take pride in my writings and my work. I hope and pray that all of you understand the man that I am and why I write the way in which I do and always will. My children, my grandchildren, and great-grandchildren, I am a true follower of the Holy Messenger Of Allah the Mr. Elijah Muhammad; he is the true and only Muhammad RasulAllah.

I have experienced many things in my lifetime good, bad, evil as well as pure wickedness, not only from the Caucasian people but from our own people and now from these different interlopers, that have come and are still coming into America. None of these people mean us any good including many of these so-called Africans. Your father, your grandfather, your great grandfather has chosen to tell the truth about all our enemies, their false religions, corrupt and evil politics. Most of the ungratefulness has come from black women and half-breed black women and most of them have babies by Caucasian men. These traitors who Mongolite our people with the seed of our enemies, these traitors, bring them back amongst us black people and now we must deal with the enemy within, that these promiscuity black women and their half breed children, by our enemies and these children are having babies by our enemies, as well. Then these foolish ignorant women believe these half originals if they are even that, are pretty because they are the children of the devil.

I must speak the truth about these false religions, and this is the reason why I have chosen to write, about the many false religions and politics which we are all living under. Friendship in all walks of life my family is gravely misunderstood by many who like to use this phase and they truly do not understand it. The only way we can have true friendship in all walks of life is when we set ourselves up to do international trade with the governments of other civilized people and cultures. This silliness that these fools are trying to pass off as friendships in all walk of life, is from those who truly lack understanding. It does not matter what their names maybe my family, these fools really do not have a clue on what is really happening; and you should not pay any **ATTENTION** to any of them.

Never my family, allow some fool to try and take advantage of you by believing that they can use your labor, to aid our enemies.

Beware my, beloved family of these fools that sound good on the surface, when you go under the surface you will discover, they are still the same sharecropping fools they always were and always will be. These fools are not like us, my family, they are afraid to go for self they will and have joined on to our enemies, to keep black people in America in a submissive state. We are not Africans! We are Asia-Attic Black People and why should we be more concern about these so-called Africans, when these so-called Africans have nothing in their hearts but content for all of us. Only an ignorant fool would join on to the enemy, of his own people.

My family this is from your father, grandfather, and great grandfather, I am dedicating this work, The to you all. Beware my family of these clowns, both male and female are never to be trusted because they are truly deceitful, they will deceive you all and lead you only back to mental slavery because they cannot figure their way out of the cage and they will leave nothing behind for their families, grandchildren, and great-grandchildren, your father, grandfather, and great grandfather is a soldier to the grave, who is not afraid to let the world know the truth and resist the subduction of our enemies.

My family, I stand strong and ready and I do not need any help or assistance from these mental slaves, who believe they are free when in truth they are more mentally dead now, then they were over forty years ago. Marrying a so-called Sunnah Muslim is no different than marrying a Christian, they all believe in a mystery god and make-believe heaven after you die and dead prophets who have been dead for two thousand years and fourteen hundred years. May the peace and blessings of Allah be upon them both.

Understand my family I am Saladin Shabazz-Allah in my very essence spirit, heart, and mind and nothing absolutely nothing will ever change me, and I cannot be bought as well. One day my family you all will understand that I am different from these others because these pretenders are afraid to make America know her sins and I am not.

To my children, my grandchildren and great grandchildren, May Allah always be please with every one of you. All my above children mention by name in this dedication May Allah always be please with you all and bless all of you, with great success. Remember my beloved family Allah visited us in the person of Master W.F. Muhammad, to whom all holy praises are due forever. He Allah raised up from amongst us His last and greatest messenger, the Most Honorable Elijah Muhammad the true and only Muhammad RasulAllah.

To My children, grandchildren, and great grandchildren I had absolutely no clue that one day, I would be able to write about the things I have experience in life. To my children I love you all although I could not show it to you in the conventional way. Being a soldier was exceedingly difficult for all of you as well as myself, So I leave this legacy for you all and everything else, I am doing. Remember this about your father he was and is sincere about everything he has done and is doing. I made mistakes because I was learning and all of you, were caught up, in this cyclone that I myself did not understand nor did I have control of. For this I take full responsibility for and I apologize to you all. None of you can ever be replace or equal by anyone.

These women with their little children with no fathers and many have Caucasian fathers and these Caucasian men or boys, only want, and get these ignorant black and half original women, for sex, they the women now have these half breed children, and these Caucasian so-called men move on. Then these silly women bring the seed of the devil back amongst us because these half breed children are not welcome, amongst the father's people. I have discovered that the women who commit these acts of treachery, have no love for black men they only pretend to have love, for black men because they need help but, in their heart, these foolish women love the devil.

My children and people we must be extra careful because we have many, enemies especially amongst these treacherous women, who have betrayed, their people; trying everything in their power, to prevent us my people from enforcing our wills on our enemies because they love our enemies, although our enemies have absolutely any love for them or their bastard children. So, my people we must guard and recognize the enemies amongst us and the ones that are very deceitful, amongst us. They these enemies have one desire and that is to deliver us all, back into the clutches of Satan The Accursed Devil.

The is about black people in America standing up for themselves and taking control, of our own destiny and stop depending on our enemies to do for us. Here we are billions of original people living on our planet and we are living under our enemies, rules, regulations, and laws which benefit our enemies. The time has come that we must enforce our own will and decide for ourselves, wives, and children our own destiny.

Long before our enemies were even made a man, we had been governing ourselves. We created our own governments, religions, politics, educational system, medical system, engineering system that work, for trillions and trillions of years. Then a mere six thousand years ago we lost or better yet had our creative minds, stolen from us.

The time is here my people that we stand up and enforce our own will as we have done, for trillions and trillions of years.

These writings will be focusing on how we are suffering under our enemy's religions, politics, educational system, medical system, social system, and governments. We must stand up my people and see there is not any good in our enemy's system, that were made to deprive original people of the basics necessities of life, Freedom, Justice, Equality, Food, Clothing, Shelter, Knowledge, Wisdom, Understanding, Love, Peace and Happiness. My people we have the greatest challenge than any people on this planet Allah Our Holy Savior in the person of Master Fard Muhammad to whom all praises are due forever. We have the greatest challenge on earth than any other people on our planet because we/true believers are the followers and students, of the last and greatest Messenger of Allah the Most Honorable Elijah Muhammad.

Once the enemy reveals themselves and the enemy will come and do come in many disguises and we soldiers' must forever be alert, so that we can recognize these enemies and deal with them all accordingly. You will discover that many are females, and they are most deceitful and treacherous, for and to black men. We must remember my people mental and spiritual poisons, are more dangerous than physical poison and this is what we must protect ourselves against and from. Our enemies amongst us are and will do everything to prevent us my people, from enforcing our wills on our enemies whom they love, and fear and they put fear into hearts and minds, of their children, for devil and turn them away the Holy Savior that came to redeem them. We must remember my people Yakub's world is not built on love at all and Yakub's world and people have absolutely no love in them for original people because they have absolutely no love, for themselves. Look at the horrors that they commit and do to themselves and children, how is it possible this world of Yakub and Yakub's makings can have any love in them, when they were made in Sin, Iniquity and Transgressions. All those who subscribe and submit to this ideology are the enemies of Allah, Allah's Holy Messenger, and all true believers.

The level of betrayal amongst these ignorant so-called Negro women and men is at critical proportion and cannot be overlook, any longer. This mongolicin of our people must be stop and the women who have participate in these crimes, of genocide, must pay for their betrayal and evil. Little girls are putting themselves on the market because of the evil, being taught to them by their ignorant mothers. At the same time these same ignorant foolish women are teaching their male children, to be soft and many cases homosexuals.

The is just that black man we must take charge and let the world know, we will no longer sit back and allow this to happen to and amongst us. The Holy Messenger of Allah taught us directly what and how to do all, that we need to do. We are living in the times of the destruction of Yakub's civilization and world and there is no stopping the violence, there is no stopping or preventing the innocent murdering, of so-called Negro men and young men. There is no stopping or preventing the rapes, perversions and every other evil, that has overcome, Yakub's made civilization. So, I say to everyone sit back, enjoy, and learn, from these writings THE ENFORCEMENT OF OUR WILL

PREFACE

These writings are about black and all original people on our planet casting off, the yoke of American and European Imperialism, which is nothing more than white Nationalism and White Supremacy; and begin to rely on our own creative minds and thoughts, that will benefit ourselves. Our enemies have super-imposed their concepts of religion and politics upon our world and our civilizations. We must all stand up together in order to defeat this evil that has grown out of control, for nearly the past five hundred years; and if we do not, then the entire plant will fill the wrath.

The Holy Messenger of Allah has taught us that we are living in a time of universal change and many of us who claim to believe, are on the side of all our enemies and these fools call this friendship in all walks of life. My people in the western hemisphere and throughout the world, this is backward thinking and will only keep our enemies ruling us all and never produce the creative minds, it will take to break free from this mental slavery.

Our enemies are in charge, of all trade routes and trade agreements that affect the lives of billions of people and the mass of people, do not even know they exist. This American and European Imperialism is the death and suffering of billions of people. This American and European Imperialism have by force and threat of death and starvation, have seized control of many of our governments thus forcing our people and their governments, to bow down to our enemies lies concerning religions, politics, education, medical and even how to raise our own children.

A uniform and posting at a certain time of the year mean absolutely nothing, except to those who are pretending to be, when in truth they are not what they are supposed, too be. Posting useless pictures which also mean absolutely nothing, and these fools believe they have escape from the cage, their enemies have imprisoned them in since fifteen fifty -five. My people in the western hemisphere and throughout the world, these are not the teachings of the Holy Savior Master Fard Muhammad Allah Almighty in person, to whom all praises are due forever; and these are not the teachings that Allah taught to His last and greatest messenger, the Most Honorable Elijah Muhammad.

My people in the western hemisphere and throughout the world these are not the real teachings at all, these are the fools that are miss-using the teachings of Allah in which He taught His Holy, Last and Greatest Messenger the Most Honorable Elijah Muhammad/ Muhammad RasulAllah. This is the reason why; Jerusalem must be taking back from these imposters/devils. My people in the entire western hemisphere and throughout the world, we must unite and denounce these false religions and politics, of our enemies unite with ourselves and build our own global economy; of true substance and not this nonsense that these other interlopers are providing our enemies with entertainment, as they did where they all came from. These interlopers who lied and scheme their selves into America and are dying to become Americans for their own purpose and evil schemes. The truth of what we must do is what I am telling, to the original people on our planet because our enemies are plotting the death of us all. What is worst my people our enemies are getting the help of these fools, here in America to murder billions of their people, for the few pieces of silver our enemies have offer to them. We are being attack through our foods, water and air and we sit back doing absolutely nothing about it; as our enemies continue to murder millions and millions, of original people with impunity. Why do I say impunity? I say impunity is because these many frauds calling themselves true followers of Allah and his Messenger, stand by and do absolutely nothing about these horrors because they are getting paid.

Instead of standing up and making America know her sins these cowardly fools, are fighting over who can grab more of the silver/crumbs, from our enemies table. I stand before the world telling the truth of what is truly happening in America and throughout the world. These fools are helping the enemies that have and are flooding America, with their false teachings, practices, and hatred for all so-called American Negroes. These simple- minded fools that are marring them are nothing but traitors, to their own people in America and throughout the world. These cowards are afraid to stand up and they use the American Constitution, of freedom of religion to dress up once or twice a year and pretend, they are following our Holy Savior Allah Almighty in the person of Master Fard Muhammad, to whom all holy praises are due forever. In fact, my people in the western hemisphere and the world these cowards are a disgrace to our leader, teacher, and guide; the Holy, Last and Greatest Messenger of Allah Mr. Elijah Muhammad.

These cowards have absolutely no place for such amongst us my people, we do not need them. This work of making America know her sins is for men not cowards. I am speaking to all my people in the western hemisphere and throughout the world, it is time we enforce our will and put an end to our enemies, enforcing their evil will upon billions of people. We must understand my people worldwide that this can no longer continue, if we are going to put an end to suffering, starvation, malnutrition, medical horrors amongst, all original people, not only in America and the western hemisphere, but throughout the world.

These writings are meant for the brave and dedicated for the liberation of billions of original people, from the tyranny of American and European Imperialism; That has been suffering for the past six thousand years and the last five hundred years have been a complete an absolute horror, for all original people on our planet from Satan the Accurse Devil. Our enemies have built great civilizations all over the planet by destroying our civilizations, everywhere they have been amongst us. Our enemies have robbed the tombs of our ancestors of the riches and even the bodies, of our ancestors. Our enemies have claimed the remains of our ancestors as their own and have them in their museums, all throughout their world. As the descendants of these great kings, queens, emperors, sultans, generals their great civilizations and all artifacts be return to us the rightful owners.

All literature that has been stolen from us should be return, to us also because it was all stolen from us, by gun point, murder, rape, and other atrocities. We must begin to enforce our will so that we can build a new world, for ourselves, women, and children. There is absolutely nothing more important than us my people, the ex-slaves, and descendants from the first slaves who were brought here aboard, the Slave-Ship Jesus in 1555; should be establishing our own culture, our own way of life that we can show the world, that we are members of the original family and civilize humanity.

Other Original people and the Caucasian Race have their various, different parades, displaying their own culture and traditions and yet we have none that the civilize world recognize because we do nothing to show the civilize world, we have a civilize culture, of our own. In fact, we allow other people to come amongst us and establish their cultures, above our own and this is very foolish on our behalf. This writing is about we my people in America, the western hemisphere and throughout the world, us as a unified people Enforcing Our Will to build our own world, with our own un-corrupt governments, religion, politics, educational system, to educate ourselves, women and children, medical hospitals to heal our sick and wounded, agriculture so that we can feed the masses of people world and set up international exchange in culinary, ideas and methods.

We must have a clear understanding of hybrid vegetables and fruits and people, filled with poisons that are detrimental to our survival, growth, and development. We must have our own land in order that we may produce, the vegetables and fruits that we all need and must have. Under this American and European Imperialism and their Governments, we can never achieve these things, for ourselves. This is what my writings are about my people in, the Western and Eastern the hemisphere all over the world. We must unite my people world-wide because we are at war with Goliath who is written in scriptures, with their mighty armies, navies and air forces and satellites, revolving around our planet keeping track on everything, what everyone is doing in secret, This work that Allah Almighty to whom all holy praises are due forever has bestowed upon me, there is none that can stop it or prevent what I must and will do. This is not work for cowards and pretenders because this is challenging this so-called mighty goliath, which is nothing more than White Nationalism and White Supremacy; also known as American and European Imperialism and the new world order. Before I was born it had been written in history by the twenty-four scientist, that He Who Has Honored The Faith would be born, to do what I am doing. So, I do this work with the authorization of our Holy Savior Allah Almighty, in the person of Master Fard Muhammad to whom all holy praises are due forever. Once again, I say to the entire world population I Saladin Shabazz-Allah am a devote follower and student of Allah's last and greatest Messenger the Most Honorable Elijah Muhammad; the true and only Muhammad RasulAllah.

My people in America, the western hemisphere and throughout the world these false religions and their interpretations of Allah, are untrue. These are the many different weapons that this American and European Imperialistic Goliath, is using to keep billions of people enslaved and under our enemy's control. It is up to us all to recognize these weapons and the agents that are working to keep this evil goliath in power. We must remember my people that this Zionist/ Christian/ So-Called Sunnah/ Hinduism American and European Imperialist Goliath and their many tentacles/governments, are true and only Satan The Accused Devil; and this is a flesh and blood devil that is not sending you to hell but keeping you in hell while you live and preventing billions of Original People from achieving Heaven while we all live.

This my people are why we must Enforce Our Own Will to prevent these atrocities from continuing to happen amongst us, while billions of people are waiting, on the enemy's made up mystery god, that never answer billions of people prayers, for Freedom, Justice and

Equality while we all live; this made-up so-called mystery god only answers the prayers of the enemies, of billions of people. My people throughout the world there is something seriously wrong with this equation. In the laboratories throughout America and Europe our enemies are creating hybrid foods and are selling these useless foods for extremely high prices, amongst us all. Why are our enemies able to get away with this? The reasons are amazingly simple; are due to us not believing in ourselves, trusting, lack of corroboration and non-unity amongst ourselves. Another reason is us believing in our enemies, false religions, and politics.

This is only possible due to us surrendering our way of life and excepting our enemies, way of life which for the pass six thousand years, has proven to be absolutely devastating and a complete horrible nightmare, for billion and billions of original people throughout our planet. We would rather corroborate with our enemies and settle for much less, when all the resources are coming from us and have come from us. We continue to rely on our proven enemies and want to be friends and lovers of our enemies, rather than be friends and lovers of ourselves. We would rather rob, steal, and cheat your brother and sister, before you try and work with your brother and sister honestly. If you have any knowledge of economics, gross national products, you will see our economy, is nothing in comparison to our enemies.

I have heard people say there is no big I and little you yet all I see is the opposite, of what is being said. This an everyday occurrence here in America and this is one of many reasons why, we do not have unity amongst ourselves here in America and throughout world, thus continuing to give our enemies the power to rule us all. Us settling for the crumbs from our enemies is nothing more than a cowardly disgrace. Us praying on ourselves like hyenas is only helping to give our enemies, the power to rule us. There are many things we must do, and we must sit down with each other, with the absence of all our enemy's presence and interferents go through life believing in lies and never really understanding the truth is much worse than never knowing the truth. To live a life believing that you are free at last, is a mockery to Allah and Allah's Messenger. America is one great big plantation consisting of fifty states and many satellites, how can anyone say they believe in Allah and Allah's Messenger and believe in American and European Imperialism, as well; this is very confusing as well as conflicting. He Allah has no association with those who disbelieve in Him and live other than the life, He has prescribed for us all. Allah Last and Greatest Messenger has no association with anyone, who disbelieve in our Holy Savior Allah Almighty and Islam. It does not matter who it may be if you are one that disbelieve in Allah, Allah's last and greatest Messenger and Islam, then how can you convince me, that you are believer; when all evidence points and lead me to see that you are only a pretender and choose to make mockery of Allah, His Holy Messenger and Islam.

I cannot remember the Holy Messenger of Allah looking for a pension from his enemies or anything else, from his enemies. So how can you be free teaching others this is what they should be seeking, in their lives. Not to become independent of our enemies but to live and depend on our enemies for their lively hood. We are still living as property to our former slave-masters due to millions of black people submitting to American and European Imperialism and refusing to get up and do something, for yourself. Millions of descendants of the slaves that tilled the soil forever, nursed their wicket children, fought in every war for our enemy's freedom, have allowed yourselves to abandon our Holy Savior Allah Almighty and Allah's last and greatest messenger.

Allah through mouth of His Holy Messenger Mr. Elijah Muhmmad, taught that the West would become a fountain of dripping blood, one hundred percent, total insanity. So why are you joining these social groups, organizations and other, to prove Allah and Allah's Holy Messenger, to be wrong and liars, for the love and praise of our enemies. Children are suffering because of the great betrayal their great grandparents, grandparents, and parents, have sold out to. There is no stopping the senseless violence in America and throughout the world because this is the destruction, of Yakub's civilization and world; and all those who believe in Yakub being their god and submit to the religions that promote this Mystery god foolishness.

My people throughout the world we need to leave all this nonsense alone and attack our problems, intelligently and seriously. Everyone who does not want to be an apart of re-building our civilization then to hell with them. This work of building our world will take hard work and dedication and we cannot have traitors amongst us. We cannot allow anyone to get in the way of what must be done, for ourselves, we must stand unified if we are going to build a civilization for ourselves. The Holy Messenger there are billions of people on our planet that are tired of living under the thumb of this American and European Imperialism and have a true desire to build a civilization for ourselves. This is an absolute fact the Holy Messenger of Allah the Holy Messenger Mr. Elijah Muhammad had no desire, to be a wealthy man, like many have adopted this American and European Imperialism attitude. The Holy Messenger was true to his missions and true to Allah and his people. Some of these so-called believers are more on the side of this American and European Imperialistic Goliath, than they are on the side of Allah and Allah's Holy messenger because they do not believe as the Holy Messenger believe, they only pretend to believe. In fact, these pretenders conduct themselves like and as masons, more than they conduct themselves as an independent Nation and Members of The Islamic World.

I never seen so much confusion within and amongst ourselves than ever before. These many and useless groups on face-book or social media is nothing more but entertainment, for our enemies. I hear more disagreement and egotistical foolishness coming from different social media and groups; the people who set up this social media are the ones controlling and monitoring, everything that is being posted. I personally stay away from these groups and I post extraordinarily little, on these social medias. It is not important that we post our personal business on these social medias many believe that this is cool, when in fact it is only demonstrates ignorance.

We must become creative in our thinking and the way we do things, one other thing I must mention, stop feeling so damn important this I say domestically, nationally, and globally. Many governments on our planet are forced to purchase these hybrid seeds, from this American and European Imperialistic Goliath, that cannot and will not re-geminate thus empowering, this American and European Imperialism to remain in control of the food, for hundreds of millions of people in the western hemisphere and the eastern hemisphere. This American and European Imperialistic Goliath are also selling hybrid beef, pork, turkey, chicken, and bunch of other animals, to many governments, on our planet; thus, causing devastating effects such as many health and mental diseases, physical deformities, learning disabilities, shorter life expectances, lung diseases, blood diseases and death included amongst new-born babies, mothers and the list goes on.

I cannot see how any of us can afford to think or believe that they are important and the right to criticize others, these are fools that are still locked in this cage of ignorance, speaking only four hundred words well. This is not the teachings of our Holy Savior Allah Almighty, to whom all praises are due forever, and this is not the Islam Allah's last and greatest Messenger the Most Honorable Elijah Muhammad, taught us all. We must understand being under the rule of this American and European Imperialistic Governments, is not being an independent nation of people. No, this only makes you a mental slave for this American and European Imperialistic Goliath to be use as their tool and a slave. This is only showing and proving that the fear of the devil is still in your hearts.

Allah Almighty our Holy Savior Himself came to raise us up to be an independent Islamic Nation, created by Him His Self. He Allah Himself raised up from amongst us His last and greatest messenger, the Most Honorable Elijah Muhammad; taught His Messenger the real Islam and you have abandon Allah and His Holy Messenger, to join onto the enemies of Allah and His Messenger; which is this American and European Imperialism. Only in American and European Imperialism do you build a business, from the top down. This is nothing but a Ponzi scheme that only fools, buy into and believe they found something good. This is completely against the teachings that Allah Almighty Himself taught to His last and greatest messenger, the Most Honorable Elijah Muhammad. You are in complete violation against Allah and His Messenger throwing in with the enemies, of Allah, His Holy Messenger, and the people He Allah, chose to be His people.

We must my people in the western hemisphere and the eastern hemisphere we must stand up together and build our own, global economic economy, media hospitals, educational system, aeronautics, navy, and everything else that a nation of people, must have in this day and time. To the entire world the teachings that Allah Almighty taught to His last and greatest Messenger, is not to be taken lightly or made fun of. There is not any changes or improvements by anyone, no matter who it maybe; they are not to change any of Allah's teachings, that He taught His last and greatest messenger, the Most Honorable Elijah Muhammad and He taught us all.

This book that I am preparing is just about that, meaning we must remain focus, committed, discipline, dedicated and faithful to the bitter end, of reaching our objective. By Allah's permission and blessings, we are supposed to be building our own, global world with the New Islam that Allah taught His last and greatest messenger, the Most Honorable Elijah Muhammad, who in turn taught us all.

INTRODUCTION

I would like to give once again my thanks to my father and mother and all my brothers and sister and especially to my eldest brother Julius/Professor Anderson and to my son Yaya who have begun, building a fishing business, in the Philippine, for us. We can never thank Allah who visited us in the persons of Master Fard Muhammad, to whom all praises are due forever, for bestowing upon us His Supreme Wisdom which trumps, all teachings including Bible and Qu-man and His last and greatest Messenger the Most Honorable Elijah Muhammad is the perfect example, for us all and there have been many. This journey has been an exceedingly difficult journey for me and to become independent, is an exceedingly difficult journey period. It has also been a lonely journey because majority of black women and men, are afraid to seek freedom, justice, and equality. This take extremely hard work, dedication, belief and focus Our Merciful All Knowing and all Wise Savior, has truly blessed us who believe, and I am extremely blessed to have been a student and follower of Allah's last and greatest messenger, Allah U Akbar There is None Worthy To Be Served, Besides You. I bear witness that the Most Honorable Elijah Muhammad is your last and greatest Messenger, the true and only Muhammad RasulAllah.

CHAPTER 1

LIFE AND DEATH

This chapter is about true life and real death for any people that refuse to honor their flag, this is real death because you are surrendering or have surrendered your independence and identity, to your enemy. Your enemies are enforcing their wills upon you, while you sit back and allow them to do so. Instead of being creative you are just like a slave living on your master's plantation, waiting for them to do for you, what you will not do for yourselves. It is amazing how people convince themselves that they are special, when they have not done a thing to show and prove that they are special, to the world population. This is mental death and I say this to the entire world population, people who think in this fashion can never bring any people life; people who think in this fashion are considered, casualties of war and absolutely anyone cares about any of them, especially us the slaves of America. We are not ex slaves of America because at least 95% of us, still believe and trust the enemies of our fathers and mothers, who have and had suffer more than any people on this earth and have given blindly to this so-called nation called America. This is not hating teachings or senseless spattering, I am just telling the truth of America, and Mr. Yakub makings.

When you see yourself, then you have made yourself the enemy to the rise, of billions of people throughout the world and especially for your own people, in which you claim to be a member of. For anyone who claims to know the truth and the best they can do is argue and bicker amongst themselves and on social media, can only bring death with them and never life to any of us. People who have such sand box knowledge and wisdom are not capable of leadership because they have absolutely no understanding at all. To be a leader you must have vision and this vision must involve and include millions and billions, of people, not only in America but throughout the world. If you are not capable, of thinking this way as all great men are capable, of doing then you can only be an instrument death for millions and billions of people, for all our enemies.

Posting your picture and imbecilic events on social media is a demonstration of a lack of knowledge and wisdom, thus there is no understanding; if there is not any understanding then there is not any life being created. Since you have given into pretending to be and yet our enemies know that you are not what you are claiming to be; you are incapable of breathing life into the dead and you cannot create life. You must understand everyone the difference between life and death because death can never enforce its will on the enemies, only life can enforce its will on our enemies. So, our enemies have taken the foolish amongst us with a minuet knowledge and wisdom and allow them to believe, that they know what they talk about; because our enemies know they are working for them and they do not know what they are talking about. So, since this is what is happening these fools are only bringing death, to the mass of people world-wide.

When you hear fools talk about things, they know absolutely nothing about because they were not trained which make them un-qualified, to even begin to be capable of operating on a governmental level and our enemies know this about these agents of death, that live amongst us, claim to represent us and are in capable, of bring life to the mass of their people so they are only capable of bringing death to their people. Going to some social event and there could be some people there from the government such as a mayor, congressmen/women, assemblymen/women, senators, judges and maybe the governor; and you are able to take pictures with them does not qualify as you are having, friendships in walks of life. If you are claiming to have made it to the store and do not know what to say once you are there, it would had been better that you were not there at all.

Since In fact you are not even truly at the store and if you were at the store you were not able to speak or understand, the language. It does not matter what uniform you have on because you are not qualified, to speak the language of government. So, you cannot bring life to the mass of people all you are able to do, is bring death to your people. It does not matter rather you do this purposely or not; what matters is that it is being done. Life and death my people in America and throughout the world, is caused by the miss-understanding of the teachings that Allah Almighty taught His Holy Messenger, who in turn taught us all. The Holy Messenger did not teach us the knowledge and wisdom of Allah for us to bring death to our people; the Holy Messenger taught us Allah's Supreme Wisdom so that we could bring life to our people and all of humanity.

There are many students and followers of the Holy Messenger of Allah that have done great things, for our people and humanity and met with oppositions from many, who claim to be students and followers, of Allah's last and greatest Messenger. Why is this so Saladin?

3

The reason is due to them not having a complete understanding of the teachings and plans of Allah. These are the teachings and plans that Allah taught His last and greatest Messenger, the Mr. Elijah Muhammad. So, they are only able to bring death to their people and no progress my people, is nothing but absolute death. And we have not seen any progress since the Holy Apostle returned to Allah over forty plus years ago. Do not allow yourself to get caught up into uniforms and antics this means absolutely nothing at all because they still cannot speak the language of government and what to say, when it is time to speak government language.

So, anyone who believe and think that these worthless pictures that are being posting on and in social media by these clowns, are working for the enemies of themselves and their people and since their understanding is so lacking, they cannot see that they are serving the enemies, of Allah and His Holy Messenger. Instead of being the helpers of Allah and His Messenger, in truth they are the helpers of the enemies of us all. The Islam the New Islam and true Islam that our Holy Savior Allah Almighty Himself in the person of Master Fard Muhammad to whom all praises, are due forever; taught His last and greatest Messenger the Most Honorable Elijah Muhammad, is not to be mixed with this so-called Sunnah Islam, Christianity, Zionism and Hinduism at all and therefore the Holy Apostle taught us, to marry one of our own.

It is Life and Death my people in America and throughout the world is what we all, must deal and are dealing with. We cannot have unqualified people representing us because they are not qualified, to speak the language because they do not know nor do they have any understanding, of said language. Since you are turning to unqualified personal to represent you, you will never have a government of your own. This American and European Imperialism is not giving up without a fight and you must understand this. This American and European Imperialistic Goliath fear only one thing or one person, I should have said excuse me O Allah. That person my people and all of humanity is Allah Almighty Himself who visited not only us, but all of humanity in the person of Master Fard Muhammad, to who all praises are due forever and this includes all Holy praises as well, His last and greatest messenger whom He Allah taught personally, for three years and four months is the Most Honorable Elijah Muhammad He is the only true Muhammad RasulAllah, so saith Allah whom wisdom the twenty four scientist, could not find an end to nor can any of these scientist of this American and European Imperialism, can find an end to either; Himself said this of Muhammad RasulAllah the Most Honorable Elijah Muhammad, is My Messenger and touch not a hair on His Head.

Life and death my people/humanity and this are what is going on right now, not tomorrow! This is happening right now! Why did you Saladin start the first chapter in these writings, as Life And Death? The reason is this my people and all of Humanity; My Sacrifice, My Life And My Death Are All For Allah In The Holy Person Of Master Fard Muhammad, To Whom Praises Are Due Forever. My Sacrifice My Life And My Death, Are All For Allah; And No Associates Has He And This I Saladin Shabazz-Allah Am, Command And I am Of Those Who Are First To Submit. I have no choice in this matter I must do what history has already written of me and that is to tell my people and all of humanity, the truth of what is really happening and what is continuing to cause our failure, as a people and this is what is destroying what is called Humanity.

How can we Enforce Our Will when you recognized these fools

or the unlearned who cannot speak nor can they understand, the language of government, as your leaders? This is impossible my people and all of Humanity, this is impossible my people and humanity; it is just impossible. We will never rise as the Original Giant that will destroy, this American and European Imperialistic Goliath that has put fear into the hearts, of billions, by the enemy chosen helpers, by listing to unqualified people because of a uniform and that is nothing more than down right foolishness; believed by fools who can only speak four hundred words well. So instead of breathing life to their people and all of humanity, these unlearned fools can only breath death to their people and all of humanity as well.

Someone anyone please tell me how these fools can ever build a government, when they all have deviated from the path, that Allah Himself taught His last and greatest Messenger, who taught us all what the correct path is. I recently read a post a post by one of these silly fools trying to explain what the five or who are the five percenters, and this idiot can barely speak four hundred words well. These are the simple-minded fools I am speaking about my people and believe me; they are not to be trusted ever I know from experience. This is what I am speaking about this simple-minded mentality can only bring death to us all because this mentality, believes they know what is really happening and they do not know. In fact, they are worst off then they were forty plus years ago this simple-minded mentality can never get anything done on their own, except report to the planation hen master tell them and leave when master tell them, they can leave. This is the extent of their knowledge, wisdom and useless understanding my people, they try to present to everyone that they are wise when in truth they are as dead as a door nail.

This mentality and I can give names, but I will not, if I do not have to; only bring death and never life because there is absolutely no life in any of them. This is the Life and death my people you must be aware of because these snakes are most dangerous, to us all and they are using the Jesus/Christ name {Master Fard Muhammad Allah Almighty} to shield their filthy religion which is nothing more than Christianity.

There have been many students and followers of the Holy Messenger of Allah, the Most Honorable Elijah Muhammad, that has done beautiful work and things that I am personally able to say, that we served together. There are also many betrayers that claimed to be students and followers, that are nothing more than traitors. All you must do is look upon their foreheads, look at their faces and you will not see the life of Allah upon them, you will only see death because they all believe in this mystery god/Yakub, this false so-called religion Islam and this un-truthful and false heaven, after you die. These are all lies my people and everyone who read my words, these are all lies no different than Christianity.

Life And Death my people are all these traitors are going to bring and can bring to us all. The true and only Muhammad RasulAllah is the Most Honorable Elijah Muhammad, everyone is a false so-called messenger, and this includes prophet Ibn Abdullah Muhammad [may the peace and blessings of Allah be upon him}. This includes ESA Ibn Yusef {may the peace and blessings of Allah, be upon him}. There is not any life in any of these traitors or those who believe in these false teachings, of a mystery god and make-believe heaven, after you die are nothing but lies. There is nothing after death so saith Allah The true and only human being that spoke with Allah face to face is the Most Honorable Elijah Muhammad. Not in just the past six thousand years but in the past sixteen thousand years; and Allah that appears every twenty-five thousand years when we renew our history, in which we have been doing for trillions, trillions, trillions, trillions and trillions of years of years. Allah Himself revealed to His last and greatest Messenger the Most Honorable Elijah Muhammad, our history has no beginning or ending. The reason why is because there is no recording of His Allah's Birth Record, so we my people have no recording of our birth record.

We must let the entire planet know what has been hidden away for trillions of years and put completely to sleep, in the last six thousand six hundred years. In the last six thousand six hundred years all religions have failed, all of humanity. More death and destruction have occurred under the title of religion and a misinterpretation of Allah/God. This misinterpretation of Allah is not from the Lord Of All The Worlds and this includes Prophet Ibn Abdullah Muhammad, of Arabia; so saith Allah Almighty Himself through the mouth of His last and greatest Messenger the Most Honorable Elijah Muhammad. It is Life And Death my people and all of humanity is what we are all face with, against this American and European Imperialistic Goliath

Life And Death my people in America the western hemisphere and all throughout the world; the only thing that exist between Life And Death is Slavery, Suffering and Death. If you are alive then you will or should have Freedom, Justice and Equality and if you do not have this, then you are being or under the control, of this American and European Imperialistic Goliath; this Goliath have you living in total fear of his/she evil, wickedness, un-mercifulness, and hatred of all original people on our planet. We must remember this and except this for us all, to institute a change of venue and we all need a change of venue because the one that we are presently on, only produces death and never any life.

We all have only experience death and never life even in the entertainment world, there is only sickness and death. The Vegan diet is designed for sick people and Dr. Sei was a student of the Holy Messenger of Allah the Most Honorable Elijah Muhammad. If one practice How To Eat Live, they will never be sick. Dr. Sei took these teachings of Allah from Allah's last and greatest Messenger, the Most Honorable Elijah Muhammad. Dr. Sei was sick and insane until he met the Holy Messenger and this Holy Messenger, the Most Honorable Elijah Muhammad Healed, Dr. Sei. Dr. Sei had absolutely nothing to offer to anybody, until Allah's Holy Messenger taught him and his wife. All one must do, is follow How To Eat To Live and you will be great. The reason why you are getting sick is due to you being taught these grafting teachings and these grafting teachings you are getting my people, is due to you all deviating, from the teachings of Allah and you have been convinced, to once again to believe in Yakub the Mystery God and these worthless religions of Yakub and this includes this worthless so-called Sunnah Islam.

It does not matter my people in America, the western hemisphere and throughout the world, how dynamic these lies may sound or the deliverer of these lies may sound, these lies are the teachings of Allah and these lies are not the teachings that Allah taught His last and greatest Messenger, the Most Honorable Elijah Muhammad; and these lies were never taught to any of us by Allah's last and greatest Messenger, the Most Honorable Elijah Muhammad.

We must stand on the Square that Allah placed us on through His Holy Messenger the Most Honorable Elijah Muhammad and absolutely no one else. These liars, these magicians and their lies called magic, have taken you all that believe and trust these magicians, off the Square of Allah the true and Living God and what Allah Himself

9

taught His last and Greatest Messenger, Mr. Elijah Muhammad and placed all back into slavery, suffering and death, of Yakub the Mystery God. Yakub is only a mystery to those who believe in these lies, being taught by these liars. Anyone who dare to teach us that Allah Almighty Himself did not visited us in the person of Master Fard Muhammad, to whom all praises are due forever; is the enemy to us all globally.

It is Life and Death my people and if you are following the lies of these traitors, there is only death for all who follow and believe these liars. The Last and Greatest Messenger Of Allah, the Most Honorable Elijah Muhammad met Allah Face To Face and Allah Taught Him from out of His/Allah's Own Mouth, For Three Years and Four Months; His Allah Supreme Wisdom which is greater than anything ever revealed to any prophet before. This includes Noah, Ibrahim, Musa, ESA, John the Baptist, Ibn Abdullah Muhammad, Imhotep, Arman-Ra and every Prophet Major and Minor, that ever walked our planet since our creator Allah; created the universe. May The Peace And Blessings Of Allah Forever Be Upon, All These Holy Men.

This is Life And Death everyone; Yakub's society is truly being destroyed and there is nothing, absolutely nothing anyone, organization, religion, or politics, can prevent this destruction; nor can anyone, organization, religion, or politics can prevent the insanity, that has creeped into the brains and sprit of Yakub's civilization. The only ones who will survive or have a chance of surviving this devastation, are those who keep their faith in Allah who visited us in the person of Master Fard Muhammad, to whom all praises are due forever; and do our absolute best to follow Allah's Perfect Example the Holy Messenger the Most Honorable Elijah Muhammad.

Life And Death is about us all standing up against this American and European Imperialistic Goliath together. There can be absolutely no division, dis-respect, and self-hatred amongst any of us, this will only give our enemies an advantage over us all. There is much we can do together must do together we are all in a life and death struggle. When you look around every major city throughout America, black people are being excluded from all major aspect, of economic growth and participation. Other people have been embraced by this American government and given more consideration, than us. Yet we have only ourselves because we allow this to happen due to our lack, of unity amongst ourselves and corroboration amongst ourselves. We are not in control of our food, clothing and shelter others are in control of our food, clothing and shelter and these strangers amongst make sure, we receive the worst of everything.

As the Holy Messenger of Allah taught us all that our unity will solve all our problems, overnight. This is a life and death situation my people in America and throughout the world. If we want to give our children a chance at life, we must stop excepting the worst of everything, from our enemies. Once we understand how we have deviated from the right path, we can then be able to take back control, over our own growth and development, and our National and International Identity. We must begin to take full control over our economics in our own communities and stop spending our money amongst our enemies. Once we have done this then we will have control over our educational systems, throughout America and throughout the world.

The original man chooses the best part for himself; so why are we allowing ourselves to except the poor part, for ourselves, wives, and children? Why aren't we as a people are not involving ourselves in international trade, as well as national trade, with every all civilize people on our planet? Why aren't we as a people not pooling our resources together and purchasing farmland, for ourselves and kind? Why are we dying at such a young age at an alarming rate? Why are there so many sickness and disease amongst us? Why will not we recognize the flaws in the way that we are approaching things. We have no unity amongst ourselves when it comes to committing ourselves, to building our Nation for ourselves. This is Life And Death my people in America and throughout the world and we must rise to the occasion to secure for ourselves, wives, and children a much better living condition than what we are all currently experiencing.

The Destruction of Yakub's civilization and making cannot be prevented but we can provide for ourselves, wives, and children a better life than what we currently living. We must have complete trust amongst ourselves so that we can build a national treasurer, for ourselves. Whereas we can make wise investments that will benefit the mass and not the few. We must invest in ourselves and stop wasting our time, supporting our enemies, religions, politics, and economics over ourselves. It seems to be a big concern about black children being murdered and dying from these many sickness and diseases, yet nothing is truly be done about this. We must take a more serious approach and a more pro-active involvement, in our situation because we are in an extremely dangerous Life And death situation and we are trusting these organizations, that have not the power to save themselves, yet alone care to save us, my people in America and throughout the world.

We must have qualified people from amongst us to be able to do this, for ourselves. The Holy Messenger of Allah the Most Honorable Elijah Muhammad demonstrated to us all, that this can work, and it will work if we just follow the economic blueprint, that he taught us all. He the Messenger of Allah used a three-year saving program for us because he did not believe that we could be patient enough to invest in the five-year program, which other countries and people use to re-build for themselves. These other countries and people were also facing their Life And Death situations and work together in building their way of life, their economics, educational system, medical system, agriculture system, construction system and more, for themselves. Now because they have done these things for themselves, they all have risen from the ashes that this American and European Imperialistic Goliath, left behind in their wake.

Now my people in America and throughout the world why is this so hard for us to do? Here many of us are still eating bad and poison foods every day of your lives and feed this poison foods to your children. Eating meat and even too many fish, is not good for us, especially when you cannot, are not even sure of what it is. The chemicals that are being placed into the food in your community stores, is only producing death, sickness, disease and retardation, ignorance, and self-hatred amongst us all. Believing that you can take the wisdom of Allah in which He taught His Holy Messenger, the Most Honorable Elijah Muhammad and graft from Allah's teachings, will never gain any of us freedom, justice, and equality. We must remember Allah by His name in which He revealed Himself to His Holy Messenger, the Most Honorable Elijah Muhammad. If you do not know His name you should know His name and His name is Master W. F. Muhammad Allah Almighty Himself, in person to whom all praises are due forever.

We must my people in America and throughout the world understand this we should not be patronizing any of these poison foods carrying stores or eateries. We are only killing ourselves, wives, and children by following the lifestyle of our enemies. This is by designed my people and we must let our people both nationally and internationally, aware of and about these poison foods, eateries and the people who are providing our people, with these poison foods. In fact, you do not know what this substance is but what we do know is that it is pure, poison to all who indulged themselves is this nightmarish substance. This is Life And Death my people in America and throughout the world, that we all must understand. These chemical giants which make up this American and European Imperialistic Goliath, are poisoning the entire planet, through these fast foods eateries and creating hybrid foods as well. This American and European Imperialistic Goliath is poisoning the soil, in which these hybrid vegetables, are being produce.

There are so many reasons for us to unite ourselves for us to combat, the evils that are plaguing our very existence. There is absolutely no reason greater than we all, are at the cross of Life And Death. We must take an extremely hard look at our situation and recognize that what I am saying, is for real. If we all were to follow How To Eat To Live Book 1 & Book 2, we will have much better health, live longer and be more intelligent; this is what these two books will do for us all. Food is essential for our existence and health we must understand that for the past nearly five hundred years, we have been taught by our enemies to eat the wrong foods. This includes all meats, fouls and too many fish as well, is not for us to be consuming, this has been taught to us by our enemies to cause sickness, diseases, shorter life span and retardation. We must understand how important these two books How To Eat To Live Book 1 and Book 2 are to our everyday lives. Allah Almighty Himself through the mouth of His Last, Greatest and Holy Messenger the Most Honorable Elijah Muhammad, taught us what food to eat and when to eat. Allah Almighty Himself in the person of Master Fard Muhammad, to whom all praises are due forever; through the mouth of His Last and Greatest Messenger the necessity of eating one meal every twenty-four hours and the necessity of fasting, three days out of every month; in fact, Allah Almighty taught us through the mouth of His Holy Messenger that eating every seventy-Two hours, will prevent us from ever getting sick.

This is life and death my people and look at how many of us have died, dis- obeying these dietary laws, prepared, and given to us by Allah Himself. Look at how many of us are sick and dying from these poison foods, that are being sold to us every day, by our enemies. This Is Life And Death my people and many of us in America and throughout the world, are still eating these poison foods making ourselves sick and shorting our lives and our children as well. We are the students and followers of the last and greatest Messenger of Allah and there is no diet or dietary laws, greater than the ones that were taught to us by Allah's Holy Messenger.

We must my people in America and throughout the world understand the importance of us, making known to the world this information given to us by Allah Himself, through the mouth of His Last, Holy and Greatest Messenger the Most Honorable Elijah Muhammad. This is Life and Death my people that we all must face up to and deal with, therefore we must strengthen our unity amongst ourselves so that we can begin to Enforce Our Own Will and not fall victim to the will of this Evil, wicket, most diabolical American and European Imperialistic Goliath.

So, I say to everyone pay heed to what I am saying because this will save all our lives. I say to my brothers and sisters who are the followers and students of the Last Holy and Greatest Messenger of Allah the Most Honorable Elijah Muhammad; I say to my brothers and sisters from the Nation of Gods and Earth; I say to my brothers and sisters who are members of the Hebrew Israelites; I say to my brothers and sisters belonging to the Black Panthers; I say to my Nationalist and sisters; I say to our people in Asia, Africa, South Pacific, I say to my Freedom fighting brothers and sisters in South, and Central America and Cuba, I say to all of my people throughout the world; It is time we form a national and international alliance, to combat this American and European Imperialistic Goliath and all of this Goliath partners. This is Life and Death everyone and we all must stand together, to Enforce Our Will of Freedom, Justice and Equality for us and all of Allah's creation that is good. Remember my people and all living beings on our planet, the entire planet has been judged and there is no escaping the judgement.

CHAPTER 2

THE SOLDIER'S MEAL

The First thing I want everyone to understand is that I am not challenging what Allah's last and greatest Messenger taught us all, In his How To Eat To Live Book 1 and Book 2. I have only learned from the Holy Messenger how to use the ingredients that is provided to us, in his books How To Eat To Live Book 1 and Book 2. I truly learned the importance of good food and how to best, prepared them, for all soldiers and anyone that care to experiment with the foods, that Allah, has provided us with. Many of these of these vegetables can be combined to produce a soup, stew and even sandwich, that will replace the necessity of using any meat, chicken, or any other type of flesh. Many beans can also be incorporated together that will produce a wonderful and most healthy, meals for anyone that will use them and be prepared at home.

There is more harmful food out here that many of us are still eating by visiting these restaurants, that are only concerned with mass production. Many of us believe that we are eating good and even healthy, but this is not true my people, we are only deceiving ourselves and making our enemies richer. Even this so-called Halal Food is very poisonous because these Arabs are meat eaters and so this makes this food, very unhealthy. We should be moving away from all flesh eating because these animals are genetically produced and are very harmful, to us all. The further we get away from all flesh eating is the better health we will all enjoy, and this will help us all to be able to Enforce Our Own Will. We must understand the importance of How To Eat To Live Book 1 and Book 2 truly are to us all, not only in America but throughout the world. I am speaking about physical food everyone which will help to lead all who try, to a much better and rewarding diet.

The time has come that we should be producing our own foods and recipes designed or better yet, created by us and we can share to the world as part of our culture, our way of life and the Islam that Allah Almighty brought and gave to us, through His Holy Messenger. These thieving Arabs are trying to claim the Bean Pie as their creation, and we all know that they are liars and thieves. So, we must protect ourselves from all these thieves and we must stop eating their poison foods. This chapter The Soldiers Meals are a creation by of one of your own with all respect, to Our Holy Savior and His Holy Messenger the Most Honorable Elijah Muhammad. We must understand the importance of using various spices and herbs and incorporating them, into our foods; that will only enhance our receipts and will demonstrate to the world, we have own creations of foods that will pro-long, longer life span, greater health and intelligent; as well as taste extremely good. This American and European Imperialistic Goliath has taken this away from us and we must put an end to this; whereas this evil Goliath portrayed to the world, that we have absolutely nothing of good or usefulness, to contribute to the world.

We my people have plenty of good to offer to all cultures and people worldwide, if we just use our creative powers for ourselves. We must put protection on ourselves to prevent these thieves, from stealing from us and try to claim it for themselves. We cannot any longer afford to trust any outsider or traitors amongst us because they will and have betrayed us all. The Soldiers Meals are created to help improve our soldiers and the single brothers and sisters with children, how they can help themselves to get away from eating any flesh, that only brings harm to all, that refuse to stop eating this poison foods. There are many different herbs that can be incorporated into our food to offset, the poisons in the foods that are being dumped, into all black communities not only in America but throughout the world.

When we stop trusting our enemies to control our food, we will be closer to once again, becoming an Independent Nation Of People. We must stop trusting these outsiders with our food and we must stop supporting these outsiders and their wives and children. Listen my people when you eliminate meat of all kind, foul, lamb, goat, and everything else; this includes all fouls and eat less fish also, your food bill will decrease and thus giving you more money to spend on produce, that will increase you are your life span, health intelligence and thinking, not only for ourselves, wives, and children; but for the world population.

We must stand up before the world and let the world know that we are not laying down, any longer and that we have elegant foods and cuisines, of our own. We must also make the world aware of the many different soups and stews absent, of any land meat or foul; and filled with plenty of fresh vegetables, spices and herbs that will help cure ourselves and promote longer life amongst everyone. We have been redeemed by Allah Himself and Allah Himself raised up from amongst us, His last and greatest Messenger. He Allah Almighty

Himself through the mouth of His Messenger, revealed to us a new and improved Islam, a new way of life and our own culture. So, there is not any reason for us not to be creating our own cuisines and everything else, a Nation of People must have, for themselves.

We must show to ourselves and to the world that we have the power to heal ourselves, through our food. That we have the knowledge to heal ourselves through our food, herbs, and spices and to heal others, of the many ailments, diseases, and mental retardation. We must let ourselves and the world know that we have our own food and will no longer, be purchasing the poison products of our enemies. The Holy Messenger of Allah taught us that food is substance for us, and food will take you out of here once you began to abuse food; by eating three or more times a day and by eating the wrong food.

The mass production of these restaurants, eateries, and fast-food joints one will find out how filthy their kitchens are, and the people are, who are handling the food. We must not become over-whelm by the taste of these stranger's food because they use many chemically filled ingredients, for fast production. You will also discover that they are using many can products and foods that sit in the open. So, we must take control of our own food and the preparation of our food, this may not sit well with many, but this does not matter at all we must use what Allah has given us through His Holy Messenger and you will find it in How To Eat To Live Book 1 and Book 2.

The Soldiers Meals, Sandwich, Juice, and Tea are created to help us all, to have decent meals and juice that will keep them healthy and alert. The Tea is a medicine that should be use every day, for preventive measures. We must always remember that eating once every twenty-four hours, is a necessity and fasting anywhere from forty-eight to seventy-two hours, once a month will prevent one from getting sick. If you can eat once every forty-eight or seventy-two hours, this will serve you even better; you will also discover that your food supply will last, much longer. We must understand that we take control of what we are consuming and not leave this in the hands, of people who have no love or respect for any of us at all.

We must reject all the poisons that our enemies are selling in our communities such as tobacco, alcohol, beer, drugs and the many poison foods, dump upon us by this American and European Imperialistic Goliath. These chemically treated foods have caused an unbalance within our children and many adults as well. Nothing but a complete change in the diet will began to cause a change, them which then in time, will bring about a spiritual change in them all. This is something that we all need not only in America, but throughout the world amongst ourselves. Knowing the proper vegetables, fruits, spices, and herbs how to cure them with vinegar, is a necessity that we all must know and how to use. How To Eat To Live Book 1 and Book 2 clearly explains what we should be eating and how they can be prepared.

This is especially important that it be understood by all our young men that are soldiers and perhaps living alone, as they struggle through this wicket, evil and most diabolical American society; how to survive through this hellish nightmare we are all living. This is especially important for elder soldiers and men to know how to prepare, these foods for themselves if the situation, may call for it. The Soldiers Meals, Soup, Stew, Sandwich, Juice, and Tea can be taken to work with you and can be eaten, without warming if there is not any way to warm them, absent of any meat, foul, or meat by products. It is extremely important that we have vegetables, fruits and bread that is baked by oneself or check out all the ingredients, if you must purchase your bread. I find the flat bread is much better than the loaf bread because the flat bread is easier, to digest and does not rest heavy on the digestive system.

To Enforce Our Will, we must eat the proper foods and more important is knowing what foods, one should be eating and how one can prepare their meal. We must also understand this as well do not cheat yourself when buying your vegetables, fruits, spices, and herbs because this for you and maybe even your families. Buy the absolute best for yourself and do not use can or frozen vegetables, to replace fresh vegetables and fruits, as well as your spices and herbs. Put the best into your bodies and believe you will notice the different from these foods, that these enemies have been and still are selling us, throughout our communities my people and all of humanity. When you take a conscious look and concern for yourself, you will begin to understand the importance of what I am saying and offering. This is especially important my people that you sisters and women with children understand what I am saying because this is especially important, for you and your families, as well. This is what I have learned from How To Eat To Live Book 1 and Book 2, and I just want to share it with, you all, In America and throughout the world.

Once you condition yourself to eating one meal a day or every other day or every seventy-two hours, that breakfast and lunch meal will no longer exist, or be needed. Your energy level will increase, your flexibility will always be there, your alertness will increase, your ability to think and analyze, will be greater and you will physically look great, as well as be great internally. Everything about yourself will increase more than ten-fold and everyone you encounter, will never be able to tell your age. The aches and pains will then begin to leave your body and you will have no more headaches, as well. These three meals a day are nothing but a bunch of lies made up by our enemies, to commercialize capitalize on these un-necessary activities, that cause the mass of people sickness, ailments, pains in all their joints, suffering and death; are not needed or wanted.

These Soldiers Meals are most surely needed amongst my people here in America and throughout the world. We must understand what was done to us, what was taken from us and still being taken from us, Allah gave it back to us through His Holy Messenger and food is just one of Allah's, many gifts to us that Allah Holy Messenger taught us all. We should not take anything for granted when it comes down, to our food and our food consumption it is especially important indeed. When you are on the proper diet you will have absolutely no body fat, in fact you will lose, this un-necessary weight that causes you your ailments and eventually death.

The elimination of all meats, foul and meat by products and the reduction of the fish intake, have you in a better state of health that will seem miraculous and this is the benefit of eating as such. We must appreciate these wonderful Books How To Eat To Live Book 1 and Book 2. If not for these two books and the Holy Messenger of Allah who taught me these wonderful teachings, I would be completely blind, deaf, and dumb, to these most valuable and important wisdom brought to us by Allah Almighty Himself. We should always be grateful to Allah and Allah's Holy Messenger for teachings us this wonderful and most needed truth. We should embrace these wonderful teaching and give all praises to Allah for bringing them, to us all.

We must stand up for ourselves and the Islam that Allah bestowed upon us all, through His Holy Messenger; every bit of this Supreme Truth that our leader, teacher and guide the Holy

Messenger Of Allah, the Most Honorable Elijah Muhammad taught us all. Obeying the dietary laws taught to us all is not being truly being observed, by many of the followers, students, and believers of the last and greatest Messenger, of Allah and the results are plainly seen upon them. Once you begin to prepare your own foods for yourselves this will be a wonderful and mighty achievement, for all who practice this to heart. Remember everyone there would not be a Vegan diet or a Dr. Sei if not for the Holy Messenger of Allah the Most Honorable Elijah Muhammad; so, if you are practicing these teachings, they came from the Holy Messenger Elijah Muhammad.

I said earlier how important that we take this very seriously because these teachings of food, will save your health and your life. The Soldiers Meals, soup, stew, sandwich, juice, and tea will carry any soldier for days or any family with children, for days. If you are practicing one meal a day or one meal every other day or one meal every seventy-Two hours, you will have plenty of food, for everyone. In fact, if you are by yourself you can even begin to store it away because there will not be any animal fat or dairy products, that can and will spoil in these foods. Every ingredient in these foods is pure organic and absolutely nothing from and land animal, be it foul or anything else. There is absolutely no fish or fish by products, in these foods as well. These Soldiers Meals are strictly Vegetarian and that is all, that is in these meals.

I have been perfecting these meals for some time and I have created something particularly good, healthy, and tasty, that any and every-one can enjoy at home, at work, at school or on the move. You can deeply appreciate the beauty of these meals because of the time, it takes to prepare them and all the different vegetables that goes into them. The juice as well will be enjoyed also because of all the different fruits, that go into it. The preparing of these Soldiers Meals takes absolute concentration and dedication, without any interference from anyone. When you are finish, I guarantee that you will not be dis-appointed, for the efforts you will be investing of your time. These Soldiers Meals take hours to complete so I must make sure I have all the necessary ingredients, that will be needed, for these creations.

These Soldiers Meals, Juice and medicinal Teas I take great pride in creating and preparing because I know there is nothing better. You will find out that the hydrochloric acids in your system, will work less thus saving the intestinal walls. You will also notice that your bowels movement will be softer thus removing any strain, when having a bowel movement. There are many advantages when eating These Soldiers Meals, the soups, stews, sandwich, juices, and the medicinal teas, will serve a great purpose for everyone that indulge themselves, and partaking themselves into these wonderful creations, that Allah has blessed me with. I am very extremely grateful for these wonderful blessing from Allah I cannot thank Allah enough, for them all.

What we all must recognize is that many of the elder followers that I was raised under did not follow How To Eat To Live, very strictly and later became more laxed in their diets. Therefore, many of them have passed away and many were very sickly. I do not say this out of dis-respect I am pointing out the necessity of following How To Eat To Live and therefore I have created these Soldiers Meals, Juice, and Medicinal Tea, to help my people who may be living by themselves, to have a better diet. It is extremely important that everyone understand that it is extremely important, that you take at least one day out of every two weeks to prepare your own food.

I named it the Soldiers Meals, Juice, and Medicinal Tea because you can march our soldiers, anywhere with these meals. Once you have gain control of your food intake every twenty-four hours, every forty-eight hours and every seventy-two hours, The Soldiers Meals, Soup, Stew, Juice, and Medicinal Tea, will and can carry everyone until their next meal. These meals are extremely good for children as well for lunch and dinner. Even our children should be condition into controlling their food intake, as soon as possible and this will put an end to an ever-growing obesity, amongst children. Therefore, I also created these Soldiers Meals to make it easier to move everyone away from flesh and foul eating because this flesh and foul are causing many sicknesses amongst everyone and yet still have the substance, the body may require. Just because you may have stop eating pork does not mean that you have cleared, the danger zone. No, my people and all of humanity you are extremely far off the mark because there are tons of life threating foods, that are on the market and many households are falling victim to these products.

There are plenty of sea foods that are not fit for human consumption and yet the entire world population, is consuming these poisonous foods from out of the sea as well. Also remember everyone this American and European Imperialistic Goliath has been conducting nuclear experiments, in the oceans, seas, rivers and lakes. Thus, poisoning the life in these bodies of waters and here is another reason why, we should be cutting back on eating fish and sea life period. Also remember everyone that our foods meat, poultry, foul, and fish, are being control by our enemies. Thus, we do not know how long it has been there and many of us do not even know how, to pick a decent piece of fish.

So, armed with this reality has inspired me to create these Soldiers Meals, Soup, Stew, Sandwich, Juice, and Medicinal Tea. The soup and stew can even be a topping for rice or even a side dish, even as a vegetable. There are plenty of uses for these meals and the sandwich can be use, for lunch meals. The important aspect we all must remember is the elimination of meat, poultry, foul, and poison sea foods, from our diets. The more organic vegetables and fruits we eat the better off, you will be. The more our children are taught and trained to resist these poisonous foods, the better off they will be, especially in the long run. I also want everyone to understand that I am not saying that my creation is better than anyone else creation, I am saying that my creation is extremely healthy and practical for everyone, including children and can be used for any meal, at any time.

These Soldiers Meals, Juice and Medicinal Tea are also extremely good and convenient, for not only for men but for working women, mothers, and pregnant women as well. The Soldiers Meals are particularly good for weight control during and after pregnancy and the meals are extremely healthy, for the baby as well. Remember everyone the women are soldiers also. So, controlling one's weight and reducing body fat is a major concern, here in this American and European Imperialistic Society. Staying away from these poison meats, poultry, foul, and poison sea foods when pregnant, will produce a stronger, healthier, more intelligent, more alert, and wiser baby. The weight gain will not be as much as if you were eating these poison foods, I have just mention. The losing of these extra pounds will not be difficult along with, a workout routine.

Remember everyone you want to stay away from all drugs and pills that are being pumped at everyone, promising weight loss and you can still enjoy these poison foods. The Soldiers Meals, Soups, Stews, Sandwich, Juice, and Medicinal Tea will do more for everyone, than any pill can ever do. It is especially important that men, women, and children understand that these candies, potato chips and all the rest of these junk foods, will destroy your health. Cakes, pies, and all sorts of pastries will also destroy your health and appearance, as well. Eating these poison foods will also destroy your skin and appearance, as well. These Soldiers Meals, Juice and Medicinal Tea will only improve your overall health, skin, and appearance because they are all organic and have absolutely no meat, poultry, foul, or poison sea food, in any of them.

Once again, my people and all of humanity all that I have learned about what to eat, when to eat and fasting, came from studying How To Eat To Live Book 1 and Book 2; given to us by Allah who visited us in the person of Master Fard Muhammad, to whom all holy praises are due forever; through the mouth of His last, holy, and greatest Messenger, the Most Honorable Elijah Muhammad. Here is something everyone should understand these bagels, butter rolls, bacon and eggs, ham on a bun all this American traditional breakfast foods, will only lead to extremely poor health, a life of in out of the hospitals, suffering, obesity and finally death.

We, who have been raised up by the last, holy, and greatest Messenger of Allah have a duty, a sworn oath to teach the truth that Allah's Holy Messenger taught, us all. We must do everything in our power to teach the truth as we have been taught and teaching our people what they should be eating, is an extreme must. Creating healthy and much needed creative meals are an extreme must also. So, since this path has been chosen for me, I must follow this path. I have been blessed with the creating of the Soldiers Meals which consist of Soups, Stews, Sandwich, Juice, and Medicinal Teas. This is a mighty achievement for the simple fact I can bring something of physical necessity, for all people. These Soldiers Meals, Juices and

Medicinal Teas are special that will save lives and promote healthier living, for we and humanity if they except them, follower and use them. By following How To Eat To Live Book 1 and Book 2 the entire world will experience, greater health and longer life.

The Holy Messenger Of Allah had and still has many sincere followers who are, working no creating rather than just talking and demonstrating nothing. In fact, you will discover that many will not even take the risk, of the possible hardship one will encounter. I have decided to bring to our people in America and throughout the world, the truth. This book I am engaged in writing is about The Enforcement Of Our Will, is especially important. It does not matter what I will continue my writings because this is what I must do. I never saw how much envy and jealously I would receive because they, cannot do this work and our Holy Savior did not bless them, with this gift but I have been blessed with this gift and responsibility.

These Soldiers Meals of Soups, Stews, Sandwiches, Juices and Medicinal Teas, which can be used in different applications, are being shown to me or revealed to me, by Allah. Every book I write it will and is recorded in Americas Library Of Congress and will live forever; so, I am not bother because I am leaving a legacy behind, for my children, grandchildren, and great grandchildren. I never realized how much envy would come of what I am doing, and I am just getting a glimpse of what the Holy Messenger of Allah, had to endured from his peers.

These Soldiers Meals anyone can eat with any salad of their choice and enjoy their meal, children included. These are the meals we all should be eating instead of eating, these poison foods that many, many are eating. So, it is extremely important that everyone remembers these names The Soldiers Meals, Juices and Medicinal Teas, for males, females, and children.

CHAPTER 3

THE SOLDIERS SOUP & STEW

Butter Nut Squash Chopped Into Chunks

Acorn Squash Chopped Into Chunks

Spaghetti Squash Chopped Into Chunks

Yellow Squash Chopped Into Chunks

Pumpkin Chopped Into Chunks

Egg Planet Chopped Into Chunks

Apparatus Sliced Into Thirds

String Beans Sliced Into Thirds

Spinach Chopped Up

10-WaxYellow Turnips Chopped into Chunks

11-White Turnips Chopped Into Chunks

12-Red Cabbage Sliced Into Thirds

13-Beets Chopped Into Chunks

14-Radishes Chopped Into Quarters

15-Parsley Chopped Up

16-Basil Chopped Up

17-Scallons Chopped Up

18-Salantra Chopped Up

19-Mint Chopped Up

20-A Clove Of Garlic Diced Up

21-Ginger About An Inch In Length Dice Up

22-Sweet Onions Diced Up

23- Red Onions Diced Up

24-White Onions Diced Up

25-Celery Chopped Up

26-Tomatoes Chopped Up

27-Red Peppers Chopped Up

28-Green Peppers Chopped Up

29-Yellow Peppers Chopped Up

30-Orange Peppers Chopped Up

31-Hot Peppers Diced Up

32-Pallopina Peppers Diced Up

33-Sweet Peppers Diced Up

34-Thyme

Four Pieces Hold And Four More In the Last Hour

Beans

1-Chick Peas

2-Black Beans

3-Navy Beans

4- Split Yellow Peas

5-Split Green Peas

6-Lentils

All Beans And Peas Should Be Soaked Together For Twenty-Four Hours In Which They Will Ferment And Cooked Together, Remember To Stir Them Often To Prevent Sticking.

OTHER INGREDIENTS AND SPICES

1-Black Rice One Cup

2-Black Salt Two Tablespoons

3-Cloves Two Tablespoons

4-Grape Seed Oil, Advocator Oil or Olive Oil Half Cup

5- Maringa Two Tablespoons

6-Slippery Elm Two Tablespoons

7-Calumus Two Tablespoons

8-Lemon Pepper Two Tablespoons

9-Curry Two Tablespoons

10-Cayenne Pepper Three Tablespoons

11-Powder Sage Two Teaspoons

12- Sage Root One Tablespoon

13- Bay Leaves Six

14-Cloves Root Two Tablespoon

HOW TO PREPARE THE
SOLDIERS SOUP AND STEW

All the Spices should be mixed up together and grinned into a powder and Well mixed together. They, the spices should be added into Soup/Stew into One third Inclement. Half of all vegetables should be added in the beginning and the Remaining half added in at the last hour, then allow a half hour to suttee Remember to stir constantly to allow all the beans and peas to burst and Prevent sticking to the bottom of the pot. Once beans and peas begin to boil Reduce flame or heat from high, to between medium and low. Remember this Soup/Stew should be cooked in a larger pot with cover during the entire process The Difference Between The Soup and the Stew Is The Amount Of Water, That Is Added. Once I have completed this process is completed, I will have a most wonderful creation that is healthy, to and for anyone who consumes it. You can eat this with bread I recommend a flat bread instead of loaf bread because the flat bread, is easier to digest, I recommend Whole Wheat Bread That Is Gluten Free And Should Be Flat.

THE SOLDIERS SANDWICH

Red Cabbage Sliced

Carrots Sliced

Egg Plant Sliced

Pumpkin Sliced

Butter Nut Squash Sliced

Yellow Squash Sliced

Acorn Squash Sliced

Spaghetti Squash Sliced

String Beans Kept Hold Just Remove The Tips

10-Apparatus Kept Hold Just Slice Of About One Inch From The Stork

11-Two Beets Sliced

12-Four Radishes Sliced

13-Spinach Rolled And Sliced

14-Yellow Wax Turnips Sliced

15-White Turnips Sliced

16-Four Tomatoes Sliced

17-Celery Four Storks Cleaned and Sliced Into Thirds

18-Garlic Half A Clove Sliced

19-Ginger Half Inch Worth Sliced

20-Red Onion Sliced

21-White Onion Sliced

22-Sweet Onion Sliced

23-Half Of A Hot Pepper Diced Up

24- Parsley Cut Off End Cook Hold About An Eighth Of Bush

25- Basil Cut Off End Cook Hold About And Eighth Of Bush

26-Mint Cleaned About An Eighth Off A Bush And Cook Hold

27-Salantra Cut Off End Cook Hold About An Eighth Of Bush.

28-Olives

SPICES

1-Black Salt/Kosher Salt Half Of Teaspoon

2-Cloves Root Quarter Of A Teaspoon

3-Cloves Powder Quarter Of A Teaspoon

4-Slippery Elm Powder Eighth Of A Teaspoon

5- Maringa Power Eight Of A Teaspoon

6-Calumus Eighth Of A Teaspoon

7-Cayenne Pepper Eighth Of A Teaspoon

8-Lemon Pepper Eighth Of A Teaspoon

9-Powder Sage Eighth Of A Teaspoon

10-Sage Root Eighth Of A Teaspoon

11-Four Bay Leaves Crushed Up

12- Four Pieces Of Thyme

HOW TO PREPARE THE SOLDIERS SANDWICH

Heat Grape Seed Oil/ Advocator Oil/Olive Oil Until Heated on Medium Flame, Until Hot A Quarter Of A Cup. Place The Cabbage In First And Begin Cooking It. Once you Begin to Special The

Cabbage Then Place the Rest of the Vegetables In, Along With Two Tablespoons Of The Spices And Remember To Mix Them Often To Prevent Sticking. Use A Big Frying Pan with a cover Also For The Entire Process. Always Remember once the oil and Cabbage become hot and you add the all the other vegetables, reduce the flame between medium and low flame/heat and remember to turn the Vegetables constantly. This process should take a few hours because we do not to ever cook our food fast. The slower you cook your food the better the food will be and taste.

After about an hour, the vegetables are suttee during the entire process, add three more Tablespoons of the spices into food mix and turn the vegetables until the spices, integrate into the vegetables completely. If you feel you may need more oil remember to add no more, than an eighth of a cup of oil. Stir the vegetables in ten minutes increments. Also remember to mix your spices together particularly good into they become integrated. As I said before, always give your food time to cook because we are not in a hurry and this is not some cheap fast food. Once the food become completely suttee and are now soft, add the rest of the spices and allow another half hour to forty-five minutes, for the vegetables to suttee again in the rest of the spices. All the ingredients will be integrated into each other and will present such a wonderful, sandwich that will keep whoever eat one will be very full, content, and happy.

This is a sandwich that America, Europe, or the world, has never known and the only food in which the Soldiers Meals, Soups, Stews, Sandwiches, Are Created From; Is From Allah Almighty Himself In the Person Of Master Of Fard Muhammad, To Whom All Holy Praises Are Due Forever; Through The Mouth Of His Last, Holy

And Greatest Messenger The Most Honorable Elijah Muhammad, How To Eat To Live To Live Book 1 And Book2.

THE BREAD AND HOW TO USE IT. THE FINAL COMPLETION OF THE

SOLDIERS MEALS AND SANDWICH

After the vegetables are completed and done, they are now ready to be rolled up somewhat like an egg roll with a big difference. Here is the difference the bread should be at least twelve inches, in diameter made from. If not, which could depend on your situation, you may have to improvise, use a whole wheat flat bread gluten free and free from as much chemicals as possible in the situation, at your command you may possibly. Then place the vegetables into the bread evenly from front to the end; fold the bread and the ends and place them, into the oven to bake the bread into the juices, of the vegetables; at about two hundred or three hundred degrees for twenty-five to thirty minutes.

When this process is completed their will be no food or sandwich anywhere on the planet, greater and this, I put my life on. Also remember everyone the Soldiers Sandwich may also be eaten with the Soldiers Soup And Soldiers Stew or any meal one may choose, to incorporate them into or with.

THE SOLDIERS Fruit JUICE AND SALID

1-Pineapple

2-Oranges

3-Lime/Lemon

4-Kwi

5-Apples

6-Plums

7-Strawberries

8-Blueberries

9-Watermelon

10-Cantalope

11-Mango

12-Papaya

13-Bannanas

14-Rasberry

15-Advacato

16-Grapes- Red/Green

17-Maranga

HOW TO PREPARE THE SOLDIERS FRUIT, VEGETABLE JUICE

AND SALADS

All these fruits are to be juiced or blended if you want it to be more liquefied, then just add water and it will be drinkable, you use less water, and it will be a smoothly. This is not difficult to do everyone and if you use enough fruits, you will be able to produce enough for a week. This same process should also be use, for vegetable juice as well and this should be remembered, by us all. You must see how the vegetables in the Soldiers Meals and Sandwich are able to be juiced, for the better of self. What we all must understand is this; we must all take the time, to do these things for ourselves and this is the key everyone.

If you are preparing salads, you may either slice or chop the fruits and vegetables up. If you are preparing a vegetable salad one may add cucumbers, radishes, carrots, lettuce, onions, peppers, garlic, ginger, celery, advocate. All produce should be organic and if you desire dressing, then you should be able to make your own dressings. Vinegar is a particularly good source for a salad dressing and can be use, to prepare a dressing, of your own choosing and liking.

We must understand that all the ingredients that we need are all around us and we should take full advantage, of what How To Eat To Live Book 1 And Book 2 have presented for us all. There is nothing in the world that is more powerful about food and health, than these two books in fact all the teachings the Holy Messenger Of Allah the Most Honorable Elijah Muhammad, gave to us from the mouth of Allah Himself, in the person of Master Fard Muhammad to whom praises are due forever; should be in everyone's home.

THE SOLDIERS MEDICINAL TEA/TEAS

THIS PARTICULAR BREW IS FOR MEN

1-Golden Seal Powder Or Root- Two Tablespoons

2-Slippery Elm Powder Or Root-Three Tablespoons

3-Red Clover Power- Two Tablespoons

4-Cloves Whole- Two Tablespoons

5-Saw Palmetto Powder- Four Tablespoons

6-Maranga Powder- Two Tablespoons

7-Cayenne Pepper Powder-Three Tablespoons

8-Garlic Whole-Half A Clove Dice Up

9-Ginger Whole- Half An Inch In Length Dice UP

10-Aloe Vera Leaf-Chopped Up In Quarter Inch Pieces

11-Black Seed Oil-Two Tablespoons

12-Calumus Powder Or Root-Three Tablespoons

13-Sage Powder or Root- Two Tablespoons

14-Yellow Dock Powder Or Root-Three Tablespoons

15-Burdock Powder Or Root-Three Tablespoons

16-Gotu-Kola Power Or Root-Three Tablespoons

17-Echinacea Power Or Root-Two Tablespoons

18-Oregano Power-Two Tablespoons

HOW TO PREPARE THE MEDICINAL TEA/TEAS

All that is needed is a big pop and boiled the water with all the herbs, in the water, for about half an hour after it begin to boil. After the herbs finish boiling let them steep for about forty-five minutes. After they have steep and cool down to where you can transport them, into containers in which you are able to carry with you and big enough to store.

Men should drink one to two cups a day It is not necessary to wait until you come down, with something. This is for prevention my brothers and sisters therefore I have created this Tea for everyone who are concerned about their health. For the women if they choose to use the tea, the women can eliminate the Saw Palmetto from their mixture. I am not claiming that I am the only one who is doing this; I am saying that this has been working for me and it has worked for many others. As I am sure that the other people who are producing these Medicinal teas has helped many. What is more important is that we incorporate this tea into our daily routine.

With the proper diet and food, with the proper time of when to eat our meals; with the knowledge of fasting and the necessity, of fasting; we will live a much better healthier life and less visits to the doctors and hospitals. We will have absolutely no need for any of these drugs that are killing our people, at an alarming rate and causing more suffering amongst our people and the world popular.

CHAPTER 4

THE SOLDIER

This chapter my people and everyone throughout the world, is going to touch on profoundly serious events and procedures, that a soldier must take and do. Many of the so-called followers truly do not understand what it takes to uphold the truth, of Allah in the person of Master Fard Muhammad, to whom all Praises are due forever, visited us in this person. Many of the followers do not understand truly what it means to be one who was in the Temples Of Islam; when Allah's last, holy, and greatest Messenger the Mr. Elijah Muhammad, taught us all. This I consider a blessing from Allah Almighty to understand what I must do. Those who came around after the Holy Messenger departed consider yourself blessed, as well and with this I have not any problem. Nevertheless, this must be made known.

The Soldier is something that must be understood because all of us who have chosen to live life on the other side of the hedge, must realize that our total existence is by the will of Allah. To convey to our people in America, to our people throughout the world and even Yakub's Making; is a profoundly serious, task; an experience that only those who have been chosen to walk this path, may understand.

One other thing that must be remember is that only 5% and more likely 2%, have been chosen to walk this path. The reason being is this; these brothers and sisters lack the real understanding, of what Allah the Great Mahdi/the True Christ/ The True and only Son Of Man; taught His Holy Messenger the Most Honorable Elijah Muhammad. They read and many have studied, but they were not chosen, and this must be clearly understood.

The Denunciation, the exiling, the rejection, and many cases down right hatred, we must bear. You will find this all part of the road our Dear Holy Apostle, had to travel. This is the time when you must be incredibly wise because the dis-believers, you may think are with you, in fact are not with you in many, of these in many of these experiences, you will discover those who you believed were your brothers and sisters, are our greatest threat. So, using The Art Of War And now that Survival is now in play, you must understand and recognize your enemy. The enemy always reveal themselves and how you know the enemy/enemies, have revealed themselves is they believe that you believe their lies; in which you must keep your enemy believing, that you do. The most important thing to remember and to always keep in mind, is that the enemy/enemies, are liars and will manufacture lies against you and do not be surprise where these lies come from. This gives you the advantage because you know your enemy/enemies and your enemy/enemies do not know you. Your enemy/enemies will always reveal themselves once you learn how to set the trap and be a little patient, the truth will be revealed to you; on who your enemy/enemies are, without any doubt. Here is something the chosen must always consider is this; Why Must Saladin Take Jerusalem Back, From The Devil? Another Thing The Chosen Must Understand Also Is This, Who Is The Devil That

Saladin Must Take Jerusalem From? The answers to these questions are coming forth with and this I promise.

My people this young generation is so foolish and stupid it is unbelievable, and these young fools, male and female cannot see it. These fools walk right into the death camps of America, as the Zionist walked into the death camps, of Nazi Germany. Just like the Jews during World War 2 claimed they did not know, these young ignorant, foolish young black children are claiming, they do not know. These ignorant so-called black children are nothing more than 21st century desperados, without any understanding of what is truly happening. These young fools are not willing to be taught the truth, they are only interested in living the lies, of this American and European Imperialistic Goliath.

The Soldier must be stronger than everyone else because everyone is not genuinely concerned about the truth. These other pretenders are not concerned about bringing the truth about our enemies to the world, or their people; no, these pretenders are only concerned about getting the crumbs off this American and European Imperialistic Goliath table and these young ignorant, foolish Negro children are more concern with the crumbs, than they are with the truth. It is a shame that these so-called enlighten ones are using the Jesus name, to shield their dirty religion, which is nothing more than Christianity; and this is the reason why the death toll will continue to rise amongst black people in America and throughout the world.

The Soldier my people in America and throughout the world must realize that there is not many, willing to make this stance. The Soldier is not just men everyone; no, you have many women that have joined the ranks of slaying this American and European Imperialistic Dragon named Goliath and freeing our people, from its evil clutches. We need a complete and un-interrupted Freedom and not the water down version of freedom, that our enemies are offering us; and many so-called enlighten ones have settle for and embraced. You will find amongst these so-called enlighten ones is that they do not and cannot unified, themselves because the cursed of Allah Our Holy Savior, is upon them.

The Greatest blessing to any Soldier be it male or female is the blessing of Allah Almighty, taught to us all, by Allah's last and greatest Messenger Mr. Elijah Muhammad and this we all should know. The next great blessing that Allah will bestow upon the Soldier, is companionship and I am grateful to Allah Almighty who visited us in the person of Master Fard Muhammad, to whom all praises are due forever.

The Soldier My people and all of humanity is a different breed of man and woman; once Allah has blessed you with this companion, you must be wise enough to recognize this blessing and next and especially important, is to appreciate this Holy Blessing. There are many who have chosen the crumbs of this American and European Imperialistic Dragon named Goliath, as the Blessing from Allah. My people and all of humanity these so-called enlighten fools are one hundred percent wrong and are far from the truth. Not only that my people and all of humanity these so-called enlighten or righteous ignorant fools, are miss leading our people and all of humanity; and black children in America and throughout the world are dying horribly, for these so-called enlighten fools' sins.

The Soldier's life is not for the weak at heart because if your heart is weak, your mind is weak and you are just searching for away, back on the plantation; in which many of these weak cowardly so-called enlighten or righteous brothers and sisters have done and are doing.

These cowardly, weak so-called enlighten or righteous brothers and sisters our enemies know, they are not going to do anything, and this empower our enemies my people in America and throughout the world; our enemies which are the multiple heads of this American and European Imperialistic Dragon with their religions and politics, make up this Beast, name Goliath. All our enemies must do is throw these cowards some crumbs and these cowards will gobble these crumbs up, without any hesitation and our enemies know this, with a certainty.

The Soldier my people in America and throughout the world knows that he or she, in many cases stand alone, or may stand alone; yet The Soldier continues to struggle against, our enemies. The Soldier will continue to inspire our people in America and throughout the world, to fight this multi headed Dragon, their religions and politics, this American and European Imperialistic Dragon name Goliath. This my people in America and throughout the world is the and not eating the sour and stale crumbs, from this American and European Imperialistic Dragon name Goliath, table.

There are many so-called believers that in truth are not believers that are on the side of our enemies, to kill the Soldiers of Allah and Allah's Holy Messenger. I personally had it revealed to me someone awfully close to me my youngest son, conspired with my enemies, to murder me; my youngest son even provided these demons with the weapons, to murder me. This youngest son armed these so-called believers to murder me and since their plot failed, these same evil, wicket females who are into pleasuring themselves, whom he conspired with and trusted have now turned against him and are threating, him with death.

The Soldier is not walking through the valley of death my people, the Soldier is living in the Valley Of Death. The Soldier is surrounded by his enemies and the Soldier in most cases, does not even know it and therefore the Soldier must be protected by Allah Himself because our enemies are remarkably close to us.

The Soldier my people in America and throughout the world is on this American and European Imperialistic Dragon name Goliath, Hit List and that is not the worst of things; what is even worst is that the ones whom the Soldier trust, is working for this multi headed dragon named Goliath and they do not even care. These pretenders are more on the side with the enemies of Allah and Allah's Holy Messenger, than they are with Allah and Allah's Holy Messenger. Remember this my people in America and throughout the world, the Soldier is the Black Baby in which the enemies of Allah, will do anything and everything to murder, the black baby at birth. The surprising and most hurtful thing that will be revealed to the Soldier, are who these enemies are and how close they are to you; in many cases the enemy may be sleeping with you.

The Soldier my people in America and throughout the world as we continue to do the work of Allah and Allah's Holy Messenger, our enemies are working against us and plotting the Soldier's death; as they all picked up the sour crumbs from this American and European Imperialistic Dragon, name Goliath. Listen to them all and you will understand why Jerusalem must be taken back, from the devil. The Soldier is the true believer and follower of Allah's last and greatest Messenger, the rest and there are many are just liars. These cowards are nothing more than sour crumb snatchers because they must keep you believing, they have answers and in truth they are nothing more than the eighty-five percenters; I can even give you names of some and perhaps I will. There are not only males my people, but there are females included, in the ranks that love this American and European Imperialistic called Goliath.

The Soldier must always be on the alert because they are surrounded by their enemies and in most cases the Soldier does not know or believe, who these enemies are. Nevertheless, we must always be aware of our surroundings and who is around us. We are in a life and death struggle and the Soldier cannot afford to turn their backs, on our hidden enemies. These enemies and believe me my people they are our enemies are very skillful in lying, you must understand they have been educated in the arts of lying and deceit, by this American and European Imperialistic Dragon, name Goliath. These traitors amongst us are not concerned about upholding the teachings of Allah and the truth that Allah's Holy Messenger, taught us all.

There are many real soldiers standing up for the cause but there are many more that are not, standing up for the cause they are only pretending and this why Jerusalem must be taken back, from these made devils. The Soldier mission in life is not filled with pleasure, fine clothes, pictures and lies, like our enemies. The Soldier's life is filled with dedication and concerned for our people and never for the sour crumbs, from this American and European Imperialistic Multi Headed Dragon, name Goliath. Then these ignorant fools call this having friendship in walks of life and when you study these disgusting pictures that they be posting, you will see their Dirty Religion Christianity, is just oozing out of their pours. The Soldier my people is quite different from what these liars who use the Holy Messenger name, the Most Honorable Elijah Muhammad to shield their dirty religion Christianity and call it Islam.

The Enforcement Of Our Will my people in America and Throughout the world is against this American and European Multi Headed Dragon, name Goliath; we who declare that we/you want Freedom, Justice and Equality; who declare their independence from all of these false religions and these false religions politics, of this American and European Multi Headed Dragon, name Goliath; You are the Soldiers of Allah The True And Living God who visited us in the person of Master Fard Muhammad, to whom praises are due forever; and not this mystery god, whose name is Yakub Ibn Lucifer, whose civilization is being destroyed as we are all living in.

We are Soldiers for Allah the true and living God who visited us and all of humanity, in the person of Master W.F. Muhammad to whom all Holy Praises are due forever; We are the followers and students of the Holy Messenger of Allah, the Most Honorable Elijah Muhammad; the true and only Muhammad RasulAllah regardless of what these Arabs with their make believe so-called Sunnah and Parisian Islam; which they all are against Allah and Allah's Holy Messenger the Most Honorable Elijah Muhammad and the New Islam that Allah Our Benefactor, Our Redeemer, Our Protector, Our Guide and There is None, More Merciful than Him.

Who do we owe my people and all of humanity when these other false, made up religions and their evil wicket politics, of their maker Yakub to lead us all away from Allah; and Allah's, true Muhammad RasulAllah the Most Honorable Elijah Muhammad; and they all have been doing this, for the pass six thousand years, four thousand, years, two thousand years, and four-teen hundred years? These enemies have been and are still trying to convince us my people and all of humanity, to trust these demons, who are one of heads, of this multi headed American and European Imperialistic Dragon, name Goliath.

There is much my fellow Soldier we must consider because our enemies, have us surrounded and believe they are going to win and are not going down, without a fight. These sour crumb grabbers are on the side of our enemies the war of Armageddon/Al-Jihad, began ever since our Holy Savior Allah in person of Master Fard Muhammad, to whom praises are due forever; revealed Himself in the early 1930s to His Holy Messenger the Most Honorable Elijah Muhammad. I was physically birth seventeen years later and never had a clue, what I would have to do soon. To be able write is something that is not easy in fact it is exceedingly difficult because many different things, come into play. Brothers not knowing how to mind their business and thus adding to your problem. Sisters who have violated the dietary laws and all laws are trying to murder you and if they cannot get you, then murdered one of your sons and preferably the youngest son. These enemies mostly females are nothing but liars and haters of Allah and Allah's Holy Messenger; and these colored females will and are using the Jesus name to shield their religion, which is nothing more than Christianity.

These foolish deceived and mis-lead brothers who do not know the truth of what is really happening, side with the ones whose only desire, is to murder myself and my son and do not even realize what they are doing. So, these deceived and mis-lead brothers give poor representation of a father's youngest son and name sake and the son's father whom the father, never gave any authorization to anyone, to act in his behalf; all these deceived and mis-lead brothers do is play into the hands of the enemies, of the Father and Son. These deceived and mis-lead brothers give extremely poor advice to help the enemies of both father and son, caught up int this evil web of lies and deceit, of the enemies of Allah and Allah's Holy Messenger; as in the case of my youngest son in Michigan; who have lied to these brothers, deceived and got these deceived and mis-lead brothers, to aid them into their deceit and lies and even murder; the disgrace is that these deceived and mis-lead brother are unknown participants, of the un-ruthless, lying and deceitful murders.

The Soldier my people in America and throughout the world our enemies are working very diligently to murder the black baby at birth, and we must recognize not only our enemies, but we must recognize the fools who are our enemies and since these fools are deceived and mis-lead, they will lead us all, To The Alter of Death. We who have dedicated our lives to the dissemination of this truth, is against those who are many in numbers, in their conception of truth which is nothing more than Christianity and therefore my people the Soldier, Jerusalem Will Be Conquered. Lies, deceit egotism and only plain diminishment will always be exposing my fellow Soldiers because Allah Almighty Himself, protects us all from these evils.

The enemies of Allah and Allah's Last and Greatest Messenger are very vast my people these/this enemy is this American and European Multi Headed Dragon, name Goliath. We are the Soldiers of Allah Almighty; we are students and followers of Allah's last and greatest Messenger, we are not going to get any support from these pretenders, who claim to be followers and students of Allah's Holy Messenger; because these ignorant fools are only interested in grabbing the poison fruits/sour crumbs, off the enemies of Allah, Allah's Holy Messenger, and the true Soldiers of Islam; filthy and dirty table which is nothing more than Christianity.

The Soldier my people in America and throughout the world

will reveal to you, how silly these deceived and mis-lead so-called brothers are and how dirty these completely evil, witched, liars who are filthy in all their affairs, so-called MGT AND GCC. This is not a knock against the true Muslim Women of Islam; this is about these demons in Michigan and all who are like them, who claim to be MGT AND GCC and they are all, proven devils and I have absolute proof against these demons. The Soldiers must always be ready to identify our enemy and understand how to not reveal to our enemies, that we know and understand who the Soldiers are and who is not the Soldier.

The Soldier must utterly understand what we are up against and how important it is to embrace, submit and keep the teachings of Allah who visited us in the person of Master Fard Muhammad. We always thank Allah for raising up from amongst us my people His last and greatest Messenger, the Most Honorable Elijah Muhammad the Real Soldier Is the FRUIT OF ISLAM; Allah-U-Akbar

CHAPTER 5

THE SOUR AND BITTER CRUMBS

This chapter is a profoundly serious and will uncover the behavior of many people, who are not what they claim to be. The Connivers And the Spiders my people are what many of us are dealing with and the evil, that these Connivers and The Spiders bring amongst us and the Lies that follows with them. Why are these traitors doing these things Saladin? These filthy, dirty traitors do these acts of treason, for the Sour And Bitter Crumbs off this American and European Imperialistic Multi Headed Dragon, name Goliath. As we set about to let the world know the truth there are many Connivers And these Spiders are out there lying and pretending, that they are for real and this make these Connivers and these Spiders extremely dangerous to us all. I am speaking about these Connivers who claim to be and the Poisons Spiders who claim to be, are absolute liars. I am not speaking about the truthful; I am speaking about these Connivers and these evil poisons Spiders. These Connivers and Evil Spiders are all evil absolutely and mean no one any good; these deadly and evil Connivers and Spiders mean only themselves good. These evil most poisonous Spiders and Connivers there are many that are making the mass of sisters and brothers, look awfully bad and can never be trusted and this everyone must know also be able to recognize them.

I have enjoyed myself greatly amongst and in the present of sincere brothers and sisters who are devout followers and believers in Allah Almighty who visited us in the person of Master Fard Muhammad, to whom all praises are due forever; there are many brothers and sisters who are followers and students of Allah's Holy Messenger the Most Honorable Elijah Muhammad; but there are many traitors, liars, connivers, and deceivers, that are out to destroy us all.

These Connivers, and their sister Spiders who are truly Liars, claim to be that which they are not, and they use past circumstances which matters nothing, into the days times we are living in; to deceive many who are truly searching for truth and especially young mothers and their children. The Holy Quran-an tells us to take care of the widows, the offends and the wayfarers, these Connivers, these liars come in many and different disguises and we all must be incredibly careful, of who these traitors are. When you are glorifying our enemies, our enemies will always do support these Connivers and Spiders. These silly Connivers never know how to mind their own business and agree with these poisonous Spiders, if they believe they can make money, off these Spiders pray. I personally know of a Conniver and Evil Spider, planning to take advantage of my youngest son whom I love equally, as all my children. These fools the Conniver and the Spider, believed they could even change his name and call my youngest son, what they choose, to call him; how insane is this everyone.

These are the enemies of Allah Almighty and Allah's Holy Messenger and they only want to use, the Savior's/Jesus name to shield their dirty religion, which is nothing other than Christianity. I am not selling any teachings of Allah and what Allah's Holy Messenger gave and taught us. But these Connivers and these evil Spiders are trying to get rich off doing just this. The Sour And Bitter Crumbs that these ignorant fools are receiving and want to receive, is not worth your souls my people. The Sour And Bitter Crumbs these Connivers and Evil Spiders want, and some may be receiving, was not and is not important to all who stands for Freedom, Justice and Equality.

The life and death struggle for independence can never be purchased with the Sour And Bitter Crumbs, from our enemies table. How can we Enforce Our Will and depend on the Sour And Bitter Crumbs, off our enemies table? What kind of fool embrace the enemy/enemies of Allah and Allah's last and greatest Messenger? Once you denounce Allah Almighty and Allah's Holy Messenger, how can you be anything but an enemy to the rise of black people? If you are so silly to embrace these enemies, then what are you revealing about yourself. These are the Connivers And Evil Spiders who love the devil and truly hate Allah and Allah's Holy Messenger. There is no excuse for this behavior because it produces absolutely nothing of good, for the masses of our people.

The youth amongst us and the young adults as well are very mis-guided and fall into the traps, searching for the Sour And Bitter Crumbs from our enemies' table, rather than seek independence for themselves. We have many Connivers and Evil Spiders that are infecting our youth. Imagine a mother purposely destroying her daughter life and marriage with lies, deceit, self-hatred, thievery and just downright evil and wickedness. As in the case of this Evil Wicket Spider in Michigan and then claims, to be a Muslim. This is nothing more than Christianity because no man desires her because she is disgustingly fat, brazen, ignorant and above all of this, she is totally ungrateful. With such evil wicket women raising black sons and black daughters' what chance do we have, my people. What kind of Islam is she claiming, to be teaching her children depriving her daughter of her happiness and life? What level of evil is this my people? Then have a Conniver come all the way from New York to help with her evil scheme, against a young brother that had the best intentions for her daughter.

These two fools believe their own ego and believe they could control the young brother and rob him of his resources. These two the Conniver and the Spider only destroyed this evil, wicket Spider daughter's marriage, life, and any opportunity she could had have. These two fools are happy to receive the Sour And Bitter Crumbs, from this American and European Imperialistic Dragon, name Goliath.

How is it possible for us to rise my people when we have such people amongst us and claiming to be believers in Allah and Allah's Holy Messenger; and are nothing more than glory hounds using the Jesus Name to shield their dirty religion Christianity and calling it Islam. How can we possible rise my people when we have Connivers and Wicket Spiders, whose only concern is for themselves? How can we raised intelligent, wise, and decent children when you have these Wicket and Evil Spiders, lying to them about their Father? Therefore, my people Jerusalem must be taken back, from these devils. Sour And Bitter Crumbs from our enemies are all these hidden enemies amongst us, care about and you must open your eyes my people, in order that you may see these fools for what they are.

The senseless arguing, bickering, fighting, lying, and conning that these foolish evils Grossly overweight Spiders, love to engage themselves in and draw others into their web of pure evil; must come to an end. What would be even better my people is to run these evils from amongst us. These grossly overweight Spiders become enrage when any man with sense and purpose, reject them as I rejected this evil, wicket Spider in Michigan and Philadelphia; the pure venom from these Spiders, are unleash throughout right lies by these evil and wicket Spiders. You will find how these Spiders are receiving the Sour And Bitter Crumbs from our enemies and loving it. Then these Spiders, they are working very closely with these Connivers to prevent the truth tellers, from telling the truth; and rob these younger brothers and sisters of any chance in life, for the Sour And Bitter Crumbs from this American and European Imperialistic Multi Headed Dragon name Goliath.

The Teachings that Allah Almighty Himself in the person of Master Fard Muhammad to whom praises are due forever; in which He Allah taught His last and greatest Messenger, the Most Honorable Elijah Muhammad in which the Holy Messenger taught us all, is beyond a shadow of doubt the Supreme Wisdom in which I am born from and of; has absolutely no comparison or equal. We my people must flush out these traitors amongst us and expose them to everyone, not only amongst ourselves but expose them to the world. The Sour And Bitter Crumbs my people are the poisonous fruits that we must understand, is a down fall and not an upliftment for self and kind.

These Connivers will throw in with anyone if they believe that they can, receive a share of this Sour And Bitter Crumbs and these greedy Spiders be salivating for their cut. Once the plans of the Conniver and the Spider fail, they will turn against each other and begin attacking each other. This is a very detrimental situation we are in which make all black people in America and throughout the world, look very silly and unproductive amongst productive and civilized people, throughout the world. By excepting the Sour And Bitter Crumbs from our enemies are only making all of us, look like fools who are not able, to conduct business, on a major level.

The Sour And Bitter Crumbs my people are extremely dangerous to us all and how much control we as a people, surrender to our enemies. The most crippling effect from these Connivers and Evil Spiders, is how silly they make the mass of us look because these fools are not capable of representing us all on any level. When you do not have a proper understanding of international trade and business how can even think, that any of them understand business. We as a people are always arguing about anything and we never get anything done. In fact, we are only causing more confusion and separation amongst, ourselves. Now these Connivers and Evil Spiders see this as an opportunity to capitalize, off the confusion amongst us and conspire with our enemies, so they can grab any amount of Sour And Bitter Crumbs, if they believe that they got over. These Connivers and Evil Spiders are extremely dangerous because if they cannot have things their way, they will lie and resort to even more treacherous actions to have the, one or ones murdered by the government especially these Evil and Most Treacherous Spiders. These Evil and Most Treacherous Spiders are more dangerous to brothers and even sisters because they abode not in the truth. These Connivers are mainly out to rob and exploit the brothers and even sisters and they do not care. The Connivers are not always really interested in physically hurting or murdering one but keep your eyes open on them. These Evil, Vicious, Most Treacherous Spiders once exposed and dealt with, they will do anything to physically kill any man that rejects them, as in the case of my son and this Evil Most Wicket Spiders in Michigan.

The level of deceit of these Spiders in Michigan is plain and pure evil because my son refused to take care of the four hundred Mother Spider and her spider children. He refused to knuckle under her and Enforce His Will upon her; these evil and Most Deadly Wicket Spiders plotted to steal his rifles he had bought and plotted to have ATF arrest him and even have them murder him, but their plans failed. Why did their plans fail? Simple everyone Allah in the person of Master Fard Muhammad is the Best Of All Planners and Allah Is The Best Knower Of All Things. So, these Most Evil and Deadly Spiders brought the rifles, back to the gun dealers. How very stupid these evil most poisonous Siders fill because they told Michigan Police, that they did not have them, when Michigan Police came with my son to retrieve his property. It took the ATF to get involve and these evil Spiders crumbled, once they were exposed as thieves and liars.

My people in America and throughout the world must understand that these Connivers and Most Evil and Deadly Spiders, must be confronted and the Sour And Bitter Crumbs they live for, be cut off from them. All the nonsense that is happening amongst us is only happening because of pure ignorance and for anyone to engage themselves in such ridicule's nonsense, is only causing more separation amongst ourselves. In the mist of this silly confrontation the Connivers are searching and planning how can they grab a little more, of these Sour And Bitter Crumbs. We must my people in America and throughout the world begin to Enforce Our Will, so that foolishness of arguing over nothing can be put down before it even gets started. We must understand that there are many amongst us that are on the side, of our enemies; and these someone is working for and with the enemies, of their people. For what reason these someone is do these evils Saladin? For the Sour And Bitter Crumbs and the reconnection and praise, of this American and European Multi Headed Imperialistic Dragon, name Goliath.

These Connivers are opportunist and are always searching for a way to grab more Sour And Bitter Crumbs, from our enemies and these Connivers use many different avenues, to accomplish this skullduggery. One thing everyone must keep in mind is that these Connivers are searching for anyone, they believe will listen to them; once you present them with this opportunity, they begin laying their ultimate trap for you and will begin trying to manipulate you, under their control and belief in them. Remember everyone the ego of these Connivers is always their downfall, but you must be-able to see through their front of concern for you, when in truth their only concern is for themselves. They will even try to come between father and son just like these evil and wicket Spiders and poison the son love for his father as they believe that they can replace the son's father no different than these evil and wicket Spiders. What do these Connivers hope to gain Saladin? They hope to gain the Sour And Bitter Crumbs of the enemies, of their people and the praise of their people enemies.

I am speaking from experience my people and I am not making any of this up because it is all true. I am not concern about other people wanting to write a book or do whatever they choose, to do. I could sit down and write a non-fictional, book about growing up in New York and the nonsense, I was involved in at that time. It has been chosen for me to write about the truth of the times that I grew up in and the times I am living in right now. There are people on you tube making videos and doing interviews and are not telling the complete truth, about the times in which we lived through nor are they telling us the truth about the times, in which we are living in because they would not be able to receive any more Sour And Bitter Crumbs from this American and European Multi Headed Imperialistic Dragon, name Goliath.

There are very few in fact I do not know of anyone other than myself who has the courage to stand up and tell the truth, about this American and European Multi Headed Imperialistic Dragon, name Goliath. There is not anyone I know of who has the courage to tell the world the truth, about who are the partners of this American and European Multi Headed Imperialistic Dragon, name Goliath and the religions and politics of these partners, other than myself. There are many engaged in foolish debates with their brothers and sisters about nothing, of importance; but they will not and do not expose this American and European Multi Headed Imperialistic Dragon, name Goliath. We were taught by the Holy Messenger of Allah, the Most Honorable Elijah Muhammad to make America Know Her Sins. So, explain to me why this is not be done? The reason is simple my people they are all afraid terrified even, of cutting themselves off from the Sour And Bitter Crumbs of the enemies of Allah and Allah's last and greatest Messenger.

The Sour And Bitter Crumbs my people are what is preventing the rise of our people because those who claim to be upholding the teachings of Allah and Allah's Holy Messenger; are in truth using the teachings of Allah and Allah's Holy Messenger to shield their dirty religion, which was and is nothing more than Christianity examine their works, actions, and deeds very closely. How can we Enforce Of

Our Will my people with this type of obvious ignorant, deceiving us all and picking up the Sour And Bitter Crumbs from our enemies'? The Conniving women are just as dangerous and are only seeking the same Sour And Bitter Crumbs as well and they are also Spiders; but being young they have not accumulated the same amount of venom, in them but they surely on their way, of being evil and wicket Spiders; that will succeed their predecessors.

The Sour And Bitter Crumbs are what they all seek my people of truth and we must stand guard, against these enemies that are amongst us. This mentality exists not only in America but throughout the world and preventing us from rising, as a unified people. This American and European Imperialistic Multi Headed Dragon, name Goliath, have ninety percent of our people fighting over their Sour And Bitter Crumbs. These fools that are addicted to these Sour And Bitter Crumbs are extremely dangerous, and they are all liars, deceivers although they pretend, to claim that they love you, when in truth they do not.

So, my people we all must understand that seeking the rewards and praise of our enemies, only make you the enemy of Allah our Holy savior who visited us in the person of Master Fard Muhammad, to whom praises are due forever. Whomever is seeking the rewards and praises of our enemies are demonstrating that they are the enemies of Allah's last and greatest Messenger, the Most Honorable Elijah Muhammad. Whomever is seeking the Sour And Bitter Crumbs of this American and European Imperialistic Multi Headed Dragon name Goliath, are the enemies of the rise of the black nation. Whomever believe that they can prevent the mission of Allah's chosen, is the enemy of all black and original people. Whomever believe or think that they can deceive and manipulate the chosen of Allah, is the enemy of the rise of black and all original people on our planet. Whomever believe in this American and European Imperialistic Multi Headed Dragon name Goliath and sop up the Sour And Bitter Crumbs, will be destroy with this Demon. Whomever supports these phonies religions and politics of this American and European Imperialistic Multi Headed Dragon name Goliath, will be destroy with the enemies of Allah and Allah's last and greatest Messenger. The Sour And Bitter Crumbs my people in America and throughout the world, is the destruction of yourself.

CHAPTER 6

THE RE-UNION OF FATHER AND SON AND THE HONORING OF OUR ANCESTRAIL FATHERS AND PEOPLE

This chapter everyone is a chapter of love between a father and son in which I take great pride, in writing. Under this Matriarch Insane society in which we live in the destruction of father and son relationship and the Honoring Of Father, has all but been destroyed. The hatred by black women is so clearly demonstrated openly for black males and treatment until, it is a crying shame and even criminal. Teaching and doing everything in their power to separate black father and son is a way of life, under this American and European Imperialistic Multi Headed Dragon name Goliath, it is religions, politics, and Goliath partners. I know this American and European Imperialistic Multi Headed Dragon name Goliath, desires that the separation of black father and son continues because they believe the soldiers that will have the courage to oppose them, will never be birth or even born. I stand here today and proudly say our enemies are terribly wrong.

From my personal experience I know our enemies are wrong because Allah is the Best Of All Planners and Allah Is The Knower Of

All Things. Under this evil matriarch government, the murdering of the black baby has reached an all-time high and have been embraced by these so-called black women, when in truth are nothing more than colored women. These colored women are the greatest weapons used by this matriarch society, in murdering black male babies. They teach black males to hate their fathers and love them over their fathers and even teach black male children, that they and women period are superior to them. In fact, in many homes especially black the females can get away with lies, deceit and being lazy, while the males are treated like slaves. I have personally witness and experience these evils against black male children and there is nothing ever done about this injustice. The physical abuse being committed by these ignorant colored women on black male children, is criminal but this society does not care. In fact, these colored women encourage homosexuality amongst black male children, to make sure they murder the black male children. These activities are being carried out all throughout America and this Matriarch American and European Imperialistic Multi Headed Dragon name Goliath and its partners, are incredibly happy to see this happening amongst, black families.

This is how made devils are manufactured and the Island of Pelan is the so-called homes, of black families. The lies that come from the mouths of these colored women are nothing short of evil. I have experience this amongst my own children and more grossly than my younger son, who is my name sake. I submit to Allah in the person of Master Fard Muhammad to whom all praises are due forever. I am a sincere and devout follower and student of Allah's last and greatest Messenger; the Most Honorable Elijah Muhammad and I taught and teach my children this Islam and I always has. Yet the mothers of my children pretended to believe changed and began teaching them against me and began teaching them against Allah, Allah's Holy Messenger, and Islam, as the Holy Messenger taught us all.

In many cases self-included black children were placed into the system because their mothers, failed at their responsibilities in many cases due to heroin, alcohol, cocaine, and later crack. In most cases the system was against the fathers and offered the fathers, absolutely no help at all. So, these black children self-included ended up in the care of the enemies, of Allah, Allah's Holy Messenger, and Islam. What this led to is the super-imposing of the enemies Christianity upon them and the lifestyle of the enemies, of Islam. The results were that many of these children became crack dealers and dealt this chemical of death, amongst themselves and rejected Islam as many of the black heroin dealers did also and rejected Islam as well.

There is this brother making videos on you tube Melchizedekian saying that the so-called Nation of Gods and Earths, kept the lessons alive. What is not being told is that the so-called Nation Of Gods and Earth corrupted the examination of Kareem and distorted the teachings that Allah taught His Holy Messenger and corrupted the Islam that Allah taught His Holy Messenger, which had a negative effect on black people throughout America. I know this to be true because I was there and personally seen the negative effects, that produce absolutely nothing for black people. Yes, they would always say the Blackman is god but have done absolutely nothing at all, in conducting themselves as civilize and intelligent people and history will prove this to be true.

So due to the many different attacks that we all were under at the time and many came from within, caused many break downs in young newly started black families. So many of the children did end up in the system and this is not being told, as well. These children all ended up in Christian foster homes or under the rule of Christian family members and the hatred for Islam was spread amongst them. What is not also known is that in many of these cases Christianity was beaten into these children, in different ways and by different family members as well. So, the love for the discipline that Islam provided for black people, was removed from the children, and replaced with the love for our enemies. You will also discover that the male children suffered the most under these horrible conditions and taught to hate their father. So, the actual love for Islam had been removed from the males and the male children were taught to hate their fathers. This was also being demonstrated by the mothers who were on welfare and many mothers had fallen victim, to loving our enemies.

It was a complete break down because the rebellion that exist in us at that time, was use as a weapon against us because there was not any discipline, direction or unity amongst black children having black children. There was so much hatred from our parents for Islam until they would beat and force our children, back into the church and the fear of the devil, self-included. We were young in Islam and many of the young sister that were having our children, were not committed to Islam. Even though we gave our children righteous first names we never changed the slave-master name and in many cases were still practicing the Christian holidays, especially Christmas.

So many of our children grew with Christian values and could never really except, Islam. Many claims that they do but, they cannot and the mothers and grandmothers, hate many of the fathers. In many cases the fathers were caught up in the society many vices and lack any training or practical education and were not able or did not give financial aid to the mothers. Most of the mothers were on welfare and were also affected by the vices of this society and through sheer ignorance and envy of the so-called founder, forbid these children from seeking the only place where they could have changed their situation and that was by running to the Temples Of Islam. When you examine this so-called organization, you will see that they are all, very dis-organize from the very beginning. So, our children suffered especially our sons because complete fools, became teachers to the children. These fools had and lacked the true understanding of the Examine Of Kareem, in which they call lessons or the one twenty.

Many brothers had lost contact with their sons and daughters' brothers from the Nation Of Islam, Black Panthers, Five Percenters, Black Liberation Army, and other revolutionary groups and in some cases, sisters also withstood these losses. Many were imprisoned for a lifetime, many were killed, murdered, and were lost in the Abyss of Drugs, Alcohol, prostitution; and the children were gobbled up by Christianity. This is the history of this time period that destroyed two and now a third generation. The Re-Union Of Father And Son And The Honoring Of My Father is especially important that all black men in America and throughout the world, must understand. Our sons and daughters were stolen from us once again but this time ignorant colored women, were working on the side of these evil, wicket Caucasian Matriarch Women and government.

Although many had the examination of Kareem/lessons/one twenty degrees this examination had been distorted and over time became completely diluted and did more harm than good. In fact, NYPD, FBI, and other Law Enforcement Agencies were able to infiltrate black communities in New York, Chicago, Detroit, Jersey, Washington DC and eventually throughout the entire country bringing death and destruction. Being mis-guided the youth became their own instrument, of their own destruction. Due to their leader teaching them that they did not follow any rules, regulations, or laws, they lacked the necessary understanding to build a self-sufficient government, for themselves and prevented them from seeking help from their brothers and sisters, in the Nation Of Islam. In fact, they were lied to about where this examination of Kareem/lessons/one hundred and twenty degrees originated from. In fact, due to the lack of understanding from their leader, caused the death, imprisonment, and the destruction of several generations, of our people; that carry over into the days' time.

It is especially important that this is understood everyone because a great and un-necessary separation came about, which could had been avoided amongst us. This separation has caused serious damage and destruction amongst father and son and this was a new construction of the spiritual Island of Pelan, amongst black people in America and the murdering of the black baby, our sons. Many of these colored women embraced this evil, wicked, and most deadly Matriarch Rule System that has carried over till todays time. Not only does this newly constructed spiritual Island of Pelan destroy our male children/black babies; this evil Matriarch System encourage the females to become sexually active with anyone and have babies, by our enemies because these females know or believe that this evil Matriarch System will give them food, clothing, and shelter and in some cases, jobs suited, for men. It's extremely important that this mistake in 1964 could had been a good thing had this particular person had directed the youth, he had given the Examination of

Kareem/Lessons/One hundred and twenty degrees to; and directed us all back to where these teachings originated from and the true and living Allah in the person of Master Fard Muhammad, to whom praises are due forever; and to the temples of Islam under the leadership and guidance of Allah's last and greatest Messenger the Most Honorable Elijah Muhammad.

The Re-Union Of Father And Son And The Honoring Of My Father way of life is extremely important, that our sons and ourselves understand. Our sons are under such immoral acts by these immoral colored women, who are nothing more than evil, poisonous, wicket Spiders. My brothers, our sons need our help in this life and death struggle, against these evil, poisonous wicket Spiders and I am telling you from experience involving my own son. If not for Allah in the person of Master Fard Muhammad to whom praises are due forever; and His last and greatest Messenger the Most Honorable Elijah Muhammad and the real and true Islam, both me and youngest son, would be dead. Through my personal trials, tribulations, and test of faith I was able to instill this spiritual, mental, and physical fortification, in them all. Which has allowed them all to overcome the adversities in which they all, had to endure in their personal lives. My eldest son had to survive the last thirteen years at the time of this writing in Federal Penitentiary in Pennsylvania. Two other sons are surviving in Brooklyn and I pray that Allah protect them all. My daughter is doing well for herself but fall under this Evil, Wicket Matriarch System, it is my sons who are at risk.

We must understand my brothers when these evil, wicket and most poisonous Spiders cannot seduce the father, the son/sons will fill the full blunt of the hatred for their father and if they have the strength to resist this poisonous and most deadly Spider/Spiders advances; he is now hated as much as his father from the enemies, of his father. The first thing these enemies do is to separate the son from his father; then try to poison the son mind and heart against his father; while these Matriarch Poisonous Spiders manufacture lies against his father, to weaken the faith and love of the son towards, his father. My brothers we must be ready to go head-to-head with these Matriarch Demons and slay these dragons, to save our sons, from such unholy evil. If your son can survive this evil until he is able to get to his father, this son has a divine purpose in life and is chosen by Allah to do great things, in his life alongside of his father.

We my brothers must be there for our sons when they most need us and this is more important, than anything else. In fact, if your son can survive and defeat this evil, he has earned, His Right Of Passage. Therefore, this evil Matriarch System is working against the black man, the black sons, earning their Right Of Passage and you will find many colored women, doing everything in their power to prevent this from happening. The Right Of Passage is the destruction of the Matriarch control over our sons and grandsons. I can tell you from personal experience how gratifying the Re-Union Of Father And Son And The Honoring Of My Father, truly is. There is nothing more important than having the true Islam and knowing who the true and living Allah is. There is nothing more important than knowing, being a student and born into these wonderful teachings that Allah in the person of Master Fard Muhammad, to whom all praises are due forever; taught His last and greatest Messenger the Most Honorable Elijah Muhammad.

You my son/sons have absolutely nothing to be ashamed of no matter what we all had to suffered through. It was predicted before any of us were born we would be tried by fire, reason being is that we have an incredibly special gift in us that is different from others and others do not have. There are many brothers who were in the temples of Islam, or in some other organization or group; and yet they have not the gift to defeat this Matriarch System because in their heart they have always submitted to the Matriarch System of Rulership. If they play ball for the Matriarch the Matriarch will allow them, certain privileges, whereas they only look as though they are in charge; but in truth they have submitted to the Matriarch and as the Matriarch tell them what to do. The battle to save our sons are extremely important because this Matriarch System is out to make our male children homosexuals or just mentally and spiritually weak and submissive, to the Matriarch Rulership. This we cannot allow my brothers because this is a direct attack on every black man in the world. Many of these women coming from different parts of the world to America, join unto this evil wicket Matriarch System because only in this American and European Imperialistic societies, can they get away with such evil.

The Re-Union Of Father And Son And The Honoring Of Our Father should be extremely important, to all black men not only in America but all black men throughout the world. We must my brothers and all fathers stand up for our Allah given rights and not allow this evil Matriarch System, to continue to kill and murder the black baby at birth. Dragging our sons back into the churches and different occults with people and under the leadership, of men other than their fathers and creator. We black men and fathers in America must stand up together as one because this Matriarch Society has been embraced by these so-called colored/so-called black women, that allows them to murder the black baby at birth with impunity. The lies and filth these colored/so-called black women are teaching our black male children, is nothing more than diabolical crimes, against all black men and against Allah, Allah's Messenger, and Islam.

The Re-Union Of Father And Son And The Honoring Of My Father must be embrace by every black man in America because until we do, Black Male Lives Will Never Matter In this American and European Imperialistic Multi Headed Dragon name Goliath and this Goliath's Partners. It is up to us black fathers regardless of your circumstances, we must stand up against this evil, wicket, diabolical Matriarch System and Society; and the evil colored/so-called black women that have embraced it and the religions that encourage this ungodly evil, against black original men in America and throughout the world. This is especially important black fathers and sons do not allow anyone to get in your way of discovering the truth, about yourself. There are many lies about many black fathers being told, by the mothers of our children. Due to these women embracing this diabolical Matriarch Evil, the black families across America have been destroyed. No woman can teach a man to be a man or what it takes to be a man because these women are only teaching black sons to be submissive, to the rule of this Matriarch rule and sons should take a back seat, to women. This is happening on all levels, throughout America black fathers. Silly young girls are taught by their mothers that they have the power over the black male, this is in complete rebellion, of all mathematical laws. In fact, to hear these silly young girls believing that they have the right to talk down to our black sons, is disgraceful and I find it hard to believe, that these colored /so-called black mothers love their sons.

We must Black Fathers Stand Up and Enforce Our Wills On This Diabolical Supremely Evil Matriarch System and Standard. The

Re-Union Of Father And Son And The Honoring Of My Father, must be instilled in all black males, so that our sons have a fighting chance against this wicked system. Our sons are being destroyed at the whole sale level because of this diabolical Matriarch Evil System, that exist in every black community throughout America. We black fathers must rise to the occasion to make war against this Matriarch Diminishment. We must black fathers take council amongst ourselves and our sons because this evil system is out to murder all black men, in America and everywhere they go. This Matriarch System is the devil in which ninety percent of these colored/so-called black women, have embraced.

Black Fathers we must have a Re-Union Of Father And Son/Sons And The We Can Begin To Honor Our Fathers and then we will be able to destroy this Diabolical, Supremely Evil And Most Dreadful Matriarch System and Standard. Any woman that believes, think, or want to put their nose into men business, is the enemy to the Re-Union Of Father And Son And The Honoring Of Our Fathers. How can we Enforce Our Wills Black Fathers When We Will not Honor Our Fathers? How Can Our Sons Rise Up From Under The Evil Rule Of This Matriarch Diminishment, If We Do not Honor Fathers? This Diabolical Supremely Evil Matriarch System teach our sons, not have any love for black women, that are not a part of this Diabolical Matriarch System and this what these foolish, ignorant colored/so-called black women are doing. Absolutely no Muslim woman or black woman with any understanding of herself, will embrace this Matriarch Diminishment. Then lead her black sons back into hands of our enemies and their filthy, evil religions; or some other stranger leading them away, from their Black fathers. These Black Sons of ours Black Fathers will never be independent of our enemies because of their ignorant mothers, have and are delivering them into the hands, Of The Cremators; this American and European Imperialistic Multi Headed Dragon name Goliath and Goliath's Wicked and Evil Partners and their evil religions and politics.

The Re-Union Of Fathers And Sons And The Honoring Of Our Fathers is a must for every black father and son, throughout America, if our sons are ever going to have any chance in life. The teachings of Allah who came in the person of Master Fard Muhammad, to whom all praises are due forever; whom He Allah raised up from amongst us His last and greatest Messenger and taught His last and greatest Messenger the Most Honorable Elijah Muhammad, Allah's Supreme Wisdom is the only chance we Black Fathers and Black Sons can defeat the Supreme Evil of this Matriarch Diminishment and this Matriarch Government American and European Imperialistic Multi Headed Dragon name Goliath and Goliath's Partners.

I am not speaking against any true righteous sister/woman at all in fact I praise these black sisters/women. No, I am speaking about the ninety percent of these colored/so-called black women, who have embraced this Matriarch Diminishment. These colored/so-called black women have aided and abided the enemies of Black Fathers and Blacks Sons every-since we crossed the Atlantic and have intensified, since this Dreadful Civil Rights and Integration, with impunity. The situation has even escalated in the last thirty and forty years and the escalation of the separation of black fathers and black sons, is out of control. Black fathers and black sons' relationships are almost completely non-existent. Understand how diabolically evil this Matriarch System is my black fathers. This old Matriarch colored demon whom she never did anything for her daughters, except teach them to love Caucasian men and have their bastard children and much, much worst things; told her daughter's four-year-old son, he does not need a daddy. This Matriarch System must be destroyed Black Fathers and Black Sons because this is the greatest evil that we are sleeping with.

We must have a Fathers And Sons Re-Union And Honor Our Fathers because sons are being raised, without any identity or awareness, of who they are and being completely dominated by Matriarch Diminishment. Black fathers you must stand up and be accountable for yourself and have pertinent knowledge for our sons, when you are with your son/sons. Can't you see black fathers how this Matriarch Diminishment is destroying our sons and ourselves? How many more of our sons must be imprisoned or laying down in some gutter, or on some highway, before we black fathers Re-Unite with our sons and teach them how to defeat, this Matriarch Diminishment? Across this country our black sons fill they have nothing to live for because if they did, they would put more value on their lives. Stand up Black Fathers and let us all stand together and have a Re-Uniting Spiritually, Mentally and Physically With Our Sons and together We Can Honor Our Fathers and begin once again To Enforce Our Will. I will end this chapter with this prayer from the two hundred and eighty- six ayah/verse, from the Holy Quran-an. Maulana Muhammad Translation: O' Allah Do Not Punish Me If I Forget Or Make A Mistake. My Lord Do Not Lay On Me A Burden As Thou Did Those Before US. My Lord Do Not Lay On Me A Burden Which I Have Not The Strength To Bare. Pardon Me. Have Mercy On Me. And Protect Me From These Dis-Believing People. Amin.

CHAPTER 7

THE SCARS OF BATTLE IS THE RIGHT OF PASSAGE FOR ALL BLACK MEN

This chapter is also a remarkably interesting subject that I will put my all into conveying the true message, to all that read it and have experience it. The Scars Of Battle Is the Right Of Passage, for all young men that are engaged in this life and death struggle. The Scars Of Battle could be spiritually, emotionally and some cases physically, that have destroyed many young men and women. As you go through this life here in Imperialistic America there are many obstacles that must be overcome. Due to modern technology things appears easy when in truth this allows the government and our enemies, to gain access to our information and even manipulate one into things, that they normally would not be involved in. Lies and deceit are easier to disguise and hide so when you think that you are getting something good, you discover that things are untrue. This is especially true in computer dating and relationships.

When you stand up for truth, freedom, justice and equally here in this American and European Imperialistic society, this government and people will bring all its forces against you. Here is where your test begins, and this will be a great test because here is where one will earn their Right Of Passage from child to manhood and you will receive the Scars Of Battle. If you are weak in faith you will be destroyed and exposed as unworthy, of the blessings of Allah. The test will come from many different places, ways, and people. You may think that you know but in truth one does not have a clue because there is not any designed script or lesson, for one to study. Once you have received your teachings and instructions from your father who has received his teachings, instructions and has passed his Right Of Passage; you will have one that is experience in this journey and will be a great source of information and wisdom. What one must understand is that the journey is yours.

No woman can prepare a young man for this journey because they are not men and do not know what this journey, is truly about. In fact, many black women especially will do everything in their power to try and prevent, young black men from taking his journey. This is not a journey for cowards, this is a journey for the weak at heart, this is not a journey for fools; this is a journey for young men seeking to become a complete man and earn the right, to his manhood. Once he has passed his test and this test is like no other test, he is now treated with all the respect and alcaldes of a man. One thing is for sure you will receive the Scars Of Battle from this journey and there is not any way around this fact. There is no calling on your mother because she cannot help you and have no right, to interfere in any young man's test of the Right Of Passage. The

The Scars Of Battle my young brothers who survive and survive with honors, are your medals of valor and you always wear them with honor. It is impossible to pass the test of the Right Of Passage and not receive any Scars Of Battle, if you are going to be your own man and seek independence, then these scars will be your trophies that will be with you for life. The Right Of Passage is totally different because this is about being tested to be a righteous man and not some silly fool committing and endorsing foolishness and evil. There will be many things that one will have to deal with and overcome and in most cases, one will be shocked where these attacks, will be coming from and from who they will be coming from. Things will be revealed to you that will be extremely painful and, in many cases, hard to believe and except. Here is where you will begin to receive the Scars Of Battle and you will then begin to understand, what the real meaning of the Right Of Passage.

The Lies, the Deceit and the Pain will at times be overwhelming and you will find it hard to believe, how these lies will be manufactured against you. You will discover how the true enemy/enemies try and keep themselves hidden as they operate through others. In fact, my brothers who are on this journey these enemies will result in downright slander and then run to church or consider themselves righteous. The deceit that also comes will be also shocking as well and the most shocking of it, is who will be deceiving you. This will cause you plenty of pain that will rock your very essence, and this will be coming at you at an alarming rate and you must handle it all, in order to pass your Right Of Passage.

The hatred and pure venom that will come is unbelievable but believe it sons, it is for real and it will be real. The Scars Of Battle will begin to amount and this will continue, until the journey is completed. People expect you to be that which you are not, and you must not be that which you are not at any time while you are on your journey and no other time in your life. We must denounce all forms of this American way of life because it does not promote anything, pertaining to our heritage, culture, and our ancestors. In fact, the only thing we are promoting is the lifestyle of our enemies and our enemies' children. None of this will serve black people in America and throughout the world any good at all yet you will find people mostly, trying to lead you back into the clutches of our enemies. We must understand my people we cannot Enforce Our Will by supporting the nonsense of the enemies and their government, way of life.

The Right Of Passage is not an easy thing for black male children especially when you have black women beating and trying everything in their power, to keep them knuckled under this Matriarch Diminishment. In most cases these Matriarch believers and practitioners do not have a man and cannot keep a man because of the evil, they want men to submit to; in which no real man will submit to. So here in Imperialistic America a young black man has not only to fight against this American government, this Matriarch Diminishment but against his female mothers, practitioners, within his own family. Mother, sister, aunt and in many cases, grandmothers included. Not to mention all the females that are or most of the women who believe in this society, will expect black males to be submissive to them, meaning female and the lies, the misconceptions these foolish women ascribe to make the journey for the Right Of Passage, of young men that much harder.

Many young black men are very confused by the lies and deceit they are receiving from there, so-called mothers because their mothers have and are in bed with the devil and none more than these foolish, ignorant lying black women and their half breed daughters, who are also mongolicin our people. Look around us today and the evidence is right in our face and these women are never to be trusted, they are only to be used because they do not believe in Allah and they do not believe in Allah's last and greatest Messenger the Most Honorable Elijah Muhammad; these women believe they can trick and fool the true believers, of Allah and Allah's last and greatest Messenger the Most Honorable Elijah Muhammad. My people the spirit of Rebecka has been transplanted all throughout the black communities in America and throughout the world, as they give birth, to YAKUB the enemy of Allah and Allah's last and greatest Messenger the Most Honorable Elijah Muhammad. Once the trust is broken it can never be repaired and most of these women do not seem to understand this. No real man is going to or want to be around a woman that believes she has the right to raise her voice to him and even threaten him physically. Then when the man refuses to submit to her insanity, she calls the police putting his freedom and life at risk.

No matter how much good the man has done for them means absolutely nothing to them at all and I know most men know this to be true. The Scars Of Battle Is The Right Of Passage for all young black men in America. It appears to me these black women have truly fashion themselves and even believe, they are Caucasian Women; and we black men should submit to them. I have been told by young black children and the males by their grandmother, they do not need a daddy. What kind of evil is this my people from a grandmother, to say to young black male children and female children? How insane for a mother to call her daughter while she is on her honeymoon and tell lies on her husband? How insane is this same mother who has never seen me physically say that my son, is her son from New York? How insane is a mother to exclude a young man father and mother, from his wedding? How insane is a mother not my son mother tells my son, you do not have a holy name and she will give him one; when she herself does not have a holy righteous name and my son is born with a powerful holy and righteous name and my son is my name sake? What kind of mother other than absolute evil and wickedness, would wound her daughter marriage? This is the evil of this Matriarch diminishment my people and some dares call themselves righteous women and in my son case dare call herself an MGT Captain and she is a proven liar and a thieve.

Not only must we my brothers deal with a society and government that is truly against us, but we must also deal with these evils coming from those that are supposed to be our mothers; doing everything to prevent young black men Right Of Passage and leaving them with the Scars Of Battle, that will last forever. Therefore, many black male children are so emotionally scared and spiritually scared because black mothers in this day and time, have embraced this evil and most wicket Matriarch American Rule System, this evil is taught and demonstrated to young black male children to hate their fathers. This is the evil of Christianity because they are forcing black children, to believe that the Caucasian People, are god and their Savior; and most black male children do not believe or want to except this proven lie.

There are no male children and female children that are more mentally and spiritually abuse, by ignorant and selfish so-called mothers on our planet, than the so-called American Negro Children, Now Called African Americans. Any black male child that survives this Matriarch Evil and comes out with his sanity, mental faculties, and spirit, has earned his Right Of Passage and will have plenty of Scars Of Battle. There is absolutely no Islam being taught to our black children by these so-called black mothers because then this evil and most deadly Matriarch Wickedness, will not exist amongst us and the male children Right Of Passage, would happen accordingly without any interference. Also, the Scars Of Battle from this Evil

Matriarch Rule System, will come to an end; this will restore the black male children back to their rightful position in life.

It is a shame that I must say these things but what I am saying is the truth and everyone must examine, the cause and the effect of what is happening amongst our people. Homosexuality has become an epidemic amongst black people in America. Homelessness amongst our black male children has reach epidemic proportions. Substance abuse has become a way of life amongst our youth and this American and European Imperialistic Governments, cannot do anything about it? The longer we keep believing in this Imperialistic American and European the worst things will get for ourselves. You must begin to understand my people this is all by designed by our enemies, to prevent us from ever rising as a people; take control over control over our own money system, the production of our own currency and banking system; we will continue to be slaves to our enemies; this Zionist control American and European Imperialistic Multi Head Demon name Goliath. Thus, preventing our black children their Right Of Passage and all they will be left with is the Scars Of Battle.

Look at the latest explosion in Harlem On Adam Clayton Power Blvd where six people lost their lives and hundreds of black people, have been uprooted as our enemies once again manufacture lies: when it is really nothing but out right murder. The question we must ask is who profits off these murderous deeds and who suffers from these murderous deeds? If we my people we continue to submit to this Zionist implemented Matriarch System, our black male children will never have their Right Of Passage of governing themselves and will only receive many Scars of Battle. Under this Matriarch System in which black male children are raised, they will never become the Kings, Emperors, Sultans, and rulers as they once were. Any black male child that resists this evil Matriarch System is consider evil, posed by the devil, treated very badly by the mothers and in many cases taken by their mothers to the enemies and given medications, that will throw them of balance for life.

These medications are designed by our Zionist enemies to make sure these black males remain under the influence, of this evil Matriarch System and will never seek out their Right Of Passage; thus, Killing The Black Baby At Birth. The young black girls are affected also because they believe this evil Matriarch System is correct and when they have children, they sub-consciously fall into murdering and hating their male black children, that resist this evil Matriarch System. All black male children that overcome this evil will have plenty of Scars Of Battle and will have earned, their Right Of Passage. This is the Enforcement Of Our Will my brothers and sons and this is the reason why we must Enforce Our Will, so that we can take control over our own destiny. We must begin to get our male children into engineering of every kind for us black people, to build our own world physically. We must direct our children into proper banking and the minting and printing of our own currency as well. We must educate our black male and female children the importance of controlling the resources, under our feet.

We must reject this evil Matriarch System black people because it was given to us and is one of the rules and regulations of Yakub, to Murder The Black Baby At Birth, which is not mention in the 28th degree. The controlling of our resources the minting and printing of our own currency is another one of Yakub's rule and regulation that is not mention, in the 28th degree. This why the Holy Messenger of Allah the Most Honorable Elijah Muhammad, stressed upon us to get some land, that we can call our own. Therefore, the Holy Apostle taught us that our unity is the key, to our salvation as a people. This evil Matriarch System was implemented amongst us to make sure that we never have unity, amongst black people especially black male children. We are not at war with black women we are at war with this evil, wicket Matriarch System that has been super- imposed upon black people and especially black women. This evil, wicket Matriarch System has purposely caused a separation amongst and between, black male and black female. This separation amongst and between black male and black female has caused the destruction, of black families and our people.

As painful as this maybe it is the truth and this most deadly, evil and wicket Caucasian Zionist Matriarch System, must forever be abolished amongst black people in America and throughout the world. If we stay divided my people our enemies will bring us into the fires of Allah, right with themselves. If we continue this path of destruction and allow this Evil, Deadly and Most Wicket Caucasian Zionist Matriarch System, to continue to rule us, we will and are condemned by Allah. All one must do is look around us and examine what has happen since the deviation in 1975 and what is happening today. Our Enemies Have and are Enforcing Their Will Upon US; When Will We Enforce Our Will Upon Ourselves and Our Enemies?

It is a shame that black male children must have so many Scars Of Battle to obtain that which is naturally theirs, which is the Right Of Passage. How much longer as a people we are going to let this continue before we ourselves, do something about it? This is what we all should Read, the Message To The Black Man In America, The Fall Of America, How To Eat To Live Part1 And Part 2 And Our Savior Has Arrived; The Theology Of Time and all the other wonderful teachings, that Allah in the person of Master Fard

Muhammad, to whom all Holy praises are due forever, taught His last and greatest Messenger the Most Honorable Elijah Muhammad in which the Dear Holy Apostle taught us all, is absolutely a great thing to do. What will be even greater is the implementing and conducting ourselves as the Holy Messenger, taught us all for forty years and let us unite and do something for ourselves, as a Nation Of Black People.

CHAPTER 7

THE PATRIARCH

This chapter is particularly important to every original man and family not only in America, but throughout the world. Every, since we all have fell under the rule of our enemies approximately five hundred years ago and brought to the western hemisphere the Patriarch of black families, which has existed for trillions of years amongst the original people, has been destroyed by our enemies. Held in Chattel Slavery here in North America for three hundred long years and another hundred years in mental and spiritual slavery, making a total of four hundred years, our language, our history, our sciences, our creative minds, our educational system, our economic system, our medical system, our agriculture system, our aqueduct's supply and return system, our way of life, our system of governing ourselves and our unity, were all taken away from us and replaced with a most dreadful, non-productive system for black men, black families and black people all throughout the western hemisphere, we have ever known before in our entire history being on our planet. Long before Ibrahim, Yakub, to Musa, ESA Ibn Yusef and Muhammad Ibn Abdullah, were ever thought of.

This is what we all must understand is the destruction of the creative minds of the Patriarch, is what we all should be focusing on original man. We all should be focusing on the destruction and robbing from us the creative minds that have been taken away from us by our enemies, that in which we have been building great civilizations physically and the applied sciences we have been creating, for trillions of years; and by designed of our enemies the Zionist who control the Christians, Arabs and the Hindus, implement this evil, wicket and most deadly Matriarch System amongst original people in the western hemisphere and the eastern hemisphere; thus keeping the Spirit Of The Patriarch/Lion locked in a cage imprisoned for life, walking back and forth searching for the way out, of his four hundred years prison. My brothers Patriarch Our Savior Has Arrived in the person of Master Fard Muhammad, to whom all holy praises are due forever.

The Holy Messenger of Allah the Most Honorable Elijah Muhammad is the second self of Allah. Who was pregnant by Allah with a new thought, with a new mind, a new order of self-respect, a new set of parameters and with a New Islam; and this holy Messenger is referred to in scripture, as the Wonder In Heaven; He the Holy Messenger the Most Honorable Elijah Muhammad is referred to in scripture as the woman from Samaria, who came to the well to get some water, there she met a stranger who had a story to tell; that woman {the second self-} dropped her picture her drinking became richer; from the water He {Allah} gave her and it was not from the well. The Holy messenger was taught and educated by Allah for three years and four months and the water/ knowledge, wisdom and understanding; was all from the mind of Allah in person of Master Fard Muhammad to whom all holy praises, are due forever. This was the re-birth of the Patriarch System for black men in the western hemisphere and throughout the world, which was destroyed by these evil Zionist and re-placed with this most evil, wicket and most dreadful Matriarch System.

The Patriarch must once again rule amongst black people here in America and throughout the world. Until this natural order is re-established amongst black people, our destruction is certain. We black man must begin to Enforce Our Will once again as we did trillions and trillions of years before the birth of Yakub and his made people and his negative mind of thought. The Holy Messenger Of Allah has given us a very keen blueprint on what we must do re-establish the Patriarch System amongst ourselves, how we must do it and what it will take for us to do this. We must first have unity amongst ourselves my brothers and begin to work together, for one common cause. Different beliefs, ideologies and religions must be put to the side because the attack, is on us all. Our enemies must kill the black baby at birth the black baby represent Allah, The Patriarch.

We black men from every organization religious groups, political groups and social groups must come together, not for ideology discussions but for discussions on how we can build and economical machine, that will be beneficial for all black people in America and throughout the world. Organized and controlled by black men the Patriarch. We must not leave anyone out of this national and even international conference because all our lives and independence depend on our agreeing with each other in order to build this economical machinery, of the Patriarch. With this in place and with corporation from us all, we can then re-assert ourselves as the Patriarch and take back control, of our families, our people, and our destiny. One may ask who will finance such an operation Saladin?

The answer is simple we ourselves will finance this operation because this operation is for us, The Patriarch.

Black men coming together from all walks of life here in America and expanding it to our people throughout the world, will be nothing more than electrifying for the purpose of building for the Patriarch, an Economical Machinery for the Patriarch globally. We my brothers can no longer afford to allow this Zionist implemented evil and wicket Matriarch System, to rule over us any longer. Instead of producing soldiers under this evil matriarch system, this system is producing fools, cowards, criminals, homosexuals, and court jesters. Therefore, we the Patriarch must come together not only in America but throughout the world and we must build for ourselves, our own Economical Machinery. We must put to rest forever that black men in America are worthless and good for nothing. Therefore, we must all come together all black groups and organizations, must stand together rich and the poor, the educated and the uneducated we must all stand together, to prove to America and the world that this is not true at all. Through the unity of the Black Patriarch is where we then show not only in America that Black Lives Matter, but the entire world will see through the Black Patriarch Unified, that Black Lives Matter.

The Black Patriarch has many enemies without and none more dangerous than the matriarch enemies, within and amongst us; but we cannot allow any of this to prevent us, the Black Patriarch from rising to the top because we are the cream of the planet earth and father of all civilizations, so saith Allah. We must begin to Enforce Our Will because we are the Black Patriarch, that Zionist and Christian America have been walking on for nearly five hundred years and getting away with it. I say my fellow Black Patriarch the time has arrived that the Black Patriarch Must Rise and Enforce Our Will, on the entire planet. We must unify ourselves because we are the Black Patriarch in order that together, we can build for ourselves our own Economical Machinery, wherein we can then provide employment for ourselves and thus provide for ourselves and families. Other people are doing it and has done it so why can't we do it my brothers? The blueprint has already been shown and given to us by Allah through His Holy Messenger, the Most Honorable Elijah Muhammad.

Every black man in America is needed it does not matter what walk of life you may come from, it does not matter what your political views may be, it does not matter how educated or un-educated you may be, we are all needed. You may believe that you have nothing to offer or give, this is completely wrong my brothers. Your time, your involvement, corroboration, and your willingness to participate, is more precious than gold. The time has arrived for the Black Patriarch to assert himself in every phase, of this American existence. There is something everyone can help do to build our Economical Machinery, that will benefit us all, here in America and throughout the world. We must remember my black brothers that we are the Cream of the Planet Earth, Father of all Civilizations and God of the Universe; So Saith Allah Lord Of All The Worlds. We have no birth record; we have no beginning, and we have no ending. This is how old the Black Patriarch Rule is my black brothers, so it is time that we shake off this yoke made up by this Zionist Matriarch diminishment and re-establish the universal rights, of the Black Patriarch here in America and throughout the world.

So, I am saying we should have a state and local conference in every state, city, and town amongst all Black Patriarchs; in these meetings there should be elected officials to represent every state, city, and town; to a National Conference of the Rise Of The Black Patriarch; our objective is the Building Of An Economical Machinery for us all. If you are a black father or a black man, you are very much welcome to attend. This will not be a conference about religion or politics; this meeting will be about building, an Economical Machinery for us all and how to best approach this situation, for re-establishment of the Rise Of The Black Patriarch Rule, Nationally and Internationally. We all must remember that the Black Patriarch Rule have been only interrupted for nearly five hundred years which is nothing in accordance with our time on this planet, so why don't we unite ourselves and re-establish our Universal Rights of the Black Patriarch Rule?

We are kept in check due to us not uniting and building our own Black Patriarch Rule Economical Machinery, whereas we can create jobs and industries for ourselves and young black men, absent of this Zionist evil matriarch system that we all have been living under and our black male children are being abuse by it today and force to live under its evil and most deadly rule. By us working together collectively we can buy our own land and build our town or city; police and govern it ourselves whereas this Zionist Evil Matriarch System will never be allowed amongst us. This way we save both our sons and our daughters from this evil rule of our enemies.

Before being kidnapped and brought to the western hemisphere, we lived together, traded with each other without any problems because the Black Patriarch Rule was always in affect. For us to once again to set everything back into its proper order, the Black Patriarch Rule must be re-established amongst ourselves and our people, this is the natural order of things my brothers. All organizations religious and political should have at least two representatives at the National Level to represent themselves, as we galvanize ourselves into one body; our objective: The Building Of Our Economical Machinery, Nationally and Internationally for the Black Patriarch Rule Once Again.

We my brothers will face major opposition here in America because America believes and practice, Yakub's 28th degree, which is to kill the black baby at birth. The main weapon at America's disposal is that many ignorant black women and mothers, have truly embrace this evil, wicket and most deadly Zionist concocted Matriarch Rule System for black people. Thus, begin the murdering of black babies all throughout America, with impunity granted from this evil, wicket and most deadly Zionist Matriarch System. The only way we can put an end, of the murdering of our black sons and ourselves, is that we must bring back amongst us the Black Patriarch Rule System, of our Honorable and Noble Ancestors.

These ignorant black mothers that have submitted to this Zionist Concocted Evil, most wicket, and deadly Matriarch System and at least ninety percent has; has the same chance of raising a Black God, as the Moon has in drawing the waters back to her, it cannot be done ever; So Saith Allah. Therefore, we must black man re-instate the Black Patriarch Rule amongst us because our sons, women, and daughters, are being denied the light of the Sun and Son. Due to this Zionist Concocted Evil, Wicket and Most Deadly Matriarch Rule System, for all black people and that system teaches these ignorant, most foolish so-called black women and black mothers, to murder the Black Baby At Birth and many of these ignorant mothers do not even know what they are doing.

I sit here today giving all praises to Allah for visiting us in the person of Master Fard Muhammad and raising up from amongst us His last and greatest Messenger the Most Honorable Elijah Muhammad, who have educated me and open my eyes, to be able to write what I am writing Allah -U-Akbar there is none worthy to be serve besides these. You can examine history and you will find the Black Patriarch Rule System has always been our way of life and you cannot find a beginning to this and you will never find an ending to this because this is directly from Allah the Universal Creator. The reason why we are all out of whack is due to this Zionist Evil, Wicket and Most Deadly Matriarch Rule System, that has brought nothing more than death, disease, suffering and misery, to and amongst black people, for approximately five hundred years. I heard this most ignorant and foolish half original women call the fathers of her children Donors. She is so ignorant she does not even know what she is saying and has said about herself. This is a shame my brothers a crying down right shame, that these foolish mothers can be so ignorant. I understand why the prophets of old hair turned white and begged Allah, to show them no more on what things will be like, in the future because it was nothing more than horror and ignorance, after horror and ignorance, after horror and ignorance, until they could not take any more.

The Rule Of The Black Patriarch System must be re-implemented amongst black people in America and throughout the world, in order to put back the natural balance of the universe. With the makings of Yakub we have been on the negative side, of the equation of life and therefore Yakub only asked Allah the Universal Creator, for just six thousand years act as the Vicegerent {one who's wisdom and makings would rule for the next six thousand years and will be the God of this six thousand years} and his wisdom will only rule for six thousand years. This is when this Evil, Wicket and Most Deadly Matriarch System began amongst our people, in the Holy City of Mecca. After leaving the Island of Pelan and Yakub's Crew of Scientist brought their experiment amongst us, six hundred years later. It was Yakub's Making's that came amongst us spreading lies and deceit amongst us and this cause us to start fighting and killing each other, which in trillions and trillions of years, never happened amongst us before. The Rule of the Vicegerent had begun, to kick in right then. Once we recognized the problem and who was the cause of these problems, we ran them across the Hot Arabian Desert {now known as the Sahara Desert} into the Caves Sides which is now known as Europe; in which the Crew of Scientist of Yakub and Yakub's Makings, spent the next six thousand years. During this time, the women in the Holy city Mecca Hid the Devil Under Her Skirt. Yakub's makings remained in the Cave Sides of Europe for the next two thousand years, until the coming of Musa who set them free and back on their course.

It's very important my brothers that we all understand this history because the chief and leaders of our six thousand years old enemies the Zionist, surely do and they are using this history to their advantage; that the black woman can easily be led into the wrong direction and use as a weapon, to help them to try and Destroy The Black Patriarch Rule; and for the past nearly five hundred years our enemies have been successful and more successful in the past fifty years, up till this very day and time. The Black Patriarch Rule Must Rise My Brothers we have no other choice because the objective of our enemies for the past six thousand years, is to kill the Black Baby At Birth and the Black Baby my brothers in this day and time, is the Rise Of The Black Patriarch Rule System and this is the New

Islam, for the time in which we are now living in; and ninety percent of these foolish, ignorant black women and mothers are feeding our children to the Cremators {hospitals} and sticking pins {lies} into the heads of the black male children} at alarming and wholesale levels.

This truth that I am revealing we all know that it is the truth, but no one will reveal it publicly, so Allah has chosen me to do so. The Rise Of The Black Patriarch Rule System cannot be stop or adverted because this is the time for us to rise, my brothers; so saith Allah Almighty through the mouth of His last and greatest Messenger. This Zionist Matriarch Rule System amongst black people must be destroy, forever amongst us. When these Zionist started the NAACP contrived by the Rothschilds in America, black people here in America to cause black people to so-called up rise against the government, this was a smoke screen for the Rothschilds and their regime to set up their Federal Reserve Bank thus controlling the printing and minting, of America's Currency; but there was another plan of the Rothschilds and the Rothschild Regime and this was to begin instituting their Zionist evil, wicket and deadly Matriarch System amongst Black People in America. To do this portion or phase of this plan the Rothschild Regime recruited two people Ida B. Wells and W.E.B. DuBois, to help them to implement their most evil, wicket and most deadly Matriarch Rule System Amongst Black People in America. Examine the history my people it is all there. Thus, the Zionist Rothschilds and their murdering Regime, installed their agents' the doctor and the nurse amongst us to begin Killing of the Black Babies at Birth and implementing this most evil, wicket and most deadly Matriarch Rule System, in which they were guaranteed to kill off the Rule Of Black Patriarch. We can see the results of diabolical plan in the times, in which we are now living. Just examine the history my brothers it is all there therefore W.E.B. DuBois was, so adamantly against the Honorable Booker T. Washington and his self-help programs at Tuskegee Institute In Alabama, for black men because his end Ida B. Wells masters the Rothschilds and their Regime, was against what the Honorable Booker T. Washington, was doing for his people. This is all a matter of history my people just examine it yourself.

The Black Patriarch Rule System Must Rise My Brothers because the time is now. This explain why our brother and Prophet Noble Drew Ali was murder because Prophet Noble Drew Ali was in direct conflict with the agents of the Rothschilds, the Rothschilds Regime and the Rothschilds Agents W.E.B. DuBois and Ida B. Wells as he was teaching that Allah is god and was counter acting this Matriarch Rule System amongst black people and also the Rothschilds and the Rothschilds Regime, were already planning to involve America in World War 1 and they needed black men, to continue to believe in this dirty religion Christianity and Caucasian Jesus Christ, in which W.E.B. Dubois and Ida B. Wells were committed to and doing everything in their power, to keep black people believing in these Zionist lies. So, the decision to murder the Prophet Noble Drew Ali and break up his organization, was issued by the Rothschilds and the Rothschild Regime, here in America; so that black men can be used to fight against Germany in World War 1. Now the agents of the Rothschilds and the Rothschild Regime in, America headed up by J.P. Morgan, John D. Rockefeller, and the Warburg's. Now with Prophet Noble Drew Ali being murdered his organization broken up the agents of Negro Agents W.E.B. DuBois and Ida B. Wells servants of the Rothschild and the Rothschilds Regime in America, were free to spread the lies amongst black people once again without any interference, from Prophet Noble Drew Ali {May The Peace And Blessing Of Allah Forever Be Upon Him} amongst black people and get black men ready for World War 1, which was surely on the way. This is all a matter of history my brothers. The Rothschilds and the Rothschilds Regime could not have any possible risk of their major plan, which was to size all control over the wealth of America, the printing and minting of all America's Currency and establishing of their Central Bank, called the Federal Reserve's Bank.

The destruction of Black Wall Street, the death of the Honorable Booker T. Washington, the murder of Prophet Noble Drew Ali and other events like the 1907 crash as well; all accrued around the same time when the Rothschilds and the Rothschilds Regime was trying to set up their privately own bank the Federal Reserve's Bank, the League of Nations, the implementing of the Matriarch Rule System amongst Black People and starting of World War 1. This all a matter of history my brothers that can be researched at any time. The Rothschilds and the Rothschilds Regime could not allow any black own town with their own banking system to exist and therefore all these black own towns and Black Wall Street was destroyed because they all had their own banking system and were doing very well when Caucasian People throughout America, were starving, so they all had to be removed and never be allowed to be re-built. It was ignorant hateful, envious Christian Caucasian People who carried out the actual murders, burnings, lynching's, and rapes; but the orders came down from the Rothschilds and the Rothschilds Regime; the Destruction Of The Black Patriarch Rule System for black people, in the beginning of the 20th century. In my first book Saladin America's Indictment in the Bibliography section, I give a host of listing where this information can be obtained.

When you examine the history carefully and closely you will begin to understand what I am saying is the truth and you will agree with me, that this is the truth. There is not any doubt my brothers the Rise Of The Black Patriarch Rule must be brought forward, by us my brothers. This filthy way of life and atmosphere of this evil, dreadful, and evil Matriarch Rule must be destroyed and never to ever, rise amongst black people again. Every time a black man has an idea to do something for himself, you will find these so-called black women who honestly believe and are great supporters of this evil, wicket and dreadful Matriarch Rule System and are part of this evil diabolical system, of killing the Black Baby at birth. At least Eighty-five to Ninety percent of these so-called black women believe in our enemies and will do and have done everything in their power, to keep Yakub's Law On Birth Control in full effect. The Rise Of The Black Patriarch Rule System must at all cost, be put back in total affect.

I have been taught by the last and greatest Messenger of Allah the Most Honorable Elijah Muhammad the true and only, Muhammad RasulAllah not to go to war against anyone, who believes other than you; but if attack fight to the death to defend what Allah has given you. This means I am not challenging anyone's belief I have respect for this, but if you challenge my belief, f I will bring the hammer of justice upon you by Allah's permission upon you; and grind you into dust. Our goal collectedly is the Rise Of The Black Patriarch Rule System and this should be all our objective and nothing else.

We must my brothers turn to each other because there is not anyone else to turn to but ourselves. We must be able to guide our sons not only into what knowledge they must obtain, but how they must obtain this knowledge and what and how, they must use this knowledge they have obtained, to build a new civilization for ourselves. Any man that sees himself is a fool and this a person at all cost, must be avoided, by our sons. These fools will lead our sons to destruction or back on the plantation, which is a faith worse than death. These fools are not hard to spot just listen to them they always reveal themselves because they are not interested, in building a civilization for themselves. These fools do not even know what to do or ask for when they are at the store, these fools are only concern with taking pictures and posting them on social media and in truth they have not done anything, of use for our people.

So, this ignorant foolish mentality is no longer acceptable or beneficial amongst black men and for the Rise Of Black Patriarch Rule System. We must be strong my brothers and we must be dedicated to our cause and we cannot allow any fool to interrupted nor get in our way. Our lives our sons' lives are at stake we must stand united on this because this is the reason why, black men and black people are so off balance and out of place because we are living under this evil, wicked most dreadful Matriarch Rule System. We must my brothers begin to guide our sons into the technical and engineering knowledge that we all need, into re-building our black civilization. These clowns you can find these fools on social media, posting their ridicules pictures and more against the Rise Of The Black Patriarch System, than anyone else besides this evil, wicked, and most dreadful Matriarch Rule System.

This is very extremely serious business for every black man and male child in America and throughout the world. Remember my brothers it is murder the black baby at birth and we are that black baby my brothers. We must rise black man shake off the foolishness that we all have been involved in, for nearly the past five hundred years and since the coming of Allah in the person of Master Fard

Muhammad to whom all holy praises are due forever; and since Allah's last and greatest Messenger the Most Honorable Elijah Muhammad, this evil, wicked and most dreadful Matriarch Rule System and this American and European Imperialistic Government, have increased the attack om the black man and the Black Patriarch Rule System. In fact, since the Holy Messenger of Allah has left us in 1975 the black man in America situation, has become extremely grave, for us all.

We are fighting for our lives black men against a government and system that has been designed, for the destruction of black men and black men are standing back conducting themselves, as fools. Black men are acting like they have accomplished something when in truth, they have not accomplished a damn thing. Still at the mercy of our enemies and dare say they have supreme wisdom this is a disgrace and an abomination in the eyes of Allah and Allah's last and greatest Messenger. The truth must be told my brothers, and someone must tell the truth, as and for what the truth really is, regardless of whom or what and whom it may offends.

This is a subject that every black man throughout America should be interested in and want to be involve in a part of. Young black men acting and doing totally insane acts because they are tire of this evil, wicked, and most dreadful, Matriarch System. Yet since they do not have the correct knowledge of themselves nor do they have any true organization to reach to, these young black men have resorted to insane acts, that hurt all black men in America and give strength to the Matriarch System. This is all by designed black men by this American Government backed Matriarch Evil System.

You so-called black men that are on the side of this evil Matriarch System are nothing but a disgrace, to your grandfathers, fathers and to yourself. Any so-called black man that does not know how to mind their own business as they interject into another man's business and working as an agent for this evil Matriarch System, is a disgrace to all black man hood. Any black man that could not manage his own affairs and dare believe he has the right, to give advice to younger black men, as he is on the side of the Matriarch Evil System, you are a disgrace to all black man hood. Any black man that would surrender their Black Patriarch Rule, for this evil, wicked, and most dreadful Matriarch Rule System, is nothing more than a worthless coward and a disgrace to their grandfathers, fathers, black man hood and themselves. You cowards instead of working on the Rise Of The Black Patriarch Rule System, these disgraceful cowards are helping these Matriarch evil spiders try, to destroy black men at birth.

The Rise Of The Black Patriarch Rule System must happen black men our very lives and the lives of our sons, hang in the balance. This insane Spider in Michigan has tried to tell my son, he should not have any loyalty to his father and mother; he should have loyalty to her, and he has absolutely no history with her and the minute of history he has with her, has been a complete an absolute living hell. This evil, wicked, and most dreadful Matriarch Rule System must forever be destroyed amongst black people; and fat obese evil, wicked Matriarch women like the one in Michigan, must be destroyed and never, ever allowed amongst black people. We must keep our sons from out of these evil demons, control because these evil demons like this one in Michigan, will surely deliverer them to the cremators, as they have been doing for the past sixty-six hundred years.

All black men should see and understand the necessity of the Rise Of The Black Rule Patriarch System because it is most surely needed, amongst black males. Evil and my brothers I mean truly evil negro/colored women calling themselves all kind of things and these evil spiders are doing everything in their power, to teach young black men to hate their fathers and themselves and to love and worship them and this evil, wicked, and most dreadful Matriarch System. This evil Demon in Michigan is not Islam although she uses the teachings of the Jesus, to shield her dirty and filthy religion, which is nothing more than Christianity, whereas she tells lies, steal and causing trouble amongst original black people and especially black fathers and sons.

Here is something else my brothers we all must remember and be aware of; we have many so-called brothers amongst us pretending to be and in truth these cowards are our enemies. I had this simple Negro calling himself a high god when in truth, he is truly stupid; calling my wife when he believed my back was turned. What this ignorant fool did not realize is that my wife Zenobia is a woman of honor, a woman of integrity, a woman with respect for herself and myself and a woman that is able to recognize, the snake in the garden and was not able to be fool, by this clownish, ignorant, foolish idiot. This same snake deceived my son and tried to use my son, against me which failed also and this snake dear call himself an FOI. We must be careful of these enemies that are amongst us and are working with our enemies, to destroy their people, for a few pieces of silver.

Any fool who sees themselves is an enemy to and of the Rise Of The Black Patriarch Rule. My brothers we cannot have these fools around us because they will always betray us all, for their own selfish petty and worthless selves. These fools are not hard to uncover because they relish in talking about themselves, referring to themselves as positions of importance when in truth, they are worthless cut-throats amongst their people. These are the fools, male and female that are using the Jesus name, to shield the dirty religion Christianity. These ignorant idiots cause more harm amongst black people than they do good. These fools always dress up like the court jesters that they are and always want to be recognized, when in truth they are afraid to stand up in public, for Allah and Allah's last and greatest Messenger. This mentality we cannot ever have amongst the Rise Of The Black Patriarch Rule because they are not truthful, nor can they be trusted.

I personally had one of these clowns tried to under mind me and this fool calling himself a high god, tried to use lies to confuse and trick my wife, so that he could rob her and dear believe he could replace me. We must be incredibly careful my brothers because these untruthful cowards, are the enemies to the Rise of us all. Also, these cowards have been around and are in many cases are around us only to gather information, for our enemies.

We must my brothers beware of all our enemies because they are hiding amongst us, feeding others who are against the Rise Of The Black Patriarch Rule information on and about everything we do and planned to do. Many have been fooled and deceived by these traitors and many are still being fooled by these traitors therefore we all must pay close attention, to the language these cowardly traitors use, and this includes their style of dress. We cannot afford any treachery amongst us at all and these complete fools with their extremely limited knowledge, wisdom also extremely limited understanding amongst us, we just cannot my brothers of sincerity and not these make-believe clowns and their court jesters costumes, they all ware.

The Rise Of The Black Patriarch Rule my brothers is the Rise Of The New Islam, that Our Holy Savior Allah Almighty, in the person of Master Fard Muhammad; to whom all holy praises are due forever, taught the last and greatest Messenger the Most Honorable Elijah Muhammad, has taught us all if you truly paid attention, through Allah's last and greatest Messenger lectures. This is the New Islam that will take Jerusalem, from the devil. I know of this hypercritic fool who is in love with himself, on Facebook saying that mind your own business when it comes, to a couple personal business. Yet this same hypercritic fool, tried to deceive this so-called sister I was dealing with, with lies and deceit against me; believing that he could move in and take my place. This complete fool and his weak knowledge and wisdom could not fool the so-called sister at all, and she told me everything this grafted snake. These are the traitors we must rule out from amongst us and dealt with Supreme Justice and these snakes will never raise their evil heads against the Rise Of The Black Patriarch Rule, ever again. This so-called sister had proven to be the enemy of the Rise Of The Black Patriarch Rule and a true servant and believer of this evil, wicked, and dreadful Zionist American and European Imperialistic, Matriarch System as well.

Understand this my brothers in our rise there must be discipline, there must be rules, laws and regulations and there must be a uniform code, of dress. This is recognized by all civilized cultures and people throughout the world and universe. Clown court jesters' colors and clothing is not acceptable at any time and self-proclamation of one's self is never acceptable because this selfish mentality, will be the destruction of us all and this language must be rooted out for the Rise Of The Black Patriarch Rule because these fools will destroy us all; therefore, keeping Yakub's making and Yakub's wisdom of deceit and lies, to continue to rule all black men in America and European Imperialistic Society, throughout the world.

We must rise black men AL throughout America and realize

if they get me today, our enemies will get you tomorrow and there will be absolutely anyone, to avenge us, at all. So, this means we must stand ready to protect and defend ourselves, from all enemies amongst us. The ones amongst us are more dangerous than all our many enemies because they know our language and in truth, they are snakes and their nature, is of the grafted type. These are the ones that are using the Jesus name, to shield their dirty religion and these cowards are hiding amongst us and have a many of us tricked and fooled. These ignorant, silly cowards care nothing about the mass of us my brothers, they only care about themselves and how much money they can make, off all of us. You can spot them as I said previously by their language of self-proclamation and their clown colors and clothing. I do know some here in New York by Name and these silly cowards know I know who they are, by name. I also know these selfish cowards have fooled and tricked many, amongst us for the adoration of the enemies, of the Rise Of The Black Patriarch Rule and The New Islam; that Allah Almighty Himself Has Given To Us All, Through The Mouth Of His Allah Last and Greatest Messenger, The Most Honorable Elijah Muhammad.

The Rise Of The Black Patriarch Rule System is imperative my brothers and we can no longer allow ourselves, to be fooled by these fools who have been incorporated by our Zionist and Arab enemies. There is this one idiot fool who gave the exanimation of Kareem to a Zionist lawyer and is so stupid to believe, that this lawyer is his son. The truth my brothers is this simple-minded fool who dear call himself high priest, is truly working for the enemies of Allah and Allah's last and greatest Messenger the Most Honorable Elijah Muhammad.

The Rise Of The Black Patriarch Rule System Must Come into

existence, for the sake of all black men, young and old as well. We have plenty of enemies working against us and this we must be aware and conscious of all the enemies of the Rise Of The Black Patriarch Rule System These silly ignorant fools haven't a clue on the teachings that our Holy Savior Allah Taught His Holy Messenger the Most Honorable Elijah Muhammad, if they did or do then they would know that Allah came to restore, the Black Patriarch Rule System and if anyone with any understanding, can see this because Islam begins with the male and ends with the male; and there will never be an ending to the black man and black people.

So, my brothers and black people we must understand that we all have been living under the evilest Zionist Matriarch Rule System, designed to destroyed not only black men but all black people, in and throughout America and the world. Once you understand our history you will be able to see and understand how evil this Zionist Matriarch System is and has been a very instrumental component, of the destruction of the black civilization not only in Imperialistic America, but throughout the world, has been and continue to be.

As I write these writings at this present day and time, I give all my thanks and praises to our Holy Savior Allah Almighty, for blessing me with my wife and Queen, Zenobia because she is the only ease and comfort I have and I love, need and apricate her sincerely and her love for me, is truly prophetic. Nevertheless, the Rise Of The Black Patriarch Rule must take president, over all things is the New Islam for all black men in America and throughout the world, that we all must submit to, in order to save us all, our women and children included.

To convince impressionable, un-learned children and take advantage of their lack of knowledge of themselves and their enemies, is a crime punishable by death. These self-proclamation fools that are amongst black people today, are more dangerous, poisonous than any machine gun, cannon, or missile, for black people, than any weapons our enemies can launch against us all. The Rise Of The Black Patriarch Rule System is a necessity for all black men, in America and throughout the world. Knowing our history that has been kept from us all, for the past approximately five hundred years, is crucial to us all. It was doing the beginning of this past approximately five hundred years, our language, our sciences, our history, our way of life, our love unity and love for ourselves, were taken away from us all by our open and most dangerous enemies. This was the beginning of the end of the Black Patriarch Rule System and the beginning of the this most evil, most wicked, and extremely deadly Matriarch Rule System, which is an abomination in the eyes of Allah Himself, all of Allah's Prophets including Allah's last and greatest Messenger.

We must rally together my brothers and all black men in America and throughout the world, it is time we present to our many enemies that we the Black Original Man, is willing to give our lives to shake off and destroy this evil Matriarch System, from amongst us forever. Let us all black man in America and throughout the world stand together in unity and reclaim, our original position in this world and on our planet. It is important that we all understand that this the time and we are all willing, to do whatever we all must do, for The Rise Of The Black Patriarch Rule System. This is the New Islam brought to us By Allah Almighty Himself in the person of Master W.F. Muhammad, to whom all holy praises are due forever. These are the teachings that Allah Almighty Taught His last and greatest Messenger, the Most Honorable Elijah Muhammad, who in turn taught us all, who were able to understand the Holy Messenger teachings and only five percent could utterly understand, the Message from Allah Almighty through the mouth of Allah's last and greatest Messenger.

So, the time has arrived were the truly believers in Allah and Allah's last, greatest and Holy Messenger. We must galvanize ourselves together as one; and stand up united for the Rise Of The Black Patriarch Rule System in America and throughout the world.

CHAPTER 8

THE TRENCHES

This chapter is not for the weak or the un-faithful because it will be dealing with surviving, a great ordeal and what one may have to do, to survive this ordeal. One must understand that when you are the in the Trenches you are at war against an enemy/enemy's that are profoundly serious, about destroying you and this you must be aware of. Once you are placed or forced into this position you must dig in and prepare yourself for the enemy attack. The enemy will attack with confidence believing that they have the advantage and their hatred for you because you will not bow down to them, drives these fools on; what our enemies do not realize is that while they recklessly pursuing you/us, they are weakling themselves and beginning to make errors; therefore, leaving room for counterattack. Therefore, understanding how to operate in the trenches is especially important, how to survive in the trenches is particularly important and how to establish allies is especially important. A wise man or person must understand that you must keep your composer under these circumstances, is extremely important and must be embraced always.

War is war and one must know when to retreat and how to retreat from all and any enemy. Any time you are faced with an enemy it does not matter who the enemy maybe, you must be ready physically, spiritually, and mentally to protect and defend yourself. When this happen or if happens one may find themselves having to retreat, into the Trenches. In order to survive one must understand what they must physically have to sacrifice and what is not important as it may seem. This will be and is a very extremely tuff time in one's life emotionally, spiritually, physically, and financially for all who must endure this trial.

These trenches are quite different from being in the trenches of physical combat because in physical combat, one knows who the enemy is and the many weapons that are can and will be used against them. Physical combat under fire has my total and entire respect. Many of these combat soldiers that survive this physical combat and trenches, when they come home many do not know how to survive this type of war and have not been trained, on these knew trenches they must use, to survive The enemy my brothers and people are this Zionist Matriarch Rule System and eighty-five to ninety percent of all black women in Imperialistic America, have embraced. Under this Matriarch System the woman can steal from men, lie on men, be very abusive to men and men are supposed to just take. Especially if you move into their so-called homes this arrangement will last only, a short time before she will call the police, to have you remove and the police will do just that. When you try and take everything that you put or brought into their home, the police will stop you from claiming that which is yours.

Now when this happen to many men, they are devastated and become dis-enchanted and do not know what to do next. The reason why is because he believes that he lost everything and she took it all, from him. So many heartbroken men take to alcohol and drugs, trying cope with this betrayal from the one he cared about. So now you have nowhere to go and these demons have all, of your possessions and found another sucker, to do it all over again. This Matriarch System has destroyed many men not only in America but throughout the world. My brothers and people this Matriarch System are designed to destroy not only black men, but men in general.

So, once you have found yourself face or in this situation you must understand that this the time, that you must dig in and fall into the trenches in order to survive, the attacks from your Matriarch enemies. My brothers this is the evilest system made by Yakub's making empowering ignorant, hateful, and spiteful negress slaves, to love their Caucasian male masters and fashion themselves after their female mistress. This is history my people and brothers so we must be strong my brothers, in the trenches and understand and except who, your enemy/enemies are. Understand this my people this Zionist evil Matriarch System is only embrace by Negro women, who desire to aid the enemies, of their people to murder off strong and positive, black men and all young black males and men, who rebels against this Zionist Matriarch Evil.

So, you are now engaged in a struggle for your spiritual, mental, and physical life and the only aid you will receive, is from your own resilience. You must realize that you are in the trenches fighting, for your very life against the ones, the enemies who are trying to deliver us all, into the hands of the Cremator. Once one understands what is happening and who are the ones responsible for his or in some cases her traumas, are the enemies we are all fighting against. So, one must understand that feeling sorry for one's self will accomplish absolutely nothing. What one must do is except what has happened, who is responsible and deal with the situation. These are the trenches and once you understand this, then you can begin to defeat your and my enemies, from the trenches.

The trenches do not represent defeat the trenches represent a place and condition, to retreat and re-group one's self. It is from the trenches is where one will gather mental, spiritual, and physical strength, that will allow one to attack our enemies once again. The different is that you will have a greater understanding of the enemy and the means of attack, that your enemy/enemies have used and will use against you. The difference will be this my people, you will know your enemy well and their methods of attack; our enemy/enemies will not know our method of attacks and our enemy/enemies, will not know, or understand our resiliency, or our resolve. The trenches are nothing to feel sorry about my people, if one makes it back to the trenches, this one has a chance to re-turn again with great substance; thus, advantage belongs to us and not our enemy/enemies.

When one is I the trenches your conditions will not be or may not be as suitable to you, as you may like but from here you can re-group and flourish, to even greater heights; free of the deceitful person/persons that caused you to have to retreat, into the trenches. While in the trenches your enemy/enemies will begin a campaign of slander, lies and hatred because the enemy could not destroy you and you should not allow these cowards, to destroy you with their slander, lies and hate. While the enemy/enemies are wasting their energy in this matter, you begin to operate positively from the trenches. Re-building and re-strengthen yourself is and should be your only objective and nothing else. Make yourself a plan and then work you are plan, and you will be the victor because all the lies, slander and hate these Matriarch enemies have spread, will be their destruction.

Nevertheless, this all will be accomplished from understanding how to apply the science, of how to effectively use the trenches.

The trenches I am not going to deceive anyone is tuff and this is where you must reach deep into yourself because this is where and when the absolute best of yourself, will manifest what is truly in you. The trenches may not and in most cases will not be pretty in fact the trenches in most cases will be extremely hard, but it is here, where your best plans and execution of the plan, will take place. Most brothers and people will run from the chance to prove themselves and conformed, to the wishes of our enemies, before they risk it all for freedom, justice, and equality. I have personally seen these cowards crumble because they are not soldiers, they only pretend to be soldiers. To be a soldier you must be ready to prove yourself in the trenches, where what is inside of you will take you to greater heights, than what you have sacrifice.

Many have taken the easy way out and have conformed to this Zionist Matriarch System and has tried to lead others, under this evil system and are involved themselves into many evils. Keeping the mass of black men under this evil Matriarch System if they can be prosperous, others are just weak. This evil Matriarch System is designed to capture the very essence of black men, thus keeping you forever trapped, with no way out. You must be ready to denounce and fight against this evil and this will take everything within you. While in the trenches you must remember to focus on yourself and not anyone else or anyone else problems, dis-tract you from your objective. The hardship should and will strengthen you also make you completely aware, of those you can trust and depend on. These are the trenches my people that we are already in and many do not know it, nor do they care to know it. In fact, they run and hide from their sworn oath and these are the ones you must recognize and avoid.

Many become confuse and do not realize what they must do in order to survive, the circumstances, they are caught up in and many die in the trenches because they do not understand and have no-one to talk to and help them with understanding, of their present circumstances and in truth these supposed to bee's do not care about you. I am extremely happy that the Holy Messenger Of Allah, cared and was more dedicated than these so-called followers of his. If you are in a shelter you must understand that you, are in the trenches and you must turn to Allah our Holy Savior in the person of Master Fard Muhammad, to whom all praises are due forever; you should and must follow the last and greatest Messenger of Allah teachings, that the Messenger the Most Honorable Elijah Muhammad received from Allah. This will give you a great chance in your recovery and you are defeating our enemy/enemies and rising to back to rightful position in this society and throughout the planet.

Many of our black youth and men are stuck in the trenches from the attacks, of this evil American and European Imperialistic Matriarch System and they cannot figure out, what is going on or what to do. Many are having lost and are still losing their lives to this evil Matriarch System and stuck in these trenches, with absolutely no supplies or re-enforcement and no hope in sight. These are the trenches my people that we all must understand and must understand, what it takes to survive and overcome. You must my brothers and people realize that we are in the trenches and here is the time, in which we must dig in and get mentally, spiritually, and physically strong and tuff and we must let our enemy/enemies know that we have not been defeated and we still live to fight another day and always.

While one is in the trenches you must think, plan, and take advantage of every opportunity, at your disposal. Control your anger and rage; control your urge to seek vengeance, this will only lead to further destruction. You will archive greater vengeance when you re-obtain use-full producing skills and knowledge, this is what one must do while living in the trenches. One must also do away with emotional hate and regrets because this is also destructive, to you being able to overcome this set-back. While in the trenches one must re-main focus and determined to the objective and mission. No matter how hard the conditions maybe; no matter how gloomy the situation maybe; no matter how hopeless the situation may appear; these are the trenches, and these conditions are the conditions set forth, by our enemy/enemies.

While you are in the trenches my brother you must understand that this is the time, to re-build your self-esteem, your manhood and your belief, in yourself. You cannot do this by chasing behind or seeking help from these Matriarch women, this will only cause more harm to yourself. This is the reason in most cases that many black men, are in this dis-graceful position and if you do not recognize this, you will never overcome and rise from this hellish nightmare of this evil American and European Imperialistic Matriarch System.

The Rule Of The Black Patriarch Rule System and The Enforcement Of Our Will, will be established from the trenches, my brothers, and people. We are surrounded by our enemies and our enemy/enemies believe they are all powerful, but they are not my brothers and people. Seek refuge in our Holy Savior Allah Almighty In Person of Master Fard Muhammad, to whom all praises are due forever and follow the teachings and programs Allah taught to His Last and Greatest Messenger, the Most Honorable Elijah Muhammad and you will overcome our enemy/enemies. Never seek refuge in Zionism or Christianity because this is where this evil, of this evil American and European Imperialistic Matriarch Rule System; you will never gain your freedom; you will never have equality and you will never have justice, while you live.

The trenches my brothers and people will bring the best out of you if you use the trenches properly while you analyze the reason and situation, that led you here. The truth lies within oneself and you must examine and take responsibility, for what cause things to disengage. Also, while you are in the trenches take pre-cautions against feeling sorry for yourself and concentrate on re-building and improving yourself and condition. You must understand our enemy/enemies well and how they operate. Our enemy/enemies will use slander and manufacture lies against you, even spreading these lies amongst your family and close brothers and even sisters, even amongst the public on social media. When the enemy/enemies begin these absorb ridicules rantings, our enemy/enemies only expose themselves for the imposters, liars, and thieves they truly are.

While in the trenches remember and study the teachings that Allah Almighty taught to the last and greatest Messenger, the Most Honorable Elijah Muhammad. Read and remember our Holy Savior and remember Him much and always. Follow the teachings and programs that was taught to us by the Dear Holy Apostle. Do not allow the slander, lies and deceit of our enemy/enemies, to disturb you because they are truly liars and will be brought to naught by their own lies and hatred. You should speak with those who are alike in mind and spirit, for encouragement if you need so. Do not ever doubt my brothers and people our enemy/enemies, are the ones being destroy ad not you. The horrors that one may had experience being amongst the enemy/enemies, is a test of our faith. If you keep the faith there is not any doubt that you, will be the victor.

Learn to use the time you may have to spend in the trenches positively and turn this negative condition, into a positive condition. Do not waste time hating and cursing your enemy/enemies because I said before, the enemy/enemies own evil slanderous, lies, hatred, their evil hypocrite ways, have and are bringing about their own destruction. While in the trenches learn to love yourself, protect yourself, care for yourself and control your sexual desires for the opposite sex. These are the keys one must implement in order to survive and overcome the trials, of the trenches. Understand those who have fallen into the trenches and do not realize the discipline one need in the trenches, will and have been destroyed.

Social Media is a trap because there is much misinformation that exasperate your situation and not help to ameliorate, your situation. Keep others out of your personal business because in most cases, you will receive the wrong advice and will not serve a positive solution, in the re-building of one's spiritual self and one's personal self-esteem. While in the trenches one must concentrate totally on themselves and work on improving oneself and this cannot be accomplished, by outside interference that are not willing to help you, without being obligatory to any person. While in the trenches re- learn about yourself and re--learn about others, then and only then will you have a fighting chance, to recover from the spiritual, mental and in some cases, physical wounds.

The trenches are filled with many wallowing in self-pity and none has a clue, on how to get out of these trenches. This chapter is about what it takes to get out of the trenches and re-cover from whatever trauma, one had endured and suffered through and from. This chapter is about how to heal one's self and re-discipline one is self and re-formed one's self. This chapter is about how not to feel sorry for one is self and to believe in once again one's, own self. This chapter is about how to find one's self back home and where home is. This chapter is about not allowing yourself to wallow in self-pity and think about what one may have lost because in truth, one lost absolutely nothing. In truth one has only been set free from the demons, that in many cases have taken control of their mind, body, and soul and who these demons are; and believe me my brothers and people these demons are flesh and blood.

The trenches are filled with treacheries, deceit, lies and slander, from the enemy/enemies. You must understand these local demons are little demons wishing to become bigger demons, but these local demons are the servants, of this American and European Imperialistic Devilish Matriarch System. These demons many are using the Jesus name to shield their dirty religion, which is nothing more than Christianity as in the case of the fat spider and her little spiders, in Michigan and the spider in Philadelphia; and believe me there are plenty more, on the side this evil American and European Imperial Zionist Matriarch System.

This is what must be understood by all who must retreat into the trenches it most important to understand is that the trenches, are a spiritual, psychological, and physical condition and instead of creating a new avenue of healing and attacking, the fool believes that one can use the same approach to recover. Anyone who believe this foolishness is only fooling themselves and will never obtained the truth, of the trenches and will never survive the trials of the trenches. There are many who have not made it out of trenches and there are many who will not make it, out of the trenches and this is due to them not knowing what to do and how to survive, the trenches. Also wanting the wrong things for the wrong reasons, this is all negative energy and thoughts.

The trenches are filled with obstacles even disappointments and this should be expected, this is where you find out who is strong for real and who are the frauds, in a war like condition; and believe me this is war my brothers and people, the price for freedom is death and if you be afraid of death, then you have nothing to live for. While in the trenches keep your faith in Allah our Holy Savior the most merciful, the wisest, the most kind, in the person of Master Fard Muhammad, to whom all praises are due forever. Fear not these demons my brothers and people no matter how many lies they may be spreading; they are only revealing the evil truth of themselves. Be faithful to our Holy Savior Allah Almighty and follow the perfect example of Allah's last and greatest Messenger, the Most Honorable Elijah Muhammad and the new Islam that has been taught to us all, by the last Holy and greatest Messenger of Allah.

My brothers and people not only in America but throughout the world; seek refuge in the Lord Of Elijah Muhammad, we all have no other god but him. We are all in the trenches our enemy/ enemies this American and European Imperialistic Zionist designed Matriarch System and so are your righteous black woman. This Most Evil, Wicked, and most Deadly Zionist Designed Matriarch System, is out to destroy every positive, sincere, and truthful black woman in America and throughout the world. You to my righteous black sisters are in the trenches, right along with your brothers and you are different from the eighty-five to ninety-five Negro women, that are on the side of our enemy/enemies; to kill the black baby at birth.

CHAPTER 9

THE PATH OF THE ANOINTED

This chapter my people is about the true five and this day and time two percent, of the world that has been chosen, to do the real work and not this buffoonery by these pretenders claiming to be something, they will never be and cannot be. Do not fall victim to these clowns because no matter how they pretend to be chosen or anointed, believe me my people these fools are not. Their knowledge is extremely limited, their sincerity is even lest and they are not on the Road Of The Anointed. These are the pretenders and false so-called gods that will never put the work in, that it takes to aid in the rise of black people everywhere on our planet. In fact, these are the ones also using the Jesus name {our Holy Savior} to shield their dirty religion, Christianity.

The Road Of The Anointed is not for buffoons, pretenders, and these so-called gods because they are not real nor are, they are sincere because they are only concern, about themselves and their illusionary self-accomplishments, which are absolutely nothing. These phonies calling themselves so-called gods are only about petty gain, for themselves and belief that they are important. Pleasing the very enemy/enemies of our people in America and throughout the world, then dare call this friendship in walks of life. The Anointed must and has been chosen to walk a different path, then others because the Anointed are the ones that must put the work in, for all their people. Not only in America but throughout the world and against the enemies, of Allah, Allah's Messenger, Allah's Prophets and Allah's People.

The Road Of The Anointed is different than any other road because this is not a road for cowards and pretending that they believe. You will find that many believe that they care about you in truth, are afraid themselves and are not of the anointed. In order that improvement and change to happen it takes people to put their lives, on the line to save and help many of his or her own people. Many will tell the anointed to hide run do not tell the truth, about who is doing what because they themselves will not do it. Yet these same cowards will be the first in line, to reap the rewards from the work put in by the Anointed. The Anointed is predicted to come and their path has already been chosen for them before they were ever physically born. Run and hide because you could be killed is the path the Anointed must travel because the Anointed must reveal to the world, the enemy/enemies of black people and the methods our enemy/enemies uses and who these enemy/enemies are.

Cowards will never get involve helping to teach the mass of our people, no they lag as cowards do and even work on the side of our enemy/enemies, to murder the Anointed and shut down all inspiration, knowledge, wisdom and understanding, from reaching the mass of our black people. There are even real and true black women that have been Anointed and willing and putting their lives on the line, for our people. The Anointed will and are persecuted, imprison, hounded, and even be made by our enemy/enemies to be insane and troublemakers. As these cowards linger behind with all kind of cowardly excuses trying to defend, their noninvolvement. Telling the Anointed do not speak the truth, run, and hide, stop doing the righteous work and let someone else do it. I ask this question: who is the someone else that will do this work and face the persecution, imprisonment and even death? Where is this someone supposed to come from? Who will these someone is to be?

The someone is the ones putting their lives on the line for their people and have no fear, of the consequences that our enemy will bring upon the truth bearers. These someone is the ones revealing to our people and the world, the truth of these cowards that are robbing, lying, deceiving, and helping our enemy/enemies, to murder their own people the world over. We are living in the time of universal changes and the fall of Yakub's civilization and making's; so, during this time period the Anointed has already been written to come, to do a certain work and reveal the truth of the hypocrites that are using the Jesus name, to shield their dirty religion which is nothing but Christianity and trying to disguise it as Islam.

These silly ignorant fools are trying to pass themselves off as high society type with their cheap suits, pimp clothing, as they live in the ghettoes/hoods and can only speak four hundred words, barely well. These silly fools are so ignorant until they believe they have friendship, in all walks of life and they barely have friendship in the ghettoes/hoods they were born, raised, and breaded in all their lives because they can only speak four hundred words well barely. I can tell you my people these silly fools are not about nation building they are only about pocket building and the pockets they are concern with, is their own pocket and not yours. These fools are not the Anointed these fools are against the Anointed and against their own people and all black people.

Listening to people with fear in their hearts are equally useless as well because they also are looking for a payday and the Anointed are in the way of this payday. The Anointed have been sixteen thousand years before they were ever birth and this is the reason why when the Anointed are birth, they are birth with this determine purpose that is in them. The Path Of The Anointed can never be changed by anyone and yes, their lives are on the line every day, nevertheless the Anointed must and will walk the path that they He or She, have birth to walk. The insults from the fearful and those that hate the Anointed are great and sometime hurtful, nevertheless the Anointed must absorb this hate and insults from the disbelieving fearful and continue the path, they were birth to walk.

We have all been mis-led by lies and deceit and the religions of our enemy/enemies about the Angles, until we do not have any true understanding about who these Angles are. Thanks to Allah Almighty the wisest and the best and only knower of all things; in the person of Master Fard Muhammad to whom all praises, are due forever; through the mouth of Allah's last and greatest Messenger the Most Honorable Elijah Muhammad, I have been taught the truth about the Angles, the Angles my people are the Anointed and they are living and breathing beings. They live and walk around you daily and when the time comes, they will make their presence known and not before this time. These are the Anointed my people but due to the poisons of our enemies, you cannot recognize the Anointed and, in many cases, you might have known he or she all your life.

Do not he confuse or taken in by the charlatans using the teachings of Allah, taught to us by Allah's last and greatest Messenger the Most Honorable Elijah Muhammad. Do not he confuse or taken in by the court jester clothing these fools wear, the few pieces of silver they may have, the pictures they post in social media, presenting themselves, as they are successful. Do not he confuse or taken in at how they are able to deceive many and lead many of our people away, from the truth. Do not he confuse or taken in how these hypocrites sell and use the teachings, to rob you my people of your hard-earned money. Do not he confuse or taken in my people by these charlatans because you may think or believe, they are sincere, when in truth they are the deceitful. In fact, they are written in the Holy Quran-an as the lip-professors and when it comes time to risk everything for Allah and Allah's last and greatest Messenger, these cowards will run and hide under the nearest rock, they can find.

These cowards are not the Anointed and in truth, the enemies of the rise of black people in America and throughout the world. Do not he confuse or taken in by these cowards trying to play both sides of the fence, as they try and deceive the people. Of Allah Almighty and Allah's last and greatest Messenger. These charlatan hypocrites are using the Savior's teachings to shield their dirty religion which in truth, is Christianity. This includes males and females be incredibly careful of these charlatans' hypocrites, my people they are all around you and sometimes you may even be sleeping with them and have children with and by them.

The Anointed my people are the Angles of Allah and must not be confuse with the anointments of Yakub the Viceregent. You will be able to recognize the Anointed of Allah because they are willing, to sacrifice all that they own, all that is within their power, to help and save their people. Believe me my people the Anointed know the consequences of their actions and are not afraid of the consequences, of our enemy/enemies and in some cases death. Fear is for the cowards and these cowards will sell the Anointed out if they believe they are in jeopardy, or they can pick up a few pieces of silver from our enemies. The Anointed knows this as they begin their calling and work, amongst and for their people. What most of them is that they close their eyes and ignore the signs, that who the traitors are amongst them and how close these are to them.

The Anointed knows and understand that their sacrifice and their death, are for Allah and no associates has Allah. So, the Anointed operates knowing this but now the Anointed of the times in which we are now living, have a much clearer understanding of the times, the conditions, the enemies, the traitors, and haters amongst us are that are disguising themselves as brothers, sisters, believers, wives, husbands, fiancés, even children, friends, and family. The Anointed must understand their position and purpose, in their lifetime and do not make unnecessary enemies. Yet the Anointed will make enemies due to the mission and work, they must do for and amongst their people. The Anointed must always present what they say and teach backed up by facts and the Anointed must study many different things and histories; in order that they can be better equip and prepared.

The Anointed must understand that they must be in control of their emotions, in order to make wise decisions, not for themselves but for their people as well. One must understand never speak out against his people in public or to and amongst our enemies. The Anointed ones will always lister to anything that makes sense and pay no attention to foolishness. The Anointed will never carry themselves as a clown or a fool and will never spread gossip or slander, anyone that may disagree with them. The Anointed will only present facts and never about what they, may think or feel. The Anointed will give false information about anyone or anything because he or she will never confuse his or her people. The Anointed has a responsibility to his or her people and must always honor their word, but never should the Anointed put up with ungrateful and un-apricated and insults, from people that are trying to prevent or change what he or she, must do in their lifetime.

Life and death are what the Anointed live under and whereas others will run and hide, the Anointed will deal with it. The Anointed must always keep in mind that their birth is not by accident, their birth has been written in history and that knowledge has been revealed to us by Allah Almighty Himself, in the person of Master Fard Muhammad to whom all praises, are due forever, through the mouth of His last and greatest Messenger, the Most Honorable Elijah Muhammad. The Anointed must always keep prayer but what is most important is that the Anointed remember our Holy Savior and remember Him Much and always and follow the teachings that Allah's Holy Messenger taught us all; this is the only protection we have because we cannot run and hide from our enemies because they have eyes, ears, and spies everywhere. Yakub's civilization is falling my people but it has not fallen yet. The work and mission that the Anointed must do cannot be stop; but the Anointed must know and understand the limit of their mission and power.

The enemies know who you are, but you do not know who your enemies are and especially the hidden enemy/enemies, that are amongst you and may even be sleeping with you. The Anointed must never allow themselves to get caught up in silly, non-productive debates on social media, that only produces hate, dis-unity, and separation amongst us all. You must understand those who have been

Anointed that you can never allow your ego, to take control of your better judgement. This is a quite common mistake that the Anointed make and this will and has led to the death, of the Anointed in different time periods. The Anointed must study and study hard and long; also, the Anointed must pay attention to his or surroundings and the people he or she may and will encounter because the majority will deceive you and lead you to your demise.

You who have been Anointed and chosen must be incredibly careful; regarding the males you must be on your guard, from the deceitful believing Zionist Matriarch so-called black women. The tricks and deceit they use like their children, pretending to be black conscious and interested in Islam, when in truth they are not. They are only trying to sucker you back under the control, of this evil, wicked, and dreadful Zionist Matriarch System, which they these so-called black women are delivering the black babies, into the hands of the Cremator. These dis-believing women will use sex, deceit and lies without hesitation and when they discover that you will not fall victim to their lies and deceit, they will reveal the truth of themselves and you will see the demon as they truly are.

For the Anointed Females the must, be careful of the deceitful men that will be attracted to them. These men are no different than their deceitful sisters and will use the same lies, deceit, and tricks as their disbelieving sisters. Beware of the fast talk, promises and false dreams they bring because they have absolutely no intention, of ever fulfilling any of them. The fast and fancy cars, clothing and in some cases using the teachings of Allah, to deceive and miss-lead you. These liars filled with deceit will convince you that they are truthful, planet seeds in you and then leave you, caring for the seeds alone and therefore taking you away from your Anointment. Now you will only suffer the chastisement of Allah and will never fulfill your Anointment. Then you will live a life of suffering and shame and so will your children.

You must be ready to go under and through the trials of the Anointment and the Anointed. This is not easy because there are many obstacles one will encounter and they are extremely hard and only the truthful, only the chosen, only the true Anointed, will survive this ordeal. Be faithful until death and the crown of life is what one, will achieve. The crown of life my brothers and sisters are your Anointment and the proof, that you are the Anointed of Allah. The trials are extremely hard on the heart and mind and only the sincere of faith, will and can survive them. The Anointed is a special breed of man and woman they are not interested in their self needs, they are most concern about their people not only in America, but throughout the world. The Anointed are not interested in self-praise or the feebly offerings of this American and European Imperialistic Zionist Evil Matriarch System; or those who believe and serve this evil.

The Anointed are burden by so much confusion grafted teachings, false teachings mis-leading false leaders' confusion, confusion, distraction after and upon distraction, hatred upon hatred and not knowing who to trust and who can be trusted; due to the many that are using the Savior's name to shield their dirty religion, which is nothing more, than Christianity. This is what the Anointed must deal with every day of their lives. In truth my Anointed brothers and sisters the life of the Anointed is not an open life, like others and this is what makes the Anointed different than others. The Anointed does not have the pleasure of acting as a court jester and wearing silly clothing and in the meantime, trying to play both sides of the fence. These court jesters dance at the tunes of their masters for the crumbs, off their masters table. These silly fool's male and females are against the Anointed and the Anointed must keep their distance from them because they mean know good at all, to Allah and Allah's Holy Messenger, the Anointed, the Cause and the Rise Of The Black Nation Nationally and Internationally as well.

The Anointed must never doubt themselves these disappointments, pain, hurt, and suffering are part of the test no matter how much, it may hurt it is by Allah's will and neither you nor I can change, what Allah has ordained. This history has already been written before we and these court jesters, were even birth and we must fulfill the history that was written sixteen thousand years ago, before we were birth. All That is happening and will happen cannot be prevented, by anyone, any government, or these silly fools. The Holy Messenger of Allah told us that these Negroes will never rule and today if one has eyes and can see, these court jesters will never rule because in truth they are disbelieving cowards, males, and females. The rulers and owners of social media {the Zionist} see them as the fools they are and the nonsense the pictures and their post are harmless because the enemy/enemies own them all. These are not the Anointed these are the cowards that our enemies are using, against Allah, Allah's last and greatest Messenger, the Anointed and all black people on our planet.

These foolish idiots are so busy debating amongst themselves, arguing amongst themselves, telling lies about each other, spreading false rumors about each other, thinking and believing they are important with their silly you tube videos and silly pictures on social media, while the Arabs are stealing and claiming, the Bean Pie to be their creation; while these so call Veganism are stealing the teachings of How To Eat To Live and giving credit to one of the students, of the Holy Messenger Of Allah, as the creator and master teacher; as they ignore Allah Almighty our Holy, All Wise and Most Merciful Savior in the person of Master Fard Muhammad, to whom all praises are due forever; the founder and author of this awesome knowledge in which He Allah taught His last and greatest Messenger, the Most Honorable Elijah Muhammad.

All knowledge of Vegetarian and Veganism in the west hemisphere, comes from Allah Almighty our Holy Savior in which the Allah taught to His Holy Messenger the Most Honorable Elijah Muhammad and the Holy Messenger taught us all, in How To Eat To Live Book One and Book Two. The Entire western hemisphere and most of the eastern hemisphere were poison animal eaters and many still are, poison animal eaters; until Allah through the mouth of His Holy Messenger revealed to us all, How To Eat To Live. Yakub's civilization and makings except the Zionist, had absolutely no idea of proper foods to eat and the Zionist hid this from all mankind, their brothers, and sisters that which Muza had prescribe, for the ones who crawled out of the caves of Europe, not to eat the swine four thousand years ago. Therefore, Yakub's makings all of them were and many still are swine eaters and eat many vegetables not created or designed, for human consumption.

So, since these fools pretending and acting like the share cropping fools that they are and the scientists that wrote our history in advance for the next twenty-five thousand years, knew this in advance; and we are now living in the six-teen thousand years, of the twenty-five thousand years of our pre-recorded history. Allah and His twenty-four Scientist knew of these false so-called believers and that they would not have the courage, to stand up for the truth against this

American and European Imperialistic Zionist Matriarch System and its partners in crimes against all, black original people, on our planet. Therefore, Allah and His Scientist put into place the Anointed because Allah and the twenty-four scientist, knew this would be needed, regarding spreading the truth, amongst our people and all of humanity, about the enemies of Allah, Allah's last and greatest Messenger, the Prophets of Old and all of humanity.

The Anointed must understand that they can be killed and even murdered and must not be too trusting, with everyone they meet or may look like you. Be incredibly careful about sharing your ideas because not everyone has the same intentions, as you have and will steal your ideas to make money for themselves and claim your ideas for themselves. There is not anything wrong with the Anointed to gain wealth or live very comfortably; you must understand these things. It is not a crime for you seek a better way of life for yourself and your family, you can even best help to teach and show others that a better condition and way of life for themselves, without compromising the teachings of Allah that He Allah taught His last and greatest Messenger, yourself, and your integrity. You will be setting a great living example for your people in America and throughout the world.

As the Anointed are maturing into themselves and what they must and will do later in life, they must be mindful of controlling, their emotions, especially anger. Always listen before you give an answer and show respect to everyone, that comes into your circumference. There will be many distractions and disappointment even suffering and pain, from different directions and people. You cannot let any of this get and keep you down and stop believing, in yourself and what you are destined to accomplish. There are many people around you, and you may encounter, that will mean you no good at all. So, you must keep your composer and faith because these will keep you in the protection of Allah Almighty Himself. Remember to follow the teachings that Allah Almighty taught to His last and greatest Messenger and let no one lead you away from this. This is extremely important, and one should never, ever forget how important this is, during their trial period and all throughout their life.

The Anointed must be aware of the many tricks and deceit from many that will cross your path male and female, pretending they are something they are not and can be very convincing, just investigate their hearts and mind the truth of them will be reveal to you. The Anointed can never allow themselves to get caught up into the foolish and meaningless lives, of others and it does not matter whom they may be. Your calling is higher, and you owe these others absolutely nothing at all because these others are only trying to prevent your ascent, to a higher level they will never be able to obtain. So, their objective is to prevent you from ascending to your purpose in life and this makes the enemy/enemies incredibly happy and you will be incredibly sad also your life will be filled, with much misery because you chose the lesser over the greater and therefore are a disappointment to Allah, Allah's last and greatest Messenger, the twenty-four Scientist, the Prophets of old and your people.

The Anointed never get involved with silly debates about proving which of our brothers, before them is right or greater because this is nothing but foolishness and a waste of time and energy. In fact, the fools who are involved with idiocy are only aiding our enemies because they are causing more and more division, amongst black people. These YouTube idiots instead of building unity amongst black people, they are responsible for causing more division amongst black people. These you tube fools obsessed with being recognized and praised for themselves, until they all do not care how much damage they are doing and causing, amongst their own people; if their masters are pleased with the work they are truly doing; for the enemies of their people and for the few pieces of silver.

The Anointed must always keep in mind is that our enemies know us well it is our responsibility, to know our enemies equally and more so even, as well. You will not be able to do this by being foolish as these other fools, are doing. These fools are accomplishing nothing but supplying our enemies, with intelligence of black people progress and how to keep original people divided and preventing us from obtaining, any real meaningful progress. Ever since our enemies took the world off analog system and place the entire planet on digital system, this American and European Imperialistic Zionist Matriarch System and government, are in control of everything that is being said and what is being done, always.

The Anointed must understand that social media and you tube are the easiest avenues for our enemies, to monitor, control and direct, whatever direction our enemies want us to go in. Our enemies are easily able to do this due to the idiot traitors providing them with information, on everything original people are doing, when they are going to do it and where they are going to do it. The Unite States Gestapo does not have to do anything because these foolish idiot traitors and so-called high gods, are providing them all the intel the united States Gestapo needs and these fools either do not know what they are doing; do not care what they are doing; or they are on our enemy's payroll.

These ignorant fools have exposed to our enemies just how un-prepared and gutless black people are, here in America. Always fighting and arguing amongst themselves about foolishness, on a public platform and then have the audacity to call themselves god and black conscious minded. This is not only a joke this is disgraceful and these court jesters, call themselves the teachers of black youth. What chance do our black children have with such clowns as their teachers, these foolish court jesters' males, and females, are the greatest weapons our enemies have and are using against billions of black people not only in America, but throughout the world. These idiots can easily be recognized because they all want to be exalted and praise and are the greatest enemies of the Anointed and our people, not only in America but throughout the world.

They all have a share-cropper mentality and will never be anything else but a sharecropper, for their Caucasian Masters. Examine the history and you will see these clowns both males and females and they are not for the upliftment of original people, in truth they are against the upliftment of original people; they only want their few pieces of silver and their court jester clothing and nothing else. This is a shame my people because you believe these cowards are for you, when in truth they are for our enemies. They talk about what they did when they were in the temples of Islam, pay no attention to this; pay attention to their actions and deeds since Wallace D. Mohammad, allegedly tore everything down. Wallace D. Mohammad exposed all the hypocrites, disbelievers, and downright phony share-cropping idiots for what they are, always have been and always will be. These are the ones who are using the Jesus name to shield, their dirty and filthy religion Christianity, calling it Islam and followers of the last and greatest Messenger of Allah, the Most Honorable Elijah Muhammad.

This is what the Anointed is up against and cannot allow yourself, to be fooled by these court jesters of Satan the Accursed Devil, to deceived, trick you and lead you, to your destruction, for the love of our enemies and the few pieces of silver, from our enemies, which are these cowards' masters. The Anointed are not known by name the Anointed are known by their work, actions, and deeds. Each one male and female stick their hands out to provide aid, to those who may need it and they are not looking for any monetary gain, as these phones who shut their ears, to the cries of those who may need them, and these hypocrites' disbelievers do not care one bit.

My Queen who had been working all-night and was very tired encountered a sister begging for help. The sister was in awfully bad shape and needed help and she approached my Queen and asked for her help. My Queen heard her cry and plead; the sister believed she would help her. My wife stopped everything she was doing and did everything in her power to help the sister. My wife placed calls to this brother David and brother who operates a crises center, to help our people and the brother jumped right on it, without hesitation. Together my wife and brother David were able to provide our sister, with hope of healing herself. These are the Anointed my people because the truth lies in their hearts, minds and actions and their reward was that they helped their sister. Allah U Akbar Elijah Muhammad is your last and greatest Messenger and the True Muhammad RasulAllah, May Allah forever be please with them both and protect them both always.

In most cases and incidents, the Anointed does not know or understand when the Anointed, cross path. This is due to all the confusing so-called teachings be perpetrated by these phone' cowards, using the Jesus name to disguise themselves and their dirty religion Christianity. Understand my brothers and sisters that are Anointed we all want to believe these charlatans are real and they aren't; these traitors are nothing more than opportunist because they are all using the Jesus teachings, to hide behind; males and females and because the Anointed are searching for their own, any fall victim to the pretenders, hypocrites, and disbelievers; that will only see and lead us all to our death, as pray and the love for their masters, Satan the Accursed Devil their true master. Look deeply into these cowards' hearts and not their words or costumes they ware, the truth of them will be reveal to you. These pretenders, disbelievers and hypocrites are nothing more than servants, of the enemies of Allah, Allah's last and greatest Messenger the Anointed and all original people that are suffering, which is you my brothers and sisters not only in the Americas but throughout the world.

These liars, these cowards, these hypocrites, these disbelievers, are all our enemies, who are sincere to the rise of original people nationally and international. As I said before look into their hearts, their minds, and their actions, they cannot hide themselves because they only sing the enchanting songs of our enemies, to lure us all back to sleep and into the hands of their masters; this includes the Anointed also the suffering of our people worldwide; from our most dreadful enemy/enemies, this American and European Imperialistic Zionist Matriarch Wicked System and Society, that turn young black children into homosexuals, males, and females.

Once you understand what is truly happening then one will understand they will have to make extremely hard decisions, that will change your approach to life and what you must do in life. The Anointed is burdened with heart break and disappointed from the ones, they love and care for and in most cases their betrayal is so devastating, until the Anointed question's their purpose and mission in life, which is more important than everything else. The Anointed work extremely hard on bringing righteousness to their families and are met with extreme resistance and this causes the Anointed much pain and discouragement. These are the trials and tribulations the Anointed must endure and overcome, in order to achieve their purpose in life. I am not saying this is easy because it is not yet the Anointed must overcome, what these disbelieving hypocrites will, have and always will fail at because they are untrue at heart.

Be extremely careful of these fools who claim to have Supreme Wisdom these are the most foolish, of the foolish. These fools place the Messenger of Allah above Allah because they in truth, are nothing but disbelieving hypocrites. Any so call man that will not post pictures of himself, wife, and children together, is the enemy of all black people and must always be carefully watch. Ignore what these fools are saying and pay closer attention to their actions, males, and females. Look beyond the lies that they use to cover up the evil and deceit that truly lye's, in their hearts. Trust me the Anointed Ones the truth of them will always be revealed to you and everyone else. They only pretend to be unselfish this is the disguise these hypocrites use, but the truth of them is that they are truly selfish and seek false recognition, praise and will not hesitate to lie and deceive the Anointed Ones.

Anyone who will speak a lie about any of the Anointed and thus putting the Anointed life at risk, can only be forgiven by Allah because this is a profoundly serious infraction in the eyes of Allah. Anyone/Anyone is who manufacture lies and spread false rumors about the Anointed, is the enemy of Allah, Allah's Holy Messenger, the Anointed, Islam and all original people throughout the world. Anyone who would do such things and has done such evil deeds, can never ever be trusted by all original people. Taking the teachings that Allah Almighty Taught to His Holy Messenger and not give the praises to Allah, is nothing but blasphemy and High Treason. Not to address the Holy Messenger the {Most Honorable Elijah Muhammad} by his title Holy Messenger Of Allah, is absolute ignorance, ungratefulness and disbelief in Allah Almighty who visited us and raised up from amongst us, Muhammad RasulAllah {The Most Honorable Elijah Muhammad}; in the persons of the Holy One From Mount Paran, with horns of power in His hands driving nations asunder; The Great Mahdi; Christ The Crusher; The Son Of Man, for us black people and all of humanity; Master W.F. Muhammad to whom praises are due forever, is nothing more than a cowardly traitor and are the ones using the Jesus Name to shield their dirty religion Christianity; Lying, stealing and trying to master the original man and this is why we must take Jerusalem from these traitors/devils.

CHAPTER 10

THE CLOTH

This chapter everyone should study very closely because we will be coving profoundly serious biological, social science and historical facts, by the permission of Our Holy Savior Allah Almighty may He guide me through me in my writings. We must first examine the First Jamestown Landing in 1555, when God Tribe Shabazz was brought to Jamestown Virginia. For sixty-four years the Caucasian race study us because we the Tribe of Shabazz did not come over in chains, Shabazz are the ones that made the contract, with the British to receive more gold, for our labor, to teach them how to build a new civilization in the Wilderness of North America. These are the teachings from Allah to His Holy Messenger, in which the Holy Messenger taught us all.

These sixty-four years are kept hidden amongst the Shriners and the Zionist and they keep this history hidden amongst themselves. The Tribe of Shabazz currently was teaching these European Caucasian devils the science of how to build a civilization, in this wilderness, for themselves therefore establishing White Supremacy and White Nationalism, in the Western Hemisphere. The Olmecs, the Indians and the Moors were here thousands of years before the

British, the Dutch, the Portuguese, and the Spaniards, were ever made a man. The Olmecs and the Moors had built great cities and monuments, in the north and south, now known as Florida; which the Spaniards called these Olmecs and the Moors, the Aztec Indians and the Olmecs built these Pyramids of Gold, in Florida; then the Spaniards; began the un-mercifully, slaughtering of these original people. The Olmecs are original black people who were here twenty-five hundred years before the Indians were exile here, six-teen thousand years ago and before the Moors were even here. All these civilizations were destroyed by the Portuguese, the Dutch, the Spaniards and the British, and the original black people were murdered and most of their works were destroyed and the Pyramids of gold, renamed, by these murdering Spaniard Devils.

The reason why they needed us the Tribe Of Shabazz to teach them the science of how to build a civilization in this wilderness is because they did not have the knowledge or strength to do it because they did not understand mathematics and they did not set up civilization in Europe because we did this for them also. So, until we taught them, and this took sixty-four years of these devils learning and studying us, on how civilize government and people live and conduct themselves. My people these original people I have mention were on this planet thousands and thousands of years before the birth of Yakub/Israel and John the Revelator. These original people above mention were here thousands and thousands of years before Israelites, Zionism, Judaism, Hebrew Israelite, Kekic and all these other ideologies the newest on the Sean, the dreadful Christianity, were ever conceived by the devil; The Tribe Of Shabazz is before them all and the devil knew, and they know this. The Rabbis of Zionism know this is the absolute truth; The Shriners know this is the absolute truth, the Pope of Rome know this is the absolute truth; the Imams in in Mecca know this is the absolute truth; the only people that do not know this, are the ignorant black people throughout the world.

The Cloth my people is what I am writing about please pay close attention, in what I am writing about. Once they gained enough information from the Tribe of Shabazz the makings of Yakub/Israel/ John the Revelator, put into action the Trans-Atlantic Slave Trade. In the meantime, the Zionist Commissioned King James and his legion of sixty scribes, to begin changing, vialing, put into metaphors and symbols; to hide the truth of the original scriptures, while the Zionist held on to the original scriptures, from Muza and the Zionist called this book the Torah; which only born members of the Zionist can read or study it and the rest of the world population are to be given the lies of King James and spread amongst Yakub's makings, by the Pope of Rome and thus giving birth to this dreadful Christianity, to enslave black people and to make low sets of Yakub's makings that they were superior, to the original people on our planet.

Allah Almighty Himself in the person of Master Fard Muhammad to whom all praises are due forever, taught His Chosen and Holy Messenger {the True And Only Muhammad RasulAllah the Most Honorable Elijah Muhammad} and Muhammad RasulAllah taught us all, "the Caucasian People Know you well; but you don't know them well". Therefore, you have ignorant fools claiming to have supreme wisdom, are the lapdogs of these Zionist lawyers and their Zionist partners, for the few pieces of silver from their still twenty-first century masters. Therefore, these same fools who claim to have supreme wisdom are still the lion trapped in the cage walking back and forth trying to find a way out, of the grasped of their master because they still can only speak four hundred words well; after being in the present and taught by Allah's Chosen RasulAllah the Most Honorable Elijah Muhammad; and these most ignorant fools dare believe they have friendship in all walks of life.

The Tribe Of Shabazz was the only Tribe that was brought into the Western Hemisphere aboard the Slave Ship Jesus, in fifteen fifty-five at Jamestown Virginia. It was not until sixty-four years later after the Caucasian Race had made their plans, built the slave ships for human cargo, forged the chains, and perfected their weapons to hunt down black people; headed by the Zionist in sixteen eighteen and nineteen and this was the beginning of the second Jamestown landing, But this landing the auction were prepared because they had the time, to prepare themselves for a mass importing of black people, for free labor. This was embraced by the Christian British, the Christian Dutch, the Christian Spaniard, and the Christian Portuguese. The Zionist at this time had over eighteen slave ships involved, with the Trans-Atlantic Slave Trade.

Once these other tribes from the jungles now call Africa arrived here, these slave masters began breeding them with the Tribe of Shabazz, and amongst other tribes. The children were sent to other plantations throughout the south, never knowing their birth parents, brothers, or sisters. Islam 90 and 120 degrees were and for the Lost Tribe Of Shabazz. These teachings were not for all the black slaves in fact 85 to 90 percent of black people, are not of the Tribe Of Shabazz, to this very day. Although many use the name of Shabazz, they are not from nor are they of the Tribe Of Shabazz. The Zionist were not out to steal the identity or position from these other tribes, coming from out of the jungles of East Asia/Africa. The Zionist was out to steal the Heritage of the Tribe Of Shabazz. Therefore, the Zionist commissioned King James and his scribes, to change the name of the Allah/God Tribe Shabazz, to Israel the chosen tribe of Allah/God. Many may appear to look like they are part or belonging to the Tribe Of Shabazz, this was all planed by the scientist of this European Caucasian, new colony head up in secret, by The Evil, Diabolical and Supreme Deadly Zionism. The reason why most black people reject Allah Almighty in the person of Master Fard Muhammad, to whom all holy praises are due forever because they are not from nor are, they of Allah's/God Chosen, The Zionist know this, and the Shriners know that what I am saying is the absolute truth.

I Saladin Shabazz- Allah am a direct decedent of the first ones from the lost and now found members, of the Tribe Of Shabazz; that made that deadly convent with the devil that promise them more gold for their labor, in 1555. These others are not Shabazz all one has to do is investigate their hearts and look at their deceitful ways, actions, and deeds. This is the Cloth of Shabazz my people there are many around and amongst us, that are absolute pretenders. Pay attention to the words and their statements this is very crucial because the truth of these disbelieving hypocrites, lye's there. Their pimp clothing and imitation suits of making themselves feel important, are the disguises they use. The Zionist know who they are and the Zionist and their partners, fear them not because all you must do, is throw them a few crumbs and they will be overjoyed, as their masters whom they believe they are now equal and in some of these disillusioned jungle slaves, believe they are superior; and the Zionist and the Shiners know that none of them, are from or members of the Allah/God Tribe Of Shabazz.

With the mixing of these other tribes in the slave and breaking camps have produced a cloak that makes it almost impossible, to recognize the true members of the lost and now found members of The Tribe of Shabazz. We have become so poisoned and infected by these imposters and our enemy 's children and off springs, until the true believers must rise above emotion and feelings, to recognized, who are truly cut from the cloth. These twenty first century share cropping slaves working for the enemies of Allah, are not lovers of Allah and Allah's Holy Messenger. In fact, these share cropping cowards, and their progenitors are servants of Satan the Accused Devil; just examine their lifestyle. None of them have any love for Allah the true and living god and Allah's last and greatest Messenger and these cowards never had any love for Allah and Allah's Holy Messenger; although these disbelieving hypocrites say they believe, in truth they do not in all reality.

To be truly cut from the cloth one will be truly tested, and the test will come from one or those, you have truly trusted. Their betrayal is and will be truly hurtful and this is what you must rise from. Only the true will be able to rise and overcome the many disappointments, from the ones you have trusted dearly. These are the test that will prove that your faith has not been nor can it ever be shaken, by any circumstances or person or people. When one is cut from the cloth there is not any selfishness in them; there is any deceit in them; there is not any conniving in them; and there is not any premeditated lying in them; and there is not any fear in them when it comes to speaking the truth, about our enemies. The trials and tribulations that we must go through and survive has been pre-written and cannot be change. The truth of our enemies will be revealed to us all and some may be painful but nevertheless, the truth will always be revealed to us.

Allah Almighty who visited us in the person of Master W.F.

Muhammad to whom all praises, are due forever; taught his last and greatest Messenger the Most Honorable Elijah Muhammad; and the Holy Messenger of Allah taught us all that the Asiatic Blackman is god and owner, of the planet. The lesson read as follow: Who is the Original Man? The answer reads as follow: The Original Man is the Asiatic Blackman, the maker, owner cream of the planet earth, father of all civilizations and God of the Universe. The lesson does not say the African Blackman is god at all; the lesson say the Asiatic Blackman is god. So, we who believe in the Holy Savior Allah Almighty, The Great Mahdi, Christ the Crusher, the Son of Man are not African Americans; we are Asiatic Black People, and we will stand on this principle, till the day we are removed off our planet and this will never happen, so saith Allah Himself.

It does not matter what is done to us; it does not matter who turn against us; it does not matter what is said about us; it does not matter who may shun us; it does not matter who love or hate us; it does not matter how much money or lack of money we may or may not have; We are and always will be the Asiatic Blackman, the Original Man and God of the Universe so saith Allah Almighty Himself, through the mouth of His last and greatest Messenger Mr. Elijah Muhammad.

We do not answer to any so-called minister or the false prophets and so-called healers, who we know for a fact, that they were students of Allah's last and greatest Messenger; have taken the knowledge given to Allah's last and greatest Messenger by Allah Almighty Himself and claiming it to be theirs; these false prophets and so-called healers are thieves and liars. The world has stolen and abused the blessing and mercy of Allah taught to the world by Allah's last and greatest Messenger Mr. Elijah Muhammad and praise the Holy

Savior not. The people of the world who have been touched by Allah through Allah's Holy Messenger Mr. Elijah Muhammad and they the world, will not even call Allah by His name, Master Fard Muhammad Allah Almighty who visited us in person; to whom all praises are due forever. As the world and these charlatans use the teachings of Allah, to make themselves rich and gain prestige and denied Allah and Allah's Holy Messenger Mr. Elijah Muhammad.

I hear brothers talking about nation building time or I am about nation building, but when it comes time to making the sacrifice to begin building a nation, they are nothing but talk, they cannot be found, or they have one excuse after another. To begin building a nation take sacrifice, commitment, dedication, sincerity, and hard work. Building a Mosque or a Temple is not nation building a Mosque or a Temple are a part of a nation because a nation has much more intricate parts than just a Temple or a Mosque and you need many different and skilled personal, to bring this into a reality. Nevertheless, the true believer will write, speak, and encourage his people about the necessities of uniting to begin building our own Asiatic Black People Independent Nation. Only one or those cut from the cloth will dedicate their lives to keeping this message alive and pass it on to our youth. Why must we pass this message on to our youth Saladin? So that our youth who could attend these colleges and universities and acquire these skills and knowledge, understand that there is a greater reward for them when they use these skills and knowledge to build a nation for themselves, therefore, whom ever is an American and wants to be an American render unto Caesar that which belongs to Caesar. The Asiatic Blackman/People does not belong to Caesar so the Asiatic Black man/People; The Original

Man/People Must Be Rendered Unto Allah Because We Belong to Allah Almighty The Universal Creator and all life in His Universe.

The many enemies of us the Asiatic Original Blackman/People do not want this truth to be reveal to our people. It is written in there, by laws to hide the truth and they {our enemies} do exactly that and they are able to prevent the truth from ever reaching the mass of our people. Our enemies control the medium and control what the mass believe, think and practice due to them controlling the medium. Even many who claim to be aware are under the spell and control of the enemies of Allah, Allah's last and greatest Messenger and the Asiatic Black Original People. These are the ones not cut from the cloth but are against the ones, cut from the cloth and we must be incredibly careful of them because they will betray us and lead us to our death, for a mere few pieces of silver and false friendship, of our many enemies.

This disputing on social media is only revealing to us all that the ones engaging in this foolishness, are completely fooled, tricked, and deceived. Therefore, they are lacking the intelligence, wisdom, and skills to help anyone including themselves, to rise above pettiness and thus cannot possibly make any true difference amongst our people. The majority of those who were even in the temples of Islam during the time when the Holy Messenger walked amongst us, are completely without clue on what must and should be done. I have been around many of them in fact was in the temples of Islam with them and I know for a fact, many are filled with hidden agendas that suits only themselves and not our people.

These deceivers are not cut from the cloth they are only pretenders and are filled, with disbelief. They will and have sided with the enemies of our people and are working with our enemies on how our enemies can use us my people as a tool; pay us cheaply below minimum wage as these traitors filled their pockets and our enemies' pockets. In the meantime, keeping us my people a slave at the bottom of the social, economic, and educational world. If these cowards are supposed to be our brothers or represent the brotherhood, then give me my enemies; at least our enemies are not being deceitful.

If I were concerned only about myself and did not care about the mission, I would be a millionaire many times over. I had plenty of opportunities in life, but I would not surrender my Islam or the mission, to make myself rich. The Holy Messenger of Allah Mr. Elijah Muhammad did not care about himself getting rich, the Holy Messenger cared about the mission that Allah Almighty had given him, he cared about his people. Prophet Noble Drew Ali did not care about getting rich he also cared about getting the truth to his people. All these great black men that raised up in the Western Hemisphere since fifteen fifty-five, did not care about getting rich for themselves; they all cared about the mission and helping their people and many have sacrificed their lives, to do so. Just study the history my people and you will learn and what you will also learn is who are these great deceivers amongst us, helping our enemies to keep us locked in the cage of despair because these cowards do not have the intelligentsia, courage, or ability to free themselves. So, they live a life filled with deceit and lies pro-claiming that they believe in Allah and Allah's last and greatest Messenger, when in truth these liars believe not.

Study the history my people the truth is there in plain sight if one truly desires, to know the truth. The Cloth my people is not for everyone and there are many using the teachings of Allah, to shield their dirty religion, which is nothing more than Christianity; trying and desiring to make themselves rich off our labor. Sunni or so-called Orthodox Islam is nothing more than Christianity my people, servants of the Zionist Imperialistic Matriarch American and European System and governments.

Rituals have absolutely nothing to do with what is right or spiritual healing, or spiritual awareness. Every religion has their own set of rituals and claim to be right. Wars have been raged over religion and these religions rituals and these rituals have been and still are being use, to control masses of people worldwide. The only true way of life is mathematics and mathematics refute all such teachings of life after death or some invisible being and heaven, up in the sky after one die. Mathematics build civilizations while religions with their rituals, have held back civilizations from flourishing and growing. So, therefore when Allah {The Universal Creator} visited us in the persons of Master Fard Muhammad to whom praise be due forever; He did not teach the Rasul Mr. Elijah Muhammad religion or rituals; the Holy Savior taught the Rasul His Language Mathematics which is the only language of truth, holiness and accuracy and the language of the Universal Creator; and the Holy Messenger did not teach us religions and rituals; the Rasul Mr. Elijah Muhammad {the last and Greatest Messenger of the Universal Creator} taught us the language of the Universal Creator; therefore we aren't supposed to teach religions and rituals to humanity, we are obligated to teach humanity the language of the Universal Creator, which is Mathematics.

The past six thousand six-hundred years are the bloodiest, corrupt, insane, where murderous zealots and deme-gods, filled with murder, rape, lies, pure unadulterated evil in their hearts and minds; and with their concepts of religions along with their rituals, are praised and worshipped; over mathematics and this truth is kept hidden, from eighty-five to ninety percent of the world population, by religions and rituals; This is where Satan the Accurse Devil has hidden him or better yet, themselves. You will find people of science the majority reject religions and their false rituals because they know, religions and rituals defy the laws of mathematics, the language of the Universal Creator; so, none of these said religions are speaking the language of the Universal Creator and none of their so-called holy books are correct. It is impossible for any of these so-called holy books be correct because none of them, speak the language of the Universal Creator which is once again Mathematics. I'm speaking about the cloth all of humanity and it takes one who truly understand or has been blessed to have some understanding, of what the Universal Creator who visited us {Humanity} in the person of Master W.F. Muhammad; taught the true and only Rasul, the Holy Messenger Mr. Elijah Muhammad; and the Rasul, the Holy Messenger taught to us, the Asiatic Blackman in the Wilderness of North America and we must teach the world of humanity, this awesome truth, that all religions want to keep hidden from the eighty-five and ninety percent, of the planets population and has been doing so for the past six thousand six-hundred years, with impunity.

Some will say no this is not right and exact brother because we exiled the devil, from the roots of civilization, six thousand years ago into caves of West of West Asia and they recited there for two thousand years and this is true. Nevertheless, they left their seed hidden into the women and this evil germinated, inside the women. This is the history I am speaking about and this germination is the same germination that is happening in today's time; keeping our enemies, false religions and rituals ruling into the times we are living in right now. So, the same enemy that was birth amongst original people six thousand years ago, have been birth amongst original people and are still being birth amongst original people, in this very day and time. Therefore, the truth of this filthy, evil Zionist American and European Matriarch system and governments must be reveal and destroyed, along with their religions, rituals, concepts, ideas, and beliefs.

The Cloth my, most of the earth's population are not cut form although many believe they are, and they are not. These pretenders are cut from a completely different cloth and these pretenders will and have joined on to our enemies, to destroy the true five percent who does not believe in the ten percent the teachings of religions and rituals and these dumb black traitors, who are striving to be like their ten percent masters. Which only a few will obtain, and many will only pretend they have achieved, amongst the ignorant of the world's population.

These fools bring false teachings of spiritual healing, meditation, false rituals, and incantations, which is absolute nonsense and believed only by the weak in mind and hearts. Also, there are many using the teachings of humanity's, Holy Savior Master Fard Muhammad the Universal Creator who visited us in person, to whom all praises are due forever; to shield their evil and filthy religions {Christianity}; which are disguised under many different so-called religions and these so-called religions rituals; but in truth these so-called religions and their rituals, are speaking the language of Yakub; the founder and maker of imperfection. So, these so-called religious liars and disbelievers in truth, believe nor teach humanity the truth, about the true and living Universal Creator who visited us in person, so that they may live a better life off the labor and ignorance, of the many billions and billions of humanity, who are silly enough to believe and trust in them, their lies, religions, and rituals.

The sacrifice is very great indeed to achieve such clarity of the teachings that the Universal Creator, who visited us in the person of Master Fard Muhammad {Allah in person} to whom all holy praises are due forever taught to the Rasul {Holy Messenger} Mr. Elijah Muhammad; who in turn taught to us all; Us all, being the entire world population friends and foes included. The Cloth everyone must examine what truly lies in your heart and mind, to truly see if one is cut from the cloth, of the Soldiers of Truth, Freedom, Justice and Equality and you will see and learn that many who claim that they are, in fact are not.

The Holy Messenger Mr. Elijah Muhammad {Muhammad RasulAllah} did not visited the Eastern Hemisphere, to sight see. Although he visited many sights and countries; He The Holy Messenger Mr. Elijah Muhammad {Muhammad RasulAllah} visited these different places in the east including Saudi Arabia, to show forth and prove that He and He alone, met the Universal Creator in person face to face, to the so-called scholars and twelve Imams {twelve major scientist}; that He, Mr. Elijah Muhammad is the true and only Muhammad RasulAllah who has the true Holy Message, that will save humanity, directly from the Universal Creator; who face to face told and taught, the Rasul Mr. Elijah Muhammad, that His proper name is Allah besides whom there is no god besides He and the Islam that He Allah taught the true Muhammad Rasul Allah {Mr. Elijah Muhammad}, is the true and only way of life, that He, the Universal Creator chose for all of humanity and the entire universe. This is the real teachings of the Cloth everyone, that is not being revealed by any religion or their many rituals.

Light waves, to all humanity travels at One Hundred and Eighty-Six thousand miles per-second and travels throughout the University; and one light year travels one trillion point eighty-eight miles. Magnet Waves travel at Two Hundred and eighty-two thousand miles per-second throughout the Universe, so how much faster do magnet waves travel throughout the Universe, over light waves? The diameter of the Universe is seventy-six quintillion square miles; the circumference of the university is times the diameter by three point five; in the same time period covers and this explain why darkness, is there before light. Mathematics is the true and only language of the Universal Creator; no religion or ritual will ever help you find this answer.

CHAPTER 11

THE DAYS OF DECISION OF LIFE AND DEATH FOR ALL OF HUMANITY

You no doubt have probably heard so-called ministers and many so-called brothers, use this term especially while they are so-called teaching. We cannot ignore the many lying and deceitful matriarch practicing that has infected so-called original women, who also do not understand our enemies have purposely, in breaded hatred to the original woman for themselves and kind; we are now in the Days Of Decision. Yet none of them can truly explain what this mean because they themselves, have no understanding of what they are saying, it just sounds good and profound to the un-learn. Nevertheless, they themselves have absolutely no understanding of the times in which we are living in.

Facebook is nothing but an avenue for our enemies and the government to monitor, what everyone is thinking and planning. Social Media is also another means that our enemies and government, to gauge on what progress everyone is making. I am quite sure this government and our enemies are amazingly comfortable that black people, are not achieving anything, for them to be concern about or with. There is more individualism amongst black people in America for us to accomplish anything, beyond church. The teachings of Allah in which Allah's Holy Messenger taught us, has been made into a religion and masonic order, which now resembles church. I know will not like what I am saying but just examine what is happening and the lack of progress, black people have made since the Holy Messenger has completed his mission, more than forty-four years ago.

There is less unity, brotherhood, and sisterhood now then it was forty-four years ago. Rhetoric is more important than progress in this day and time and self- proclamation, are the only things that are being built, in black communities throughout America. There is not anything on the mathematical level that shows progressive unified, productive people at all. Black people must take a more serious look at themselves especially those who consider themselves, to be leaders because the methods that are being use, are not applicable in this day and time. The teachings are and always will stand but the methods being used in today's time, will never produce a progressive and productive black people, community, and an independent black nation. The leadership is outdated the thinking of these so-called leaders are also outdated because instead of advancing our people, this outdated thinking has stagnated black people to advance themselves and unite themselves, on a national and international level.

Most black and Indian people have made the decision to believe in America and trust in this Zionist American and European Evil Matriarch System. Many so-called black women have embraced this evil and teach black male children, to be like them, rather than be like their fathers. A woman can never teach a man how to be a man they only produce a weaker version, of a man who is more like them, a woman's mentality and in many cases sexual preference like their mothers. So even young black males must decide as well; to be like their fathers or be like their mothers. As we have approached some extremely critical times in history and black people in America are the most dis-functional and un-unified people, history has ever known up this present day and time. This is due to their decision making which has clearly demonstrated, is extremely poor and produces nothing of productivity and prosperity, for themselves and children, as a civilize people.

The Decision Making of any civilize people must be done by rational, logical and emotionalist, civilize thinking men. Why are you saying emotionalist men Saladin? The Reason why I say this because emotions are one of the weapons that this evil Zionist destructive American and European Imperialistic Matriarch System and Government {Governments}, ever produce, on our planet In fact throughout our planet history never have such evil existed, until Yakub's wisdom had been given the power to rule for six thousand years. Have been instilled in black and Indian men for the past six thousand years, that have been leading to the destruction of all black and Indian males, young and old throughout America and the world.

I applaud the righteous black women and mothers who do and have done everything in their power, against in surmounted forces, conditions and odds that held are still holding, as being true black righteous black women, who love their children and searching for real black men. Not these phonies pretending to be when in truth they are the enemies, of the rise of all black people in America, and throughout the world. We all must understand there are greater and most dangerous hypocrites, more poisonous than Minister Malcolm could ever be. How do you sell your people out and threaten the mother of your child, over these many African, Zionist and Arabs enemies? Imagine you claim to be an FOI and you posting pictures of yourself, wearing pimp clothing, indecent women helping the enemies of the Holy Savior who visited us in the persons of Master W.F. Muhammad; to whom praise be due forever; and the true Muhammad RasulAllah, Mr. Elijah Muhammad. None or very, very few believe or care about either one, most of them, believe in their mystery god. So how could you believe in our open enemies, for a few pieces of silver and dare say you are a believer. If a devil cannot fool a Muslim in now a day, then how are these deceivers, liars and connivers are able to deceive these so-called believers and their entire congregation? How is this possible?

These so-called believers are just that so-called believers and they will never stand up, for truth, freedom, justice and equally. There is much information that is being revealed today that everyone must study. Not from blind ignorance or blind conviction because none of these will enhance, original people growth and development. Building a nation whereas the black patriarch ruling system must rule, must derive from a knowledgeable, perspective and never from ignorant blind belief, without any clear facts to support what one is saying. Standing on street corners of Harlem, Brooklyn, Chicago, Watts, Newark, and other places, mean nothing into days society in which we live in; simply because it is not showing and proving, that the black man is god. Why isn't this showing and proving Saladin? The reason being our enemies are building homes for us; Our enemies are in control of our education and political systems; Our enemies are in control of our food, clothing, and shelter; Our enemies are taking care of our women and children; Our enemies are the ones supplying us, our women, and children with medical and health care; Our enemies are policing us, our women, and children;

Our enemies are the scientists that are building civilizations. Tell me black man what are you doing for yourself, but relying on the ones you call devil? So, when our enemies desire to murder us, rape our women and poison our children; what are you crying about? When you so-called gods, do not even care about yourself, women, and children because you will not and have not, done anything for yourself, women, and children.

This is the time for the Rise Of The Black Patriarch System Of Rulership and The Enforcement Of Our Will, which is the New Islam given to the world of original people, by Allah Almighty Himself. What are you doing black man besides wearing clown clothing and being a coward and hypocrite? Submitting to the enemies of our people and dare calling this disgrace, as having friendship in all walks of life. This and you are an absolute disgrace and the open enemies of Allah and Allah's last and greatest Messenger, Mr. Elijah Muhammad; the true and only Muhammad RasulAllah. We submit to Allah who visited us in physical form by the name of Master W.F. Muhammad, to whom all praises are due forever. Allah our Holy Savior raised up from amongst us His! Last and greatest Messenger Mr. Elijah Muhammad/ Muhammad RasulAllah who taught us all; and it is our duty and responsibility to teach to the world. The Sunnah or so-called Orthodox Islam have been living in error since prophet Ibn Abdullah Muhammad and this was approximately four teen hundred years ago; may peace and blessing be upon him.

The Messenger of Allah brought to us a perfect teachings that he received directly from Allah, for us all. He the Holy Messenger taught us through teachings and demonstration, what and how we need to do in order to re-build our destroyed nation. We have been given a flag by Allah Himself that we can fly high over our nation and the people of our nation, twenty-four hours every day three hundred and sixty-five days every year; amongst all civilize productive nations and people. Nevertheless, these teachings have been corrupted by rebellious and less learned so-called students, whose understanding has and still is, very destructive and productive for original people inside America and throughout the world. It is time of passing blame, speaking evil against each other and self-exaltation.

The miss representation of the teachings of Allah by the ones calling themselves god and many calling themselves Fruit Of Islam, to so-called black women in America; has driven our women into the hands of our enemies, along with our children. Yet! When it comes to the enemies of our people and the rise of our people, these cowards and traitors are on the side of the enemies of our Holy Savior and our Holy Savior {Allah Almighty Himself} last and greatest Messenger. I myself have made misstates dealing with our women who went through this hellish nightmare since fifteen- fifty-five and sixteen nineteen because of my lack of understanding and fear and miss representation of Allah Almighty Teachings, which Allah last and greatest Messenger, taught to us all. Due to people who I believed knew and understood the teachings of Allah {Our Holy Savior, Redeemer, Benefactor, Protector and Most Wise} taught His Holy Messenger; were corrupted, misused, exploited for self-gain, as they went about aiding and helping our enemies, destroy our own people.

These are not the teachings of the Messenger of Allah {Mr. Elijah Muhammad}; these are the teachings of Allah Almighty Himself to whom He {Allah} taught His Holy Messenger {Mr. Elijah Muhammad}. This is a great misstate that many of the so-called followers have made and are still making. Due to this misstate our people do not know who has visited all of humanity and thus allowed corruption, deceit, lying and betrayal, to walk in and to continuously, destroy our people with impunity, women and children included. Therefore, Jerusalem must and will be taken from the devil because the devil cannot fool a Muslim {God} in now a days, as they fooled them nearly five hundred years ago; to this present day and time of these writings.

Much confusion, much deceit, mush lies and betrayal {which is the cancer} that have entered the minds and body, of the lost and now found members, of the Nation Of Islam in America. Not only the Muslims in the Western Hemisphere have been affected by this disease, but also so-called Muslims in the Eastern Hemisphere have been affected by the same disease. What is this disease Saladin? Greed; Materialism; Self Exaltation; To be love loved by our enemies. What methods will many of our people and those who claimed to be our people, or claim to be Muslims use the teachings of Allah {Our Holy Savior} to achieve, their dirty goals and dare call this filth Islam? These traitors use lies, deceits, betrayal and every form and method of trickery, to disguise and hide their treachery. I ask a question how anyone could who claim to believe in Allah and Allah's Holy messenger, throw in with people who hate His {Allah} chosen people. How is this possible?

The Days Of Decision Making is now my people because the insanity amongst us, since Civil Rights and Integration, has poison ninety-eight percent of so-called black people including these so-called self-appointed ministers, claiming to be something they truly are not. Our enemies sit back and laugh at the traitors, the fools, weak understanding, and their greed, against their own people; to continue to rob black people globally and suppress the ones, who are supposed to be their own kind. Imagine this my people in America and throughout the world, traitors of us, are claiming to be followers of the Holy Messenger Of Allah; when in truth these cowards are in partnership with Yakub's Wisdom and Yakub's making, the enemies of Allah, Allah's Holy Messenger, and Allah's Chosen People.

There are many people calling themselves ministers taking and posting pictures as if they are sincere, when in truth they are not. Drama amongst our people they are the ones that are keeping it going because of worshipping the Holy Messenger of Allah and making Allah's Messenger equal to Allah, in which the Holy Messenger is not over the Universal Creator. These truly un-learned so- called ministers and others with ridicules self-proclaimed titles do not understand the worshipping of Allah's Holy Messenger over Allah; The Holy Savior to all of humanity if they would only believe; is causing the destruction of all original people and Yakub's making as well. Thus, all the foolishness on social media and foolish debates and pictures are bringing more destruction upon black people, than Wallace D. Mohammad, back in nineteen seventy-five because it has absolutely no unity or progress, amongst black people anywhere. Therefore, the upliftment of the rule of black men and the enforcement of black men rule, means nothing at all in America, Neither Amongst the rulers of civilizations and nations throughout the world.

The destruction, the chaos, the hate, the confusion, the complete one hundred percent insanity, is caused by these fools believing that these are the teachings, of Mr. Elijah Muhammad, the Holy Messenger of Allah/Muhammad RasulAllah. My people and all of humanity these are the teachings of Allah Almighty who visited us {Humanity at that time period four-billion four hundred million and in this present time approximately six to seven billion people on our planet} in the person of Master W.F. Muhammad, to whom all praises are due forever; whom wisdom will live forever; the scientist cannot find and end to his wisdom.

Mr. Yakub world/civilization is being destroyed but what is not understood is that we my people, are destroying with Mr. Yakub's civilization because of those who have set up rivals, to Allah and dare make Allah's Holy Messenger equal to Him. Pictures, uniforms, and silly debates are the enemies of humanity because these actions, are continuing to keep the hate amongst humanity living. These ignorant, foolish, and most detrimental actions and behavior are destroying all of humanity in America and throughout the world. There is not any hope for the generations to become the great scientist and builders because of the selfishness of those before them, have condemned our grandchildren, great grandchildren, and great-great grandchildren.

Deceit and lies will eat away at your heart and mind more than any cancer could and will ever do and it will overtake the body as well. When you say male or female; my word is my bond and you fail to keep your word, this person will be punished, and this must always be remembered. I don't consider myself special; I don't consider myself better than anyone; I don't consider myself wiser than anyone; I'm just a man that have been chosen by Allah to be a scribe that will tell the truth and take Jerusalem, back from the devil who is now occupying this Holy City,{Which Means Found In Peace} where Allah and Allah's last and greatest Messenger is buried; under lies, deceit, false mis-understanding and cowardice; by those who consider themselves to be true believers and followers; and in truth they are nothing more than Christians, using the Jesus name to shield their dirty religion and trying to pass it off as Islam. Thus, preventing the Rise Of The Black Patriarch Rule And the Enforcement Of Our Will and no longer submitting to this evil, wicket most destructive Zionist Matriarch System which has produce, this American and European Imperialism; in which you silly fools who dare call yourselves true believers, have and are still submitting to, too this very day today. Allah-U-Akbar Mr. Elijah Muhammad is the true and only Muhammad RasulAllah.

I love my second self the Asiatic Black Woman, but she has been mis-lead by our enemies, and therefore I am revealing this truth, to set her, our children and ourselves free from the strangle hold, of our enemies. The Asiatic Black Woman for nearly the past approximately five hundred years, have been living under tyranny and fear from our enemies and ignorant so-called black men. These ignorant so-called black men are the ones that are protecting and helping our enemies, to keep the Asiatic Black Man, Women and Children confined in this dreadful cage, of despair. Suffering because of these cowards, lack of manhood to stand up and do something for themselves. Yet, these same spineless cowards call themselves Gods, F.O.I and so-called Black Conscious people. Our enemies have a great laugh at them as they toss the few pieces of silver, to these disgraceful traitors.

We are in the days of decision between falsehood and truth the clue is being able to recognize, falsehood from truth. There are many traitors amongst us wearing bowties and F.F.I uniforms, Black Panther outfits and there are others and are the on the side, of our enemies. These are the cowards and traitors we all must be aware of and these traitors have fooled and tricked, many who genuinely believe in truth. These traitors and fools who believe in these traitors have made their decision, to be in opposition against Allah and Allah's last and greatest Messenger. Do not pay attention to their words because they are all skillful liars; pay attention to their slimy actions and deeds, which they all work hard on, keeping hidden this I know for an absolute fact.

Why does the devil keep us apart from their social equally? Once we know about them and the evil and wickedness they are involved in and apart of, we will run them from amongst us. This is not referring to the Caucasian Race, this is referring to these many hypocrites hiding under the name of Our Holy Savior, His Holy Messenger, the teachings of Allah and the Rise Of Allah's People. These fools have taken Allah's teachings and have changed them into church and dare call these churches, temples of Islam, when in truth they are nothing but churches of Christianity and the Masonic Order. How do you know this Saladin? I know this for this reason: If they believed in Allah Our Holy Savior who visited us in the person of Master Fard Muhammad and Allah's last and greatest Messenger Mr. Elijah Muhammad; there wouldn't be any division, hatred, who side I'm on; who is right and who is wrong; I believe in this one and reject this one; I going hear for Savior's Day and this so-called temple is better, than this one; this minister is better than that minister; or this temple the believers are better than these believers. This is the cancer that the Holy Messenger warned us about, in the lesson Islam in Ninety and One Hundred and Twenty Degrees; and surely it has, all come to exitance into days' time.

I want no part of none of this insanity and will not be a part of any of this insanity because this insanity, is leading us all to hell fire, with Satan the Accused Devil, the enemy of Allah, the enemy of Muhammad RasulAllah, the enemy of Islam and those who honestly believe. Original Woman you do not have to prove your strength because Allah knows your strength, trying to do something out of order of your creation, will only destroy you and everything around you [your children and family] just like the hurricanes, the great waves that destroy nations and earthquakes included. This is caused by the separation of first and second self-combating with each other, for control. Since we are now living and have been living for the pass six thousand years in imperfection, therefore the Original People are suffering; not only in America but throughout the world. Following the lifestyle that your enemies have made up my Original Woman, is and has taken you out of your Original Self and therefore you cannot find Love, Peace and Happiness and therefore there are more broken homes, dysfunctional Original Families, and self-hatred amongst Original People in America, than any other place on our planet. Couple with these ignorant fools believing they understand the teachings of Allah our Holy Savior, make things even more confusing, for the second self to understand, believe and except.

The Rise Of The Original Black Patriarch Rule and The Enforcement Of Our Will must be implemented, expediently above all other things. Allah visited us and raised up from amongst us His last and greatest Messenger. Not for the insanity that is happening at this present day and time, but to restore order amongst all Original People and put things into balance and there are many who are against this from happening because they will have to go for themselves and will not be able to receive the few pieces of silver from our enemies, and the blessing also permission, to operate as they many are doing today. My People and the entire world be incredibly careful in this day and time, be very extra careful OF YOUR DECISION MAKINGS.

CHAPTER 12

RISING FROM OUT OF THE OUICKSAND

This chapter is to let everyone that read these words know that we are all in Quicksand and the mass of people worldwide, do not even know it. The reason being is because they all are living and illusionary way of life, designed by our enemies. Our enemies have allowed these fools to believe that they have made progress when in truth, they have not made any progress at all. These ignorant fools do not own nor control anything at all except a church and they only have this because their slave masters, allow them to have. It does not matter if they call these churches temples or Mosques, they still own nothing. Rather they realize it or not their slave masters are still in control of everything they do and think, and they never operate, of what their slave master allows them to operate. In truth they are nothing, but scared cowards and they do not want this truth revealed. Yes, they will always kill one of their own kind; they will rob and steal from their own kind, yet when it comes to the enemies of their own, they bow down and cringe, at the feet of our enemies for the few pieces of silver [called paper in this day and time] and dare call this friendship in all walks of life.

According to the Holy Quran mothers and children are to be

protected those that are striving, to be up right through this maze of confusion and mayhem. There is so much deceit, lies trickery, clandestineness amongst those who claim to believe, when in truth these are the enemies of Allah and Allah's last and greatest Messenger. The Lost and now Found Members belonging to the Nation Of Islam in the Western Hemisphere, are in Quicksand and are sinking into the abyss, without any chance of recovery because they disbelieve in Allah and Allah's last and greatest Messenger Mr. Elijah Muhammad. These are the reason why the ex-slaves of America will never rise because many claiming to be believers, are nothing more than advocates, Yakub Ibn Lucifer. This is the Quicksand that is causing us all to sink in oblivion, while others are getting rich here in America. If your loyalty is not to the rise of your people then that make you a hypocrite, a trader, and a disgrace in the eyes of Allah and Allah's Holy Messenger Mr. Elijah Muhammad; the true and only Muhammad RasulAllah written of, in the Holy Quran.

Allah our Holy Savior who visited us in the person of Master W. F. Muhammad to whom praise be due forever; taught His last and greatest Messenger Mr. Elijah Muhammad in which the Holy Messenger taught us all that followed Him; that where there are no decent, intelligent, striving up right black women and mothers; there can be no decent, upright, independent self-producing intelligent black original men. If you have a child by a black woman or any woman, you are obligated to that child. When and if the mother of this child or children calls upon you and you will not make time for your child [children]; how dare you call yourself an F.O.I, God, Black Panther, Black Conscious or even a black man. No, you who have and are committing these horrible crimes are the enemy, of Allah, Allah's last and greatest Messenger, Islam, and all of humanity.

The quicksand my people and all of humanity are the lies, deceit, and cowardice, of these disbelieving hypocrites, calling themselves followers and believers in Allah and Allah's last and greatest Messenger Mr. Elijah Muhammad; when in truth they are devoted servants of Yakub and these are the made devils, hiding in disguise that are written of, in the Examination Of Kareem; Therefore, Jerusalem must and will be taken back, from these Made Devils. The cancer did not overtake Yakub's grafting or Yakub's civilization; the cancer that creeped into the body and minds, is speaking about these so-called followers and believers, of the Allah and Allah's Holy Messenger Mr. Elijah Muhammad and these hypocrites and disbelievers dare call Minister Malcolm [Al-Malik Shabazz], a hypocrite and most of them are crawling back on the plantation, of this Zionist American and European Matriarch Imperialist System, for a few pieces of silver.

The truth of what is the quicksand that is rapidly pulling millions of black original people here in America, must know longer kept secret and hidden, from the mass of people. The cowardly wolves have penetrated the defensive of the sheep and have open the gates, for the wolves and hyenas to hunt us all down, with impunity, as these cowards collect their scraps from their masters. These traitors have absolutely no love for their so-called people, as all servants they have only love for their masters and the crumbs [few pieces of silver] that they will receive from their master, for doing such a great job of deceiving their own people.

There is much proof against these traitors and hypocrites, but most people have been tricked and fooled, by these cowardly traitors. How are they able to fool those that consider themselves enlighten

Saladin? The answer is amazingly simple my people and humanity: these ones who believe they are enlighten in truth they are still deaf, dumb, and blind, to the wisdom of all of Humanity Savior that visited us, in person of Master W.F. Muhammad to whom praise be due forever. Everyone must understand that since Yakub's wisdom was given the power to rule for six thousand years, for him his wisdom to rule, he had to blind and separate the original people from all our natural energeias and self. So, now in this day and time everyone is trying to find the higher self. Many who are writing books and teaching on these subject are only mis-leading their people because they truly are not aware of where the higher energy comes from? Where the higher energy exists? Also, what produces this higher energy in oneself?

Since in the past six thousand years the truth of we, has been hidden and concealed, much literature has been written from those who are not from the creator and thus these other people, do not know who the creator of the universe is and how the creator, created Himself from the Atom Life. This Kemitic energy as many believe they know in truth they do not know because if you do not understand the deportation of the moon, then you will never be able to understand the energy of the universe, nor will you be able to understand yourself. The Kemetic powers will never and can never be achieved until the original Asiatic black man and Asiatic black woman, unite as one; then the power of the universe will be back in our control my beautiful sister, my beautiful Asiatic Black Woman.

The only way we can rise from out of this quicksand is that we work together and trust one another, or we will both drowned in this quicksand. Misunderstanding, lies and deceit is what we must rise from and above. This society and wicket system promote dis-trust and doubt amongst and between the Asiatic Black man and his second self the Asiatic Black Woman. Where there is nothing happening other than everyday survival, we make up things that does not exist; then false accusations come into existence and then hate, and contentment follows behind; and the destruction of the black family and the destruction of black man and black woman relationship. We must have trust, faith, and belief in each other for us, to defeat our many enemies.

Believe me my people these deceivers, liars, and traitors amongst us are not about re-building an independent, Asiatic Black Nation at all. These cowards are only trying to integrate into a society that does not even want them. So, these cowards are trying to force themselves upon Yakub's making, even though Yakub's making do not want them apart, of their society and world. Pretending that they are making a worthy contribution to the elevation and advancement of this society and world, when in truth they cannot make any contribution to the advancement, to any civilization on our planet.

Pretending is the way of life of these traitors and there are many on all social levels, here in America. Religions and ideologies are where these traitors hide in and behind and these are the greatest enemies, of the rise of Asiatic Original Black Nation and Islam. If we continue believing, following, and practicing the evil ways of our enemies, we will only sink deeper and deeper in the quicksand, of this society in which we are presently living in. Sorrow, pain, misery, and despair is all we will ever receive and never rise us from this quicksand, that have been prepared for all humanity; by this evil Zionist and Christian Matriarch Imperialism; that has a strangle hold on all who believes, trust and worship them.

The present Zionist and Christian Imperialist Matriarch System must be removed from all original people not only in America, but throughout the world. This system is un-natural for original people and has caused nothing but death and destruction for all original people worldwide. Until we understand what is ailing us all and what is this quicksand, that humanity is drowning in. The Answer my people is this Zionist-Christian Evil Imperialist Matriarch System; and now they have incorporated others such as the Hindus and the Arabs, who bring nothing but falsehood amongst all original people; such a system everyone on our planet will not last forever and cannot last forever. All though they are back and supported by the American government, this evil will be destroyed and everything about them as well. Everyone who is following and practicing the evils, of America and Europe religions and evil practices, will also be destroyed.

We my people and all oppressed people of the world will never be able to rise out of this quicksand, by following and believing in our enemies because our enemies only care about themselves and pleasing their masters. Although these enemy's may look like us especially here in America, they are our enemies and this we must always remember. They do not have anything in the way of knowledge, wisdom and understanding, to contribute to the upliftment of black people in America. These enemies cannot uplift where they come from, so they have all ran here, to embrace our enemies by any means necessary including selling out us, the ex-slaves of America.

Black Woman in the Hells of North America do not ever be impressed by anyone coming from Africa, Asia, The Mid-East, or Europe because you are the mother, of Muhammad RasulAllah and the mother of all civilization, and Allah has chosen you, to be the wonder in heaven if you would only believe in your Holy Savior Allah in person of Master Fard Muhammad; to whom praises are due forever. Prayer is better than sleep, but the remembrance of Allah is greater than prayer and this my Queen you must always remember. There is no woman coming from Africa, Asia or Europe are more beautiful or as strong, as you. You my black Original Queen are the strongest woman on the planet, none of the above mention are your equal. Therefore, you Striving to be Upright Black Woman in the Hells of North America, is the Wonder in Heaven and not them, so saith Allah Almighty the Universal Creator. Your place my Black Queen in Heaven has already been ordained and therefore you must rise out of this quicksand, together with your Striving to be Upright Black King from the Hells of North America. That has suffered persecution, misery, pain, starvation, deprivation, and unimaginable evil no other people had to suffer through together, for nearly five hundred years.

These fools coming from Africa, Asia, The Mid-East, and Europe are envious of you because you and only you my Striving to be Upright Black Woman who have suffered in the Hells of North America along with your, Striving to be Upright Black Man for nearly five hundred years; have been made a Wonder in Heaven by Allah Almighty Himself. Our enemies know that we neither you or I can achieve this un-united and therefore the enemies work extremely hard on keeping us separated from ourselves. So, these ignorant fools come to America claiming to be Kings and Queens and bring with them these false teachings in order to help us remain mis-guided to keep you and I away from our heavenly position. If these teachings were so powerful and correct then why is Asia and Africa are such a wreck, so devastated? If these false so-called Kings and Queens and their spiritual gifts of healing, why can't they uplift their people in Asia, the Mid- East and Africa? They bring nothing but trick knowledge logy in order that they can set themselves up as pimps in America and rob you of your money and take sexual pleasures with you.

My Striving to be Upright Black Queen who have suffered in the Hells of North America along with your Striving to be Upright Black King, for nearly five hundred years; I am warning you my Black Queen be incredibly careful when dealing with them and their woman included because they will lie to you, deceive you and lead you away from the truth. Be incredibly careful of anyone bringing these false teachings to you because they will destroy you and then take total advantage of you. There was a time when we were just stuck in the mud this mud has turned into quicksand with the diabolical insertion of these false teachings and hateful people coming into America, from Africa, Asia, the Mid-East, and Europe; with lies and deceit my Black Queen from the Hells Of North America; to rob us both of our gift and promise from Allah, to be the Wonder In the Heavens.

This is the quicksand that we are trapped in and purposely being mis-led deeper into the abyss, by our enemies and silly fools, who want to rob us of our divine heritage and the silly fools who dis-believe that we are the chosen, by Allah Almighty Himself. Things go wrong because you are running from yourself rather than turn to yourself. Running to our enemies for answers is dangerous to your life and the life, of your children, wives, husbands, and family. We are living in very crucial times and there is no mystery god or energy. There is no one from outside of America that can bring any life-giving teachings or energy, that will be of any use for our elevation or survival; only we ourselves are able to do this for ourselves.

We my people in the Hells Of North America Have been chosen

by Allah to be His People because we, are the people that have been in a land and world and society, of Sin, Iniquity and Transgression since fifteen fifty-five and no other people on this earth, have fulfilled the prophecy of Ibrahim lost seed. Not these so-called Africans of today; Not these ones coming from Asia; Not these ones coming from the Mid-East or Mitterrandian or Europe; are the lost seed of Ibrahim; especially these lying thieving Zionist. All the above mention people are doing everything in their power to keep us my people, buried in the Quicksand of the Abyss here in the Hells Of Yakub's world and society.

CHAPTER 13

THE DEPT

This chapter my people and all original humanity and those who want to know the truth, about what is happening in this day and time; must examine very closely, what is the Sure truth. The Holy Messenger of Allah Mr. Elijah Muhammad {Muhammad RasulAllah} has made it very plain and simple to us all. We my people in America and throughout the original family of the world, are living in an Abyss and do not recognized because all the misinformation that is flooding social media, and the silly clowns that are promoting this misinformation, also the misconceptions of this Allah forgotten and un-forgiven society and world.

I sat back and spoken with my youngest son and he has brought me into a reality, that I must face and get away from. Lies and deceit are all around us the chosen, by the ones who claim to believe, and they believe not. Murder the black, baby at birth is in full effect in this day and time. The complexing part of this most diabolical plan is who are the helpers of this evil. In this chapter I will reveal to the world who these monsters are. Why did we take Jerusalem from the devil? Which devil was Jerusalem taken from, the grafted devil or the made devil? Who is or are they made Devil? This is a very guarded secret especially in this so-called said Nation of Islam, in North America.

We must keep our entire focus on Allah who has no equal nor any associates. We must all think and use our abilities of critical thinking and analyzation, to separate truth from falsehood. We cannot use methods that were used fifty or more years ago, to solve our problems in today's time. The Holy Messenger of Allah Mr. Elijah Muhammad {Muhammad RasulAllah}, mission was to wake us up, from our four-hundred-year slumber in which he did. If one chose not to except the teachings of Allah through Allah's last and greatest messenger, then that is on you. If one is stuck in yesterday that also is on you. To say you have supreme wisdom and then there is absolutely, no visible progress, then the question is this; What Supreme Wisdom do you have and what are you doing with this supreme wisdom? To say that you are god and yet not building anything tangible the question once again is how you can be god and do not build anything for yourself? How can you be god and another man must build homes for you, feed you, cloth you and your families, and give you employment? What Supreme Wisdom do you truly have when you are still conducting yourselves as ignorant slaves, on your Caucasian Masters Plantation? I am not an African: I did not come from Africa: I and from the Roots Of Civilization ever since, the planet was found or recognize after the great deportation sixty-six trillion years ago, the Roots of Civilization has been in Arabia; not this so-called Africa; name Africa by a homosexual Alexandria, after his homosexual lover Africana.

Allah instructed the lost found members of the God Tribe Shabazz, though the mouth of His Allah Holy Messenger Mr. Elijah Muhammad; not to marry or dress like these African traitors, the part-takers, in the kidnapping and enslavement of his chosen people, the Tribe or Members of the Shabazz People also called, The Tribe of Shabazz; who are members of the Nation of Islam; In fifteen-fifty-five. He or she who do this are enemies of the Holy Savior, Allah's Holy Messenger and the once lost and now found Members, of the Shabazz Family. Anyone who does this and mates with these so-called Afrikaans Traitors male and female included are not our people and does not belong to our family.

This land now named so-called Africa is not the Motherland this a complete lye, this is the jungles of East Asia of the True Motherland, Arabia. If not for the Arabs these savages would have never known anything about Islam because they were all savages, living a jungle way of life. It was these so-called Africans that aided the Dutch, the Spaniards, The French, the British, the Portuguese and the Arabs, to build the slave ports in Senegal, Ghana, and Mali because West Africa, was the closet way by sailing, to the western hemisphere. So, in truth these so-called West Africans were and are co-conspirator, in the kidnapping of Ibrahim seed, the Members of the Shabazz Family or Tribe of Shabazz. Also trying to claim that the jungles of East Asia now called Africa by a homosexual, to be the Motherland; These are all lies by our enemies.

If you are a true Member of the Family of Shabazz, then it is a disgrace to call yourself a so-call African. If you marry any of them and have children with them you are a disgrace and a disbeliever, Having children with these West African traitors, is no better than having children, with the grafted devil; because these Western Africans or so-called Africans period, are Made Devils. So, if you are silly enough to marry and have children with them, how dare any of you call Malcolm X a hypocrite. Also, if you allow any of these traitors to come amongst you for Savior's day, thank you for not inviting me because you all are greater hypocrites, greater then Minister Malcolm because you are all defying the laws and instructions of Allah, to us by His Holy Messenger, Mr. Elijah Muhammad, who need friends, brothers, and sisters such as you I know I do not. The Holy Messenger himself instructed us that Allah did not want the True Members of Lost and Found Members of the Tribe of Shabazz; The Holy Messenger also instructed us by Allah's command; not mix with them nor are we allow to even dress like them.

Examine the times and events in which we are now living in with this so called, Coronavirus in which have claimed the lives of Kevin Abdul Hafeez and five others, from Masque #7 is letting everyone know that we all are touchable. If you are violating the Laws of How To Eat To Live, you all will pay with your lives. The Holy Messenger of Allah {Mr. Elijah Muhammad} had warned of this day and time and many, have rejected his warning for a false so-called prophet; that tells the mass of people nothing but lies. There is no life aboard the Mother Plain these are lies no different than seeing Jesus in heaven after you physically expire. These lies are taught to the mass of people {85%} to control their minds and their purses, by the enemies of the Holy Messenger, using the Jesus name to shield their dirty religion, which is nothing more than Christianity disguised under the name of Islam or under some other name, or philosophy, believed only by the 85%. Easy Led in the wrong Direction and extremely hard to be led in the right direction.

We are living in the beginning of the destruction of this evil most dreadful Zionist, Christian, Arab and all other participants, in this evil Matriarch Rule System which is Yakub's society. This

Pandemic that we are living under in this day and time, is the end of this most serious dreadful evil and the people who made this evil system, the ones who support this evil and the ones who abide by this evil system. I have absolutely no empathy or sympathy for anyone who is in support, of this evil, wicket and most dreadful system. I say to the world the worst is yet to come and there will be more destruction, more decay, more decline, and more devastation on the way. This evil, most wicket system that we have been living under for nearly the past five hundred years, is now being destroy by the Universal High Power, who' proper is Allah Almighty Mighty. He Allah promised us this through the mouth of His Holy Messenger Mr. Elijah Muhammad, that these plagues on Yakub civilization, was on the way and now they have arrived. Praise Be To Allah The Justice and The Destroyer, Of Yakub Civilization and People.

Everyone well mostly everyone that comes to America fall under the spell, of America especially women because America is ruled, by this evil Matriarch system. It does not matter, what religion or ideologically any original man may follow, it is still brother against brother. Even in this said Nation of Islam this evil exists I personally have experienced this evil, from within. This is happening due to black original men will not rise and enforce their will. Why won't they rise and enforce their will Saladin? This is due to them not having any will of their own and subconsciously, are still under the spell of this evil Matriarch system. So, no matter what they profess to be or believe in, they will sell out their own. Thus, giving other than their own the power to rule their own. Therefore, preventing the rise of black men back to power, self-rulership, and independence.

We are now living in the beginning of the fall of Yakub's society and world and there is no place to run and hide. This pandemic in which the entire planet is suffering from and under, makes it useless to believe that you can escape, that which has been predicted to come and is now here. The entire planet is living in fear, insanity and social media displays this every day, how the people of our planet have lost their minds. The ones who say that they believe in Allah and that they followers of Muhammad, are the most insane because they do opposite of what Allah's Holy Messenger taught the world. Envy, jealousness, and plain hatred are the order of today, by those who claim to believe and are righteous. If one sees things differently or choose to do other than what they believe are right, then you are caught off. This self-righteous mind set will never produce the Rise of the Black Original Patriarch and the Enforcement of His Will.

The holy messenger of Allah Mr. Elijah Muhammad said, "I met face to face with god as Musa met face to face with Jehovah". Yet we do not call Musa the Honorable Musa. We do not call ESA the Honorable ESA. We do not call Ibrahim the Honorable Ibrahim. We do not call Prophet Muhammad 1,400 the Honorable Prophet Muhammad. So why are you so-called followers of the Holy Messenger of Allah Mr. Elijah Muhammad, calling him the Honorable Elijah Muhammad. Do you not know that you reducing him in rank and status? I cannot believe that you who claim to have supreme wisdom and that you are god, are all making a grave error, and therefore people throughout the world, have absolutely no respect for you and what you claim to follow and believe in. There for you cannot make any progress in uniting as a people because in truth you are all still Christians and believers in Yakub.

You lie to one another, you deceive one another, you steal from one another and you have absolutely no love for one another. How can you claim to be god and have supreme wisdom and the ones you claim to the enemy, are the ones building homes for you? The ones you claim are the enemies are the ones building schools for you and your children. The ones you claim to be the enemies of you are the ones, with government for you. The ones you claim to be the enemies and inferior to you, are the ones who have built hospitals for you and themselves and have made marvelous advancements, in this field and other fields that keeps civilization, going. You claim to be righteous people yet do as much evil as the ones you claim to be un-righteous, amongst and to yourselves. Standing on the corners, using social media, dressing like pimps and fools, to shield your evil ways. How can the Black Original Patriarch Rise and Enforce Their Will upon the world, with clowns such as you? In fact, it is fools such as yourselves that keeps this evil Matriarch Rule system, in power because you dis-believe in the message that last, holy and greatest messenger Mr. Elijah Muhammad, taught us all.

I know without any doubt many of you will disagree with me and argue with me but nevertheless, this is the absolute truth about yourself. We are not Africans and Africans are not the Original Black People. Allah's last and greatest messenger Mr. Elijah Muhammad taught us we are the Asiatic Black Man. During the slave trade many of us came and passed through the slave ports, of Africa which led to the Atlantic Ocean and we ended up in the western hemisphere. So, Africa is not the Homeland Africa is the slave ports in which many of us, passed through and many so-called Africans hate us and do not claim us as their people or one of them. The Holy Messenger of Allah said Mr. Elijah Muhammad "that in the end his true believers will only fill up a taxicab". We are surely living in this and time because the majority that set in the temples of Islam, have reverted, to the following of Mr. Yakub his teachings and lifestyle. They all like to quote the lessons and teachings of Messenger Elijah Muhammad, but very, very few are willing to live according to the Messenger teachings. They boast about what they have maybe a little farm and about their little civic gathering, but none are practicing on the grand level or scale, that produces a productive people. Thus, there is no Rise of the Black Original Patriarch System of the Enforcement of the Original Black Will; There is nothing more than Christianity and a bunch of still slaves of a mental death and power.

This so-called Black Mafia is one of the most disgraceful part of Black History in America and for black people, in America. These foolish so-called black gangsters were nothing for than the angles of death for their own people. This so-called Black Mafia was formed by a regrade from the Italian gangsters or Mafia, Crazy Joe Gallo. The Italians Mafia referred to him as Crazy Joe Gallo because he stayed in conflict with his own people and then went outside of his own people, to build his own family not of his own people. So Crazy Joe Gallo incorporated these ignorant and foolish black men and un-least this Heroin Expedient, amongst black people with the help of these foolish negro men. Thus, producing amongst black people such people as Super Fly, Gold Finger, Iceberg Slim and other names, all of them were and are, angles of death and destruction for their people.

These angles of death aided the genocidal destruction amongst their own people without a second thought and un-least generations of what are known as trick babies. These babies are born from mothers who ran the streets selling themselves, for drugs. These women and girls would be having babies by anyone and then bring them back to their so-called man or husband, claiming that they were the father, when in truth they did not know who the father might be. I myself had got caught up in this nightmare whereas this street whore brought children back to me, were not of me. I have only one child that is of me and this child is my only son. The rest of them even though they carry the slave master name, are not my children and are not of me. This process has been passed down by women through the pass two to three generations, amongst so-called American black people. This history must be told in order to understand what happened amongst us, that keep us in the condition which we are in.

The American government embraced this destruction amongst so-called American black people, now called African American. This is a monumental Disgrace of the first order as the American government took care of these whores, bringing back these trick babies, amongst the so-called black people in America. The American government knew without a doubt that these babies, will grow up to oppose the ones being accused of being their father. I speak through experience everyone, that lends an ear. This is a truth that is being kept hidden amongst so-called American black people, that no one want this truth to be revealed. I Saladin Shabazz-Allah am revealing this hideous truth about America and the so-called American black people, now referred to as African Americans. The Holy Messenger of Allah Mr. Elijah Muhammad tried to make and build a place amongst civilize society, for these people; and have been rejected by these people because they love the devil cause the devil gives them nothing.

There is no heaven when we all die; there is no special place where anyone go to after death overtakes them. You live on in the memories of others or some work you may have left behind. Only the fools remember the enemies of themselves and his or her people and glorify them, this is not intelligent behavior at all. So, this so-called Black Mafia and the damage and hell they have brought to their people, they should be scorned for the evil they have all done. They are not heroes and people that should be admired regardless to whom they might be, male or female; these are the enemies of black people in America and the instruments and Angles Of Death, for their own people. We as a people and individuals are still suffering the effects, of these traitors from amongst us that has produced generations, of these Angles of Death. Where should such people be everyone? What should their punishment be everyone? Why should we embrace these murderers amongst us everyone? They are most surely never to embrace the Rise Of the Black Original People and the Enforcement Of Our Will and this has been proven; So, what need do we have of them?

There are so-called brothers out they are that are very envious of me writing a book and claim that I want to make money, from the teachings. They are very wrong indeed I am just bringing about a much-needed understanding, to everyone. There were followers of the messenger of Allah and then there are students, of the Holy Messenger of Allah; I am a student of the Holy Messenger Mr. Elijah Muhammad. Many of the so-called followers of the Holy Messenger have felled back into the practices and worshipping, of Christianity. All one must do is examine the everyday living and what they associate, themselves with. There is no integrating Christianity with Islam if anyone is doing this this makes that person, a Christian. If anyone is supposed to be born in the Nation of Islam and she dress like a Christian woman, she is the enemy of Islam, Allah, and Allah's Holy Messenger.

There is so much self-hatred, animosity, envious and loathing amongst the ex-slave of America until it is placed, into the universe.

This self-hatred has come back to us with a divine chastisement. The so-called black man of America is now being represented by homosexuals, as the so-called American Blackman of America. There is no justice for the so-called African American because they do not deserve any justice, due to their self-hatred for their own self. They run to others and help other than their own self to use their own people for their gain and prosperity. They seek to make slaves of their own people for other people for a few measly dollars. There-fore preventing the rise of the Original Black man and the Enforcement of their will. These traitors are incredibly happy of the self-hatred they have for themselves.

These actions tell me that they did not understand the message of the Messenger from Allah's Holy Messenger and this is clear proof, that these phonies are using the Jesus name to shield their dirty religion. When one examines the truth and the reality of what is happening, and one have learned also understand the message given to us by the Holy Messenger, then this taught one must draw the same conclusion. A student sits before his teacher and master to learn for them to pass on, what they have learned. A follower is one that has been programmed to conduct themselves, in a certain manner. When the programmer is no longer there to program them, these followers will fall back to conducting themselves, like their formers. In the case of so-called American Black People and especially the so-called followers, they have reverted to practicing the ways of their former slave masters, amongst their people and love also worshipping the devil because the devil gives them nothing. These ones are easily led into the wrong direction and extremely hard to be led into the right direction.

As I approach my 69th birthday from the time of this writing on

September 27th back in March I suffered a serious medical condition, whereas I was hospitalizing for eight days; not a one of these so-called brothers have come to visit me, or even called me. Yet I have been there for them in many ways, when and if they called me. This includes my blood sister, brother, and so-called children. If not for my son Ibn-Saladin, I would had been totally alone as I fought back for my life, from this ailment. I will and am forever grateful for his concern and devotion to myself and his mother, who had taken ill at the same time. My eldest son Niheem would call me from prison but could do nothing, to help me. During this time and my stay in the hospital I had time to consider and see many things, about this so-called brotherhood. I learned that this s-called brotherhood is not real at all and that Allah is with me because He Allah strengthen, my will to survive. Lying and deceiving is the way of life for those who claim to be righteous and are striving to be up right, amongst our so-called people.

There appear to know chance for of recovery for the so-called American black man, woman, and child. Due, to the fact that easy 95% of them has rejected Allah and Allah's Holy Messenger, for the pleasure of this world and society. Therefore, no other people on our planet are killing their own, more than these so-called American black people, now referred to as African Americans. No other people on our planet have as much self-hatred, loathing and content as these so-called African Americans, for themselves. There appears to be no rise amongst the mass of these now called African American people. There is no waking them up because they enjoy the evil of this world, society, and people.

If Allah has blessed one with a gift then that one must use his or her gift, by telling and speaking the truth. It does not matter how much money you make, and it does not matter what anyone might say; you are still responsible to tell the truth. I wish no one any harm and I have nothing to say negatively about anyone. Whatever one must do then one should do it, to the best of their ability. I am in the greatest test of my faith and I still stand and tell the world that Allah Almighty Visited us in the person of Master Fard Muhammad to whom praises, are due forever. I still stand and tell the world that Mr. Elijah Muhammad is the true Muhammad RasulAllah and Allah's last Messenger, as we are witnessing the destruction of Yakub's world and society. This is the Dept that we all owe to Allah and Allah's last and greatest Messenger Mr. Elijah Muhammad.

We are living in a very, very desperate time period and everyone should be aware of this time. We must begin to adjust the applications in which, we are currently using because we are currently failing, at the raising of the Original Mind Set and people. All religions talk about the day of judgement and now that it is making itself known, the entire religious world, is trying to prevent Allah's will of destruction for their sins. There is no preventing the destruction of mankind, as we have known it to be. All the evil that has been presenting their selves as righteous, is now being destroy before our very eyes. There is no mercy coming to relieve you of your burdens; the manifestation of disbelief is known by Allah and Allah's prophets. It does not matter what name one may call this supreme energy and force, this energy, is bringing about Universal Justice, to every living being on our planet and it cannot be stop or delayed by anyone.

The debt that we owe is to Allah and all of Allah's prophets and no one else. It is the deceit of those who claim to believe and in truth these, hypocrites are the enemies walking amongst us daily, spreading their evil throughout the world. As Allah's Holy Messenger

Mr. Elijah Muhammad taught us all; We cannot blame anyone for the condition of the so-called ex-slaves of America, now referred to as African Americans; the ex-slave of America now referred to as so-called African Americans must take responsibility, for their own actions, decisions, their belief beliefs. There is no love, consideration or caring, come from that, which you or we, have created Mr. Yakub and this filthy world, religions, beliefs, and hatred, for humanity and self. The history will always be on the side of the ones who understand and seek justice, for everyone on our planet.

It is not fear of the so-called unknown that have everyone frighten; it is the fear of the known evils they had and are still participating in and must face; this is what is truly happening. There is no so-called religion or ideology that can protect you because in truth, the life that one can have in this society is very pleasing, to the ones who claim to be righteous, but in their hearts, they are not capable of such and your day is in the arrival is at hand.

CHAPTER 14

THE PANDEMIC

This is a very terrifying chapter because of all the horrors and deaths that is happening not only in America, but throughout the world. We have been taught by the scriptures and by Muhammad RasulAllah, Mr. Elijah Muhmmad himself, the last and greatest messenger of Allah. So, Allah's waft is now affecting and touching everyone, on our planet. Every religion, ideology, and whatever else, everyone one tells the story, of the great destruction of this society, religions, and politics. Now that some of the signs are being made visible and feeling Allah's waft, most of the planet's population is trying or believing, they can prevent the destruction, of Mr. Yakub world and society. If one does not have the strength to see exactly what is happening, then all is lost. What is happening cannot be stop or prevented not if humanity, continue this course of self-annihilation; of the world mass of human life by a minority greed and insane desire for power of life and death, is no longer acceptable by Allah.

With the changing of the earth's axes there will be continue stories by people, in different regions. Every twenty-five thousand years the planet takes on a new and different shape. So, on the scientific scale through mathematical formulas begin to explore these changes around them and throughout the world. Every religion can and will say this is by Allah will and doing because of this and that and this is said by all religions and their religious scholars. Yet when Allah's wrath starts to manifest itself; you so called religious scholars are the first to defy Allah and Allah's prophets and Allah's last and greatest messenger Muhammad RasulAllah.

We must understand the time period in which we are now living and the time period in which we are now living in, cannot be ignore nor can it be forgotten. We must keep records of what we were doing in fact we must the history of this time and what part do you play in this making of history. There is only yourself to blame reason being is that you will not stand up for self and are content for others, to do for you, that which you are afraid to do for yourself. This message is for the 85% to 95% of the world's population because our political and religious leaders have failed and betrayed our trust.

This Pandemic in which we are experiencing at this present time is about sterilization, of an ignorant people, who does not have the capability of understanding the times, in which we are now living. Biological warfare is now being used against all humanity and the mass of people, cannot believe what is now taking place. Many go to their place or house of worship and they still do not understand, the dreadful times, in which all of humanity is presently living in and under. Every religion speaks about Allah sending plagues, fire, water, and hatred, upon this civilization. Now that Allah's will and the predictions of all of Allah's prophets and Allah's last and greatest messenger Mr. Elijah Muhammad, made it absolutely clear to us all; So, absolutely no one on this planet cannot say that they did not know, and chose to ignore Allah's. last and greatest messenger, Mr. Elijah Muhammad. My people and all of humanity only the waft of Allah is increasing, upon humanity and Allah's waft is inevitable. There is nowhere to hide because the entire earth population is having been judged and found guilty of loving the devil as the devil continues to give them nothing.

During this Pandemic there have been reports of people dying by the thousands, hundreds of thousands and even millions, worldwide. There is no preventing the destruction that is now plaguing the entire planet. Every life form on our planet is feeling the effects of the wrath of Allah and there is no escaping this. So now the former President Mr. Donald Trump has lost the election and America now has a new President Elect Mr. Joe Biden, believe me everyone President Elect Mr. Joe Biden is not the answer because him and his administration, cannot prevent the destruction that is now upon us. Every government on our planet is totally confuse because they do not have the power or intelligence, to prevent the destruction that is plaguing our planet.

To be living in the times of the beginning of the destruction of Yakub's civilization, world, and people, is incredibly special because you are living out the prophesies, we were taught from the scriptures {Bible, Holy Quran, and the Torah}; ever since we were birth and all our lives. We are now facing the inevitable and humanity does not know to do because humanity have been lied to, deceived and mist led, for thousands of years. My younger brother Mahdi made me realize that lessons, are for students so that the student may continue the journey of life; and seeing how he or she may contribute to aid humanity by making and disseminating all information accessible for the upliftment, of all humanity.

Humanity at this time is confused and it is a pitiful site to see how confuse humanity is. This confusion has attacked every so-called religion and every religious sect, on our planet. This state of confusion has attacked every political organization, throughout the world. The pitiful acts to demonstrate love, is not fooling Allah and are not excepted by Allah. To all of humanity remember that it does not matter what name you call the Universal Creator, It is the person that all religions, call upon and teach in the mosques, synagogues, churches, temples, and everything else, Allah revealed himself to his last and greatest messenger, Mr. Elijah Muhammad; that He W. D. Fard Muhammad is Allah in person and the physical to whom all praises are due to.

This Mighty One and only He, has the power to know what is in everyone's heart and their mind, not only on just our planet whose name is originally Asia but throughout the entire universe. The confusion is so thick the entire humanity has fell victim to the lies, deceit and false promises, Satan The Accused Devil has given them. This is so plain to see during this controlled So-Called Pandemic, and it is a shame. To see good people in their hearts, succumb to the wishes of all of humanity, Satan The Accused Devil which is this 10% also known as the Illuminati. Knowing and understanding who makes up this devilish regime of international terrorist, murders, and thieves, is more important than anything. Knowing how to control yourself in all situations is even more important, for all of humanity's survival. It is extremely hard to have a relationship of meaningfulness and truth matters, here in this Pandemic. The mass of humanity is very confused and truly do not know what to do, so primal instincts begin to kick in and everyone feels their survival depends upon one's self. The mas of humanity does not know why what is happening is happening, so they fall into searching and believing for that, which does not exist as the history has revealed itself because everything, continue to fail the mass of humanity.

In fact, everyone you must understand or begin to question the validity of the poison foods {information} that you are ingesting and what you are teaching, the children. What you may believe is in correct because surly one can see, this world and society of Mr. Yakub is being destroyed, right before our very eyes. This time period in which we are now living is an incredibly stressful time, for all love ones because we live in a society and world, where love, mercy and truthfulness do not really exist. The pretense of love is greatly except because this society and the many distraction, makes it impossible to love oneself, so how is it possible to love someone else.

This American government and society taught the ex-slaves of America to love only them and not themselves. After giving their enemies what they wanted which was total submission to their kind and many black men and women, always had attitudes and self-hatred and the men took their frustrations and hatred for their enemies, out on their wives and children. This is still happening today my people and all of humanity, right here in America and many other parts on our planet. The entire planet of humanity must understand that we are now living, in the destruction of Yakub society.

The so-called founding father and mothers of this American Society or nation, were so evil especially the women included their evil made the prophets of old, fall and cowered in fear. If one new what the so-called founding fathers and mothers did, I cannot see what they are proud of because their ancestors, were and are nothing but demons. I know from personal experience that that the so-called founding fathers and mothers and their decedents, taught me to hate myself, my original woman and Queen and my children, father, mother, brothers, and sister. So, in truth I walk around filled with hatred all my life and was afraid and did not know how to love and show, my original black queen I love her. Not this American homosexual version, of love which have destroyed black families all around our planet.

In truth I say to the world and every human being on our planet what I and my ancestors had to endure here in America, It is impossible for me to have any love or forgiveness for America and this wicked government who is at the helm, of Mr. Yakub society and world.

This Pandemic or so-called Pandemic has taught me no matter how close I and his mother, was looking at death our creation together was their watching and protecting, over both of us. if not for Juliana Ruth Brooks giving birth to our son Ibn- Saladin Shabazz- Allah my youngest son and baby and name sake, we both would be dead and forgotten Allah U Akbar, Elijah Muhammad RasulAllah. There is absolutely nothing in this entire universe is worthy to be serve, beside you. My eldest son Niheem {Alfa} and my youngest son Ibn {Omega} demonstrated, their love for their father and Ibn mother.

This so-called Pandemic or Pandemic has shown me that my two sons, love me and are concerned about me and it has shown me other things, as well. I love a woman an incredibly beautiful woman from Jersey but since I was abused by this American society and government in every aspect, I failed because I had no love for myself. How could I understand how to love, an Original Black Queen?

I want and need the entire world to understand that I was born into a world in which it was breaded into me and all of slaves, that I and my kind are nothing; but what we [the Enemies of yourself and kind] want you and your kind to be; so we [your enemy and the enemy of freedom, justice and equality] give you Jesus {A mystery god}, The Enemies Of Our Ancestors] we give you make believe so-called religions, belief and so-called written religions, scrolls and books other than what the Original Creator, wanted for all of humanity; not Mr. Yakub makings and his grafting's.

For us original people it has been taught to us all, that Home Is where; The Hatred Of Self And Kind Began and started; by our enemies, the same enemies of our Fathers and Mothers and ancestors, by this hateful American government, people and their Supreme Evil of Zionism, Christianity and every other religion and claim, that your religion is from the Universal Creator, is an absolute lie.

What kind of religion and government would teach, encourage, and put under a death penalty, the ones who cleared up this wilderness and made this so-called America government, exist today; to hate themselves and kind? To hate their fathers, mothers, brothers, sisters, wives, and children? This is what this supremely evil American government and people, did to us the original people, whose history transcends Abraham, Muza, Jesus and Muhammad of Arabia included, by trillions of years.

We the ex-slave and descendants of the first original people from the eastern hemisphere, where brought here to bring America into existence, in 1555 this includes South America as well and everywhere else in the western hemisphere. We never called ourselves Africans because we are not Africans, we are by nature the Original Asiatic Blackman and woman. This world and society have purposely destroyed us whose history here in America, is nearly five-hundred years; three hundred years of chattel slavery and the next one hundred years of mental and spiritual slavery.

This evil world and society have done so much damage to dark people here in America and throughout the entire planet, until over 95% of the world population are doomed. The destruction of Yakub's world and society cannot be stopped, avoided, or escape because this is not Hollywood. Your religion will not help you, your belief in these wicked politics and demons you love and support, has sealed your faith and gain you a seat in the fires from Allah. Another thing everyone if you have evil in your mind's hearts, in this day and time, what religion can save you. So, everyone must understand that Allah knows what truly lies in every life form not only on the planet Earth, But every life form in the entire universe.

I have an exceptionally beautiful Queen whom I dearly love but this American government, society, and people, do everything to make sure that we do not love our Original Asiatic Black woman. This and all the drugs and alcohol make it impossible for us to love our wives and children. If a man does not love his wife and children, this is a man who have absolutely no love for himself. It took me many years and a bout with death, taught me how valuable she is and how much I need her, how much we need each other. Such a society, government and people must pay for their diabolical sins.

I discover true love from my Original Asiatic Black Queen. This shows the supreme evil of this American government, Mr. Yakub world and makings and all these so-called religions. My Queen Shakara [Zenobia] deserves to be treated as the Queen and I have learned to love, appreciate, trust, enjoy and depend on; to the entire humanity I say this; "there isn't a woman on this planet who is more worthy than my Queen, [the Original Asiatic Black Woman] deserves to ascend into the heavens, where I and she was created.

The atrocities, ignorant, disbelief loathing for self and kind, prostitution and every other evil in America, have been compacted into black communities throughout America. Everything of evil with no end in sight everywhere one may traverse throughout America, this evil is now at a boiling point condition, in black communities throughout America and the world. This evil has spilled into every community the death toll is staggering and have all of humanity, gripped with fear. These so-called religions it does not matter what name they may go by cannot save humanity, due to all the evil that has been committed by these so-called religions of god. These so-called religions claim their so-called holy books Bible, Torah and Quran, are from god; yet judging from all the actions by the people who say they believe and follow these said religions, none of these religions are worth having and they cannot save humanity because they are all liars and have betrayed, their oath to Allah [God].

People may not like what I am saying nevertheless what I am saying is the truth and I will never stop, telling the truth. As I have said in my other writings, I am a student of the Last Messenger of Allah Mr. Elijah Muhammad. He Muhammad RasulAllah, is responsible for me what I am today, and I am forever grateful to Allah who visited us, in the person of Master Fard Muhammad. Allah thou art the greatest and there is none worthy to be served besides you Allah U Akbar Mr. Elijah Muhammad, the true and only Muhammad RasulAllah.

Beware of these ignorant fools disguising themselves as so-called followers of the Holy Messenger, when in truth they are still the ignorant field hands and house slaves they were when they came to America, aboard the slave ships. They have the same mentality as they had when they were on the plantation and that have not been so long ago. They claimed to be followers of Muhammad RasulAllah when in truth their mentalities, are rooted in Christianity. These so-called followers' ways and actions are like the snake of the grafted type and our enemies knows this about them because their scientist of human behavior, have been studding them, ever since they crossed the Atlantic.

There is absolutely no progress of building or policing their neighborhoods while our enemies are still, dumping their toxicity waste throughout every black community in America and many other places throughout the world. This evil American government made up Zionist, Christianity and so-called Sunna Islam who had recently, joined this club of iniquity the American government. The American government has never set us free we are 'not free today. We have no land of our own, we do not produce or manufactor anything for ourselves. We do not have our own farms to produce food for ourselves; we do not warehouse and silos to store and protect our crops; we do not have any hospitals for ourselves; we do not have any schools for our children; why the only thing we receive is self-hatred, loathing, ignorant and every other evil that one cannot imagine in black communities, unless you are one of these demons or you are servant to these demons.

If any Black man and black woman that have a higher spiritual love for each other, here comes this devil and its black looking servants, doing everything to destroy us and our heaven. We have absolutely no land of our own, culture or customs of our own, we are celebrating the customs and barbaric culture of the enemies of our ancestors and ourselves. We do not even have a language of our own. All the above mention is what comes with Freedom once you understand this, you will see we have never been free; only freedom our enemies gave us is the freedom to worship them our enemies, their false religions, and useless politics.

My people and all of humanity must understand is that we have been living under Pandemic Conditions, ever since we crossed the Atlantic or was brought here by our enemies in chains. The jungles of East Asia now called Africa have been under and in Pandemic conditions since the early fourteen hundreds and they do not or cannot recognize this truth and reality.

Yet you ignorant so-called African Americans still love the devil although the devil continues, to give you nothing; not even the pleasure of loving and respecting your other half and children. I here or I had heard brothers say in this day and time we are going fishing, or we are going to raise the dead; how can a dead man or person raise the dead when they themselves, are still dead to the reality of the times, in which we all are living in? It is impossible for anyone to raise the dead because raising the dead, is not their mission; that mission belongs to the Holy Messenger of Allah Mr. Elijah Muhammad. Our mission is to re-build a righteous government and nation for ourselves that is our mission. How can you convince me that you love the Holy Messenger of Allah and Allah Almighty, but you call Allah's last and greatest Messenger the Honorable Elijah Muhammad? By calling him the Honorable Elijah Muhammad you who claim to a follow of the Holy Messenger by calling him the Honorable, you who claim to a follow of him are the ones that are reducing the Holy Messenger to nothing, but a regular human being and he is not. Mr. Elijah Muhammad is in fact, Muhammad RasulAllah.

The dictionary if you truly have study it explains the difference between Mr. and Honorable and which is why American government referred to him as Mr. Muhammad and never the Honorable. If one has truly learned then one should know the different and this why I always refer to the Holy Messenger as being, Mr. Muhammad.

I refuse to follow or let anyone other than my own self, to think or decide for me because none of them are qualified to think or speak for me. I am disappointed those who claim they are followers of MuhammadRasulAllah and have not even tried to carry out the plan that the Rasul, has left us. Instead, you so-called followers are more incline to build churches and temples. The temples are structure after the Masons lodges prescribed and built, by Mr. Prince Hall in 1790. Even Prophet Noble Drew Ali designed his temples after Prince Hall because this was very affective, for housing, social gatherings, political discussing and educating his people.

The Holy Messenger Of Allah mission was to deliver the Message from Allah, in hopes that He could raise all his people. The Holy Savior [Allah in person] knew that his Holy Messenger would not be successful yet because of the love of his people and the re-establishing his people, amongst humanity as intelligent, righteous and a productive civilize people; so, our holy Savior Master Fard Muhammad [Allah in person] allow His Holy Messenger [Mr. Elijah Muhammad] to try. Allah knew he would not be successful because eighty-five to ninety percent of His people, are disbelievers. The Holy Savior also knew that eighty-five to ninety percent of those who claimed to follow the Holy Messenger, were in fact disbelievers and would not carry on with the plans of Allah, to build a Nation For Themselves.

The Holy Savior [Allah in person] knowing that His Holy Messenger would not be successful but because of love and sincerity towards his people and the love Allah has for His Messenger, Allah allowed the Holy Messenger to tried. During the time period from 1934 the Muhammad RasulAllah, was birth and began His mission of educating his people and building a Nation and Home, for his people. As time went on the Holy Messenger realized why Allah was reluctant in granting him, this request. These are facts everyone that can be examine at any time if one dares to know the real and actual truth.

It is not my desire to cause trouble amongst this now said Nation of Islam, I am just revealing the truth that is being hidden, by these hypocrites. Having a better understanding of the Teachings of Allah through the mouth of His Messenger [Mr. Elijah Muhammad] has made me a supremely much better man and I thank Allah for visiting us and showing us His Mercy, Kindness, and love for us, in the person of Master Fard Muhammad [W.D.Fard Muhammad Allah U Akbar there is none worthy to be served, but Allah. I thank Allah for choosing Mr. Elijah Muhammad to be His last and greatest Messenger because Mr. Elijah Muhammad never wavered and delivered the teachings he received, form Allah and the Holy Messenger gave these teachings to all who would lend an ear.

The only way the so-called African American can have a chance of survival is that there must be complete unity and Ruthless Pragmatism. When these so-called ministers begin to understand this, then they will be able to properly guide congregation. As it stands, I have not met a minister or so-called follow who understand this, therefore they are opening lodges and they call it a temple, when in truth these are nothing but lodges. It was the Holy Messenger of Allah who was mission by Allah to build and open temples, for a place of learning, doing and how to do, in unity and pragmatism.

I said before we the so-called negro now called African Americans have been living under Pandemic conditions, for nearly five hundred years. These traitors amongst us these religious and political traitors working with the enemies, of their supposed to be people; have purposely led back into our enemies and the enemies of our ancestors, for selfish gain.

In fact, if there is any un-rest in the black communities throughout America, these religious and political so-called representatives of the black communities throughout America. Are summoned to the enemies' court [the white house, congress, the senate, and house of representatives] and then are giving instructions equipment and funds, to rock the black communities throughout America, back to being passive and trusting the enemies, of black people in America and throughout the world.

The Pandemic conditions black and red people [Indians] have been living under for close to five hundred years, are now being felt by our enemies. The Holy Messenger of Allah Mr. Elijah Muhammad; told us that Allah promise to remove fear from our hearts and put it on those, who have put it on you [us]. This nearly five-hundred-year Pandemic we all have been living under has ripped away from us our very essence of love for ourselves, our children parents, self and kind. This nearly five-hundred-year Pandemic has even ripped every Once and grain of Moral fiber, from us all my people and replace in us all, to embrace this Demon, that our enemies call Jesus. This nearly five-hundred-year Pandemic has extinguished our quest for learning and knowledge and replaced by buffoonery and ignorance. This nearly five-hundred-year Pandemic has destroyed and wiped from our memories, that we come from and are the Kings, Queens, Princes and Princesses; not just the Eastern Hemisphere but the entire planet and replaced with false images of the thieves and murder and whores, trying to claim our History and Heritage.

This nearly five-hundred-year Pandemic has robbed us of our beautiful complexion, skin and even our beautiful teeth, by feeding us the same foods our enemies fed to the pigs and hogs they called it slop; the ignorant amongst us called this soul food and till this very day these fools still call it soul food; the only food on our planet, that absolutely has no nutritional value and produces poor health, ignorance, total savagery physical suffering and an un-merciful, painful death.

This nearly five-hundred-year Pandemic we were forced to live under has destroyed our ability to communicate and love our second self, nor can we even recognize our second self. Fathers hating sons, sons hating their fathers; mothers hating daughters, daughters hating mothers, death, destruction, filth, diseases, murder, rape, pedophilia, drugs, alcohol, in every black community throughout America and the world. Truth be told black communities in America and throughout the world, are sewage, waste deposit of every inconceivable evil, has been flushed by this society, world, people, religions, and politics, into every black community in America and throughout the world.

This nearly five-hundred-year Pandemic that we have been forced to live under has completely Demoralized, us all. These false religions all of them also have mis-led us and added on to our Demoralization. These worthless politics through all of the false promises that our enemies come up with, is part of waste being harvest in black communities throughout America and the world. These agents of our enemies come around during election seeking our vote, never having any intention, of fulfilling the lies that they all are o-called telling us and this includes these so-called negro politicians, who are servants of our enemies. Also, my people be aware of these false religious leaders quoting scriptures telling us they represent god; read this book because it came from god, none of these liars are telling us the truth because they all want to rob us and use us a tool, to keep themselves, wives, and children in heaven; while they all are on a mission to keep us locked into this cage, of ignorance, suffering and death. Never knowing the truth about anything, especially our enemies and the lies, deceit, treachery, and murderous intentions concerning the original people; not only in America but throughout the world.

This nearly five-hundred-year Pandemic has left black and red people in capable of doing anything for ourselves, wives, and children, without the approval, intervention, and micromanagement, by our enemies. You are not motivated to do anything of good for self or anyone else because your creative scientific mind, has been stolen and lost, by our enemies. So, since you know longer can think positive for yourself, wives, children nor the society in which we live in today. You have absolutely no respect, love or patience for your woman and you treat her like garbage; yet you treat the woman of our enemies like she is a Queen and in truth our enemy's women are just as evil, diabolical, and filled with hatred, for us and our kind.

Examine the history and current events and stop running to our enemies for interpretation or understanding because our enemies, will lie to you, deceive you and mislead you without any hesitation at all. Rather it be a so-called religious person or a politician both are working for our nearly five-hundred-year-old enemy, since being kidnapped and brought to the Western Hemisphere. My people and all of humanity the past nearly five-hundred-years we have been living under Pandemic conditions and we have physically survived. We must not forget our survival abilities because that is all we have, and it has not failed us. We my people must stop disillusioning ourselves wife, children, and people, in general because nothing is going to save us, but ourselves. There is no so-called heaven as our enemies have taught us somewhere in the sky or elsewhere; these are lies concocted by our enemies. There is no seat on the Mother Plain for any of us because the Mother Plain is a war ship, not some luxury cruise ship for the dead, these foolish mis-guided people are also lying, my people. There is only one Universal Creator called by many different names but nevertheless, He is the Universal Creator. So, get a better knowledge of the Universal Creator and be incredibly careful when reading or studying any of these so-called holy books and be incredibly careful who you ask for interpretation, meaning and understanding because our enemies' control all these so-called religions and our enemies as always, will lie to you, deceived you and lead you to your demise; as the past nearly five-hundred years have taught us, since being in the Western Hemisphere.

CHAPTER 15

THE TWENTY-FIRST CENTURY ILLUMINATI

When you travel around America and throughout the world and talk to people you will discover, that ninety to ninety-five percent of the world population has absolutely no clue about the Illuminati, or what is this Illuminati is. Who are players, what are goals of this Illuminati, who are the members of this Illuminati and what is the purpose of this secret organization? Who are the leaders of this secret organization, how old is this secret organization? Where did this secret organization originated from?

My people as well as all humanity never seek knowledge, wisdom and understanding, from fools and clowns because they have absolutely no concept of what is, taking place. Religions and politics are control by this Illuminati and have been controlling politics and religion, since the Civil War. The Illuminati origin began in Europe and since has spread to America and throughout the world. The Illuminati is about power and controlling the entire planet resources as well as printing of currency, by all nations on earth, the Illuminati is in control of it all. Baron Von Rothchild is originator of this secret organization ever since Napoleon Bonaparte began conquering

Europe and invasion of Russia in the seventeen- hundreds. Baron Von Rothchild was diabolical and supremely ruthless, in his thinking and planning because he envisioned himself as the puppet master, he was manipulating world events since the seventeen-century.

It was the Illuminati that built Wall Street and controlled the stocked market and anytime they chose to cause depression or recession, they did it without the approval of any government, anywhere on our planet. Since the Civil War and all the wars in Europe, this Illuminati invested and took control of arming America's military, by controlling every arm production plants, in and throughout America. This includes the Army, Airforce, Navy, Marines, and the Coast Guard, this also included the space programs not only in America but throughout Europe and Russia included.

Every army that invaded so-called Africa, China, India, the Mediterranean, Manchuria and everywhere else, were financed by the Illuminati; in fact, this Illuminati would finance both sides, to make sure the Illuminati would always be on the winning side. The list of men that made up this Illuminati were a few men passion and objective, was global domination of every bank throughout the world and the controlling of the world's resources, also the manufacturing of arms and weapons and ship building.

This is the power that Baron Von Rothchild understood and he passed this information along with his plan, to conquer the world and get others to do it for him. To crush the Confederate world the Illuminati through President Abraham Lincoln, the North [Union Armed Forces] instituted the Green Backs thus making the Confederacy currency, nothing more but monopoly currency and the Green Back is the currency of the Union, all America and recognized by the international community, as the legal and only currency, of America.

This Illuminati destroyed nations and people to achieve their goals, of world domination by any means necessary. Ever since the Industrial Revolution in the nineteenth century and early twentieth century, this Illuminati has been and still are controlling every aspect of life, in this society and world; giving this Illuminati absolute control over the lives of all humanity. This Illuminati seized control over all manufacturing of all goods, foods, housing, and real estate, everywhere on our planet. This Illuminati controlled the coal mines, smelting of Iron ore, copper mines, oil wells, gold mines, silver mines, nickel mines, led mines, every resource the country produce. When the country produced the Atomic Bomb financed by, the Illuminati and this Illuminati was involved then and after President Truman gave the order to bomb Hiroshima and Nagasaki. The Illuminati after seeing the affect and power of these two bombs, the Illuminati took control of all nuclear plants, and material throughout America and Europe.

You must remember my people and all humanity the Illuminati does not operate out front the Illuminati always have a front man and, in some cases, a woman. This Illuminati rule the president and all military forces and act with total impunity, the Illuminati answers to no one. Who do you think brought down this so-called Mafia/Costa Nostra it was the Illuminati, who brought them down and why? To let this so-called Mafia /Costa Nostra know, that they are not the real power, here in America or anywhere on our planet. The Illuminati operates in secret their identities are kept hidden their membership is kept hidden, from everyone in today's time. But understand my people and all of humanity the Illuminati has been exposed by Allah Almighty Himself and revealed to us all by Allah's last and greatest Messenger, Mr. Elijah Muhammad.

Who do you think made the decision to wipe out the Black Panthers and every other revolutionary organization, here in America and throughout the world? It is this Illuminati that gave the orders to J Eagar Hoover, the President, Congress, the Senate, the House of Representatives, and every Law Enforcement Agency including Interpol, FBI, CIA NSA Homeland Security, and every Police Force, throughout America. Politics is the weapon the Illuminati uses to enforce their will, policies, and ideas not only on American citizens, but every living being on our planet because the Illuminati has open it ranks to a few new members; from all over world, leaders from different countries and nations, have sworn an oath to this secret society and have joined the ranks of this secret society called the Illuminati. Religions are the dope and drug that this Illuminati uses to keep ninety to ninety-five percent, of humanity deceived and misled to the truth, of this Illuminati. Keeping ninety to ninety-five percent of humanity searching and waiting for this Mystery God, to come and save them.

The evil lies in in your places of worship because the lies about Allah the Universal Creator, cannot be seen by Humanity. This is believed by ninety to ninety-five percent of humanity and this is how the Illuminati, can hide themselves in plain sight. This Illuminati is extremely confident in their abilities to escape detection and mislead Ninety to ninety-five percent of humanity, to their destruction, starvation, physical suffering, mental slavery, and a horrible death, never realizing that the religions and caretakers of said religion, has lied to them all.

We must remember my people and I say this to all humanity;

When Allah visited us in the person of Master Fard Muhammad to whom praise are due forever, He Allah raised up from amongst the slain, the despised, the ignorant His last and greatest messenger Mr. Elijah Muhammad [Muhammad RasulAllah]. Allah did not teach His messenger or give his messenger any religion, for His chosen people. Allah the Universal Creator Lord and Master and the best knower; set up temples of learning the truth and not places of worshipping this Mystery God {Yakub}. Once Allah's Holy Messenger began his mission back in nineteen thirty -four, the Holy Messenger began building Temples of Learning for his people throughout America and this is the reason why the once lost and now found members of the Nation of Islam, set our Temples up for a place to learn the truth and to explore the sciences of life and the universe once again.

This scared the Illuminati to death because the Illuminati knew their time and the time of their maker {Yakub}, was now up. Now here is the love and mercy of Allah for us my people; Allah gave us his chosen people fifty-and twenty-year extinction, to clean ourselves up and return home. Yakub's makings, society and world had an opportunity to change their world, society and people and perhaps receive some compassion from Allah. But this evil, wicked, and diabolical Illuminati chose to honor their father and maker Mr. Yakub, reject the true Universal Creator, and persuade a life of evil, lies, deceit hatred and trying to master the Original Asiatic Blackman, woman, and child. And bring death, destruction, and chaos to all humanity. All anyone must do is first stop believing in this mystery god and false religions, then begin to search out and study the truth. The truth this Illuminati has been keeping away and hidden from all humanity, for the past near two hundred years, here in America;

it is more like four-thousand years because they spent two-thousand years, in the caves West Asia now called Europe.

This Illuminati and its members are not spirits, they are human beings that walks, talks, sleep and eat, just like every human being on our planet does. In fact, this lustful Illuminati has an over zealousness for sex with men, woman, little boys, and girls. Mothers and Fathers pleading for justice from this Illuminati who uses the American government and all governments on our planet, to bring death, destruction, chaos, hatred, suffering, starvation, and death, to enforce their evil will and diabolical thoughts upon all humanity. How ridiculous it sounds to hear these foolish so-called African Americans believing black lives matters. When history clearly demonstrates that black lives do not matter, black lives have never matter and black lives will never matter, amongst this Illuminati, government, and people. Your religious and political so-called leaders are lying to you all their nor? Then explain to me why these lying hypocrites are still teaching that Homosexual Caucasian boy, is the only child of the Universal Creator? Explain to me why these lying hypocrites teaching you to worship a mystery god, that you will not be able to see him, until you die? Why are these lying religious hypocrites from every religion, are telling you about this mystery heaven and twenty virgins, waiting for you.

This Illuminati and all its members know for an absolute fact there is nothing waiting for you after you die and there are no twenty virgins waiting for you either. Heaven is created by you while you live on this planet and you cannot create heaven without your second self. If you have no spiritual love for your second self, you cannot have any love for yourself, the Universal Creator or His Messenger. So, the only thing you have left is the hell this Illuminati, government and people have made and given to you and then they tell you god is watching over you and believe in something, that has never come to your aid, your wife aid or your children aid and never will.

What gives the heads of this Illuminati the ultimate confidence is that they have the truth of who, maker is and the instructions their maker left behind to his making. The Illuminati knows for an absolute fact that there is nothing after one dies and the Illuminati refuses to share this truth, with the mass of people including their own kind. Therefore, this Illuminati grab, steal, murder and commit every type of evil that a righteous person could never conceive. This Illuminati is Diabolically Ruthless in everything they plan and carry out on all of humanity, without any hesitation. You may hear fools talk about the Illuminati like they know what they are talking about, but in truth these fools do not have any clue on what they are saying or talking about. Especially the fools who claim to have supreme wisdom and they are the worst of the lot and more dangerous, to their own kind and humanity because these fools will and have threw their people under bus, for a few pennies and false friendship from the enemies of all humanity, as well as all life form on our planet.

Through Ruthless Pragmatism and unity are the weapons we need to implement against this Illuminati, for ourselves and all humanity to have a chance to survive this destruction that is certainly, over taking this Illuminati and the world they have made for themselves and kind. My people and all humanity these are not hate teachings these words I am speaking are to enlighten my people and all humanity, how to defend and protect themselves from the hate teachings, of this Illuminati and the world they have made. The propaganda machine stretches everywhere in America and throughout the world and this Illuminati will and have launch it against anyone, who may know the truth of them, and dare revealed this truth to his people and all humanity. I am a student of the Holy Messenger of Allah Mr. Elijah Muhammad {MuhammadRasulAllah} and I say this with great pride and honor. I serve Allah the Universal Creator Lord and Master and there is none worthy to be serve, but Allah and there is none liken unto Him. Allah visited His chosen one to be His Messenger {Mr. Elijah Muhammad} in the person of Master W.F.Muhammad, to whom all praises are due forever.

I have been taught go to war with no one about their so-called religion and will not let any of these false religions, attach that which Allah has given and taught me through the mouth of His {Allah} last and greatest Messenger Mr. Elijah Muhammad. Allah U Akbar there is none worthy to be serve besides you. The Holy Messenger taught us that Negroes are not going to rule, and this is true indeed. The real key my people is to be able to recognize these Negroes and frauds, when you see them because these Negroes and frauds have cloaked themselves, in the garments of the members of the Nation of Islam and other religious factions. Many of you are fooled by them and trust them when in truth, they are only out for their own self gain and false image.

Why can't these fools raise the dead Saladin? The reason being is that they are still dead, this why we must take Jerusalem, back from these Negroes and Frauds in order to put an end, to lying hypocrites. These Negroes and Frauds are in truth working for the Illuminati at an exceptionally low level and dare call themselves, the High Gods; what insanity is this in fact, this is downright disgusting and nothing more but out right Treason against Allah, Allah's last and greatest messenger and Islam period.

This Illuminati and their extremely well educated and well-trained scientist of human behavior know that I am telling the truth and they do not want me or anyone else, to reveal this truth. Study, observe and listen to these Negroes and Frauds they are revealing themselves constantly and they cannot stop or prevent the revealing of themselves. The reason why I am telling everyone this truth is to alert my people and all humanity how persistence, diabolically calculating, focus and determine, this Illuminati truly is because they know their Negroes and Frauds because they made them, nearly five-hundred-years ago. This is the reason why these Negroes and Frauds can only speak four-hundred words and these Negroes and Frauds, are not capable of speaking these four-hundred words well at all.

This Illuminati test, re-test evaluates and re-test again before they implement their most evil and diabolical plans, that will cost millions of lives and affect every life form on our planet, including every life form in the oceans, rivers, lakes, and streams. This Illuminati is headed by the Zionist and Christians and thirty years ago they have incorporated the Arab world and their religion, in which they call it Islam during the first Gulf War in which the destroyed the government of Iraq and people. It was the rulers of Saudi Arabia who struct up the deal that the Arab world along with their so-called religion of Islam, was invited to join this supremely evil and diabolical Illuminati and stop serving Allah. Since the Saudis joined up many other Arabs so-called nations, have also joined the ranks of this Illuminati with Saudi Arabia. This is all true just examine the history and current events, the truth is there, if one has no fear in their heart of this Illuminati and its newly acquired Arab members. The Hindus had already joined up with this Illuminati and was in complete agreement, with the diabolical plans, of this Illuminati and this is when the Illuminati using the American government

Mr. Woodrow Wilson was the President at this time, had enlisted Mr. Chang kai Chek for the Illuminati and the Illuminati began importing Opium from China to America. This is the early twenty-century when all this was taking place.

My people and all humanity the truth is out there all one must do is study and embrace, truth that this Illuminati wish to be kept hidden, from all humanity. The Monks in China fled North into the Mountains in order to protect the teachings, given to them by the Prophet Buddha. The Monks were also protecting the teachings of Mr. Confucius a great and brilliant Chinese Scholar and philosopher, for his people and humanity as well. The Monks were also protecting the teachings of Sun SU Art Of War. It was President Mr. Chang Kai Cheuk that was giving these precious works or allowing America and Europe, to steal them from his people. The orchestrators of these diabolical plans are this secret organization called the Illuminati.

Wallace D. Mohammad did not destroy his or tried to destroy the teachings that Allah Himself, had taught and gave his father, for us all. It was the ones who claims tb be followers of Allah's last and greatest Messenger Mr. Elijah Muhammad, are the ones who sat back and did nothing because of their disbelief and fear. The sad part about the whole thing is that these same disbeliever believe they are doing the work, that the Holy Messenger had did because they built a so-called temple and call themselves raising the dead. The truth be told these fools have and are leading themselves and people, further away from Allah and the teachings that Allah taught and gave His Holy Messenger Mr. Elijah Muhammad.

I have heard constantly from these so-called said followers of the Holy Messenger, "these are the teachings of the Honorable Elijah Muhammad". This statement is completely and totally incorrect!

There is absolutely no capital in this statement because this statement demonstrate that you have no idea on what you are saying and that you were not paying attention, to the lectures the Holy Messenger of Allah Mr. Elijah Muhammad was lecturing us on. This seriously in accurate statement these so-called followers continue to boast about, has allowed this Illuminati to infiltrate, the temples of Islam here in America and manipulate control over ninety-five percent, of the congregation and spread dissension and interrupted the unity amongst these so-called followers, that Allah had mission His Holy Messenger to re-establish amongst us Allah's chosen people . Thus, giving Wallace D. Mohammad the power to swoop down and rob the National Treasury, of the eighty to one hundred million dollars, siege control over all the resources without any opposition and extraordinarily little resistance at all. Wallace D. Mohammad was an agent of the Illuminati by way of Saudi Arabia and this so-called religion they call Islam. These so-called followers of the Holy Messenger also believe that the temples of Islam here in America, were infiltrated by the F.B.I. What these so-called followers did not know or understand, was that the Illuminati was on top of everything that was taking place and was giving the orders to the President, the Director of the FBI Mr. J. Edgar Hoover, the Attorney General, the so-called United Nations and every other Law Enforcement Agency in America, this include the CIA, Homeland Security, ATF, the NSA, the entire Media and all of America's Military Forces; this is how powerful this Illuminati is back then till this present day and time, in which we are now living.

Clarity my people and all of humanity included is what the entire planet of humanity must have, if there be any chance for humanity to survive this destruction of Mr. Yakub's world, society,

Mr. Yakub's makings and this Illuminati, who he left in charge, to rule for six-thousand years. Another name or phase for this Illuminati is as follows, "Satan The Accused Devil". The truth of all things, all people, all religions, and corrupt evil politics, must be revealed to the entire world. If you ask any so-called follower of the Holy Messenger of Allah what happened in nineteen- seven seventy- four and nineteen seventy-five, these so-called followers will not tell you the truth or they still do not have the ability nor capability, to understand what really happened and who were the architects and the orchestrators, of this diabolical, evil and wicked plans to wipe out the Teachings of Allah, the reality of Allah and the true Holy Messenger of Allah {Muhammad RasulAllah}, Mr. Elijah Muhammad. This is the only truth that has the power to save all humanity if humanity would only submit to His Allah's Will.

There are absolutely no Negroes or so-called African Americans that are members of this Illuminati, these Negroes now called African Americans are only the servants of this Illuminati, its members, and associates. We must regain back from this Illuminati, there members and associates, all scientific knowledge of all things and life on our planet, that they have stolen from us. We my people and all humanity must with draw ourselves from all these false religions because these false religions have ninety to ninety-eight percent of all humanity, strung out on this religious dope which is more powerful than any drug in all the hospitals worldwide, that are under the control of this Illuminati, their members, their associates, and Negro so-called African American Flunkies, worldwide. This Illuminati their members and associates pledge and oath, to their maker {Mr. Yakub} to fight to the death before they surrender. Therefore, they have an insurmountable stockpile of nuclear weapons and many different methods, of delivering these weapons of mass destruction on earth and into heavens for the purpose of trying, to destroy the Mother Plain. This is referred to as the Battle In The Sky. As Allah taught His last and greatest Messenger Mr. Elijah Muhammad and Allah taught us all throughout America, Africa, and other parts of world, through the mouth of His Holy Messenger.

This Illuminati is relentless in the pursuit of staying in power at any cost and who knows better than we, who felt this unholy regime wrath for nearly five-hundred-years. I love my wife, my Queen, second self on a supremely higher spiritual level that brings us both joy and happiness that we found and now have each other. We both realize that we are gifts from Allah to each other and here is where the true heaven is and this diabolically, evil Illuminati with all their members and associate, will never get in our way or prevent the Asiatic black man and woman from loving each other and all our children, from achieving heaven while we live. Allah U Akbar there is none liken unto you or your equal in any shape form or fashion and this includes all your prophets including your last and greatest Messenger, Mr. Elijah Muhammad. I am forever grateful Allah for you visiting us in the Holiest person of Master W.F. Muhammad, or I would not be the man I am today. All Holy Praise Be Longs To You Allah and absolutely no one else.

A man who has nothing to die for is a man who has nothing to live for and this is a crying shame because at least ninety-eight percent of the world population, is in this condition and this includes these so-called said followers of the Holy Messenger of Allah Almighty. I refuse to allow this Illuminati and its American government to control and dictate to me, how I should love, treat, and respect my wife, my Queen and my second self as I am to her. I will not live-in fear of my enemies this Illuminati and all its so-called superpowers, to the point that I am afraid to demonstrate sincere love, respect, and appreciation to and for my Asiatic original Queen and wife, whose beauty surpasses all other women, on our planet and given the chance her intelligence, her spirit to live and overcome the diabolically evil plans to destroy us and our children, are far greater than any other woman, on our planet. I would rather die on my feet fighting and defending her, all our children and our way of life, in face of the most powerful Beast, our planet has ever known. I have everything and every reason to surrender my life for and this is the reason, I have everything and reason to live for.

Every time my wife Shakara {Zenobia} and our children look at me they all know, they are looking at Allah in the physical and I am her husband, and she will never let our children forget, who their father is and what her husband and their father is about; and that her husband and all our children know that I could not be bought and would never sell out his heritage as many of these so-called said followers have done; for a few pennies. These twenty-first- century want to be pimps, trying to sell my wife, my Queen, my second self the MGT and GCC handbooks I put a swift and immediately halt on this foolishness. My wife is not a Muslim Girl in Training! My wife knows how to act at home and abroad because she is born a righteous Asiatic Original Black Queen and she is the wife of Saladin Shabazz-Allah and I Saladin Shabazz-Allah am her husband. Most of these so-called said followers of the Holy Messenger of Allah Mr. Elijah are so confused and mis-led by this Illuminati, without even knowing or realizing they themselves are acting on behalf of this supremely diabolically, evil Illuminati and these fools claim to have Supreme Wisdom.

I wanted to point out how diabolically crafty this Illuminati is because this Illuminati will attack from every avenue possible, has attack from every avenue possible and if necessary, create a situation or stage an event to possibly open a new avenue or platform, in which this Illuminati can launch another one of their supremely diabolically evil plan of total and complete domination of all humanity and all life forms, living and existing on our planet. The Illuminati that are ruling in today's time are not physically the same physical beings let us say four hundred to nearly now five-hundred-hundred- years, we are dealing with the descendants of the first Illuminati established here in the Western Hemisphere.

The history our history my people and all humanity should pay extremely close attention to what I am about, to reveal. The history of all Original Asiatic Black men and Original Asiatic Black women have been destroyed and distorted, by this Illuminati, their American government, their public educational system, and their people; until you will never find the truth of ourselves, in their history books. In fact, our enemies in the Western Hemisphere since Christopher Columbus, Ferdinand Magellan, the Pilgrims and Plymouth Rock and the Jamestown Landing in fifteen-fifty-five, up to the explosive mass migration of Europeans to Elis Island, have all participated in our destruction and distorting of our history not only in America but throughout the world.

So, then who will do everything in their power to reveal and help to restore our history, to our children. Every other people on our planet love their scholars that they have produce, for themselves except these ignorant so-called African Americans and especially the ones who claims to be followers, of the Messenger of Allah. The envy, the wickedness, and evil things these so-called followers about the scholars that have been produced from amongst themselves. These foolish silly so-called African Americans are their own worst enemies and this why there is not any unity amongst themselves. In fact, even amongst those who claim to be followers of the Messenger of Allah have fell into tribalism because they argue amongst themselves, compete against each other, they lie and deceive each other and for the life of them, they have not earned the trust and blessings of Allah because at least ninety-eight percent of them, have rejected Allah and Allah's last and greatest Messenger Mr. Elijah Muhammad. This Illuminati, all their governments, members and associates know that what I am saying is the absolute truth. The Holy Messenger of Allah Mr. Elijah Muhammad taught us that " we must speak the truth even if the truth condemns ourselves, the truth must be told". This was taught to all the students and so-called followers of the Messenger of Allah, this supremely diabolical and supremely evil so-called secret organization or society called the Illuminati, all their governments, members, associates, and people. He the Holy Messenger of Allah {Muhammad RasulAllah} Mr. Elijah Muhammad said "I am the Messenger of Allah to you all meaning all humanity on our planet.

So, if you do not like what I am saying tells me you are not a believer in Truth, Freedom, Justice and Equality; you are only pretending to be a believer and Allah knows exactly what evil lies in your minds and the evil that lies in your hearts and Allah cannot be fooled or deceived, by anyone or any life form in the entire universe. So, everyone who claims to be righteous and evil lies in your minds and hearts, be aware Self Deceit is the greatest of all deceits. Until one stop deceiving themselves and face up to the evil, they have committed and are still committing, it is impossible for you to serve or believe in Allah and in truth were never a believer or follower, of Allah's Holy Messenger Mr. Elijah Muhammad. If one cannot admit or see the envy in their hearts because another one was given the ability by Allah, to do something they cannot do or achieve, what this one is achieving and this is due to nothing but self-envy and hatred; this is not Islam at all, this is nothing but that slave making religion Christianity and you fool only yourself. While this Illuminati, governments and people view you as absolutely no threat to there on going rulership. What you ignorant foolish so-called followers of the Messenger of Allah could only realize that you all believe, you have deceived Allah and deceived the Holy Messenger, when truth be told all of you are only doing and have done is deceiving yourself and kind; therefore, aiding the enemies of Allah and Allah's last and greatest Messenger Mr. Elijah Muhammad, to wage war against Allah and Allah's last and greatest Messenger.

What you are trying pass off as friendships in all walks of life is truly nothing more but eternal submissiveness to the enemies of Allah, Allah's Holy Messenger, and your so-called people. There is nothing more rewarding than Allah bestowing this gift of writing and disseminating, the truth that Allah has taught me and the world through the mouth of His last and greatest Messenger Mr. Elijah Muhammad {MuhammadRasulAllah} and I am able to record this truth, for future generations. It is not about the money it is about leaving something behind for others and to hell with everyone else, who maybe against me and are against what I am doing. Who falsely accuse me of things they make up in their own heads, while they are the guilty ones, selling the teachings of Allah for self-profit? While they are guilty of selling the publications of Allah's Holy Messenger Mr. Elijah Muhammad, for self-profit and self-gain. I thank Allah for revealing these ignorant and foolish disbelievers to me and removing me from their mist. I thank Allah forever for revealing to me the truth of this Illuminati, who makes up the heads of this Illuminati, where this Illuminati received their instructions from and the purpose of this Illuminati being in existence. I am forever grateful to Allah for revealing to me through the mouth of His Holy Messenger the members and associates of this supremely evil Illuminati are. I thank Allah our Holy Savior in person for revealing to me the truth, about all these failed religions and who is truly controlling all these false religions and how this Illuminati use this religious dope, to drug and keep ninety-eight percent of all humanity completely drugged up and ignorant to the truth. I thank Allah for visiting us in the persons of Master W.F. Muhammad, to whom all praise is due to forever. I thank Allah eternally for choosing and raising up from amongst me and my people, His last and greatest Messenger Mr. Elijah Muhammad. I thank Allah eternally for revealing these ignorant fools that are using the teachings of you Allah, to shield their dirty religion Christianity and trying to pass it off as Islam. I thank you O' Allah for revealing my hidden enemies to me. There is none worthy to be serve besides you O' Allah and there is none your equal and there is none liken unto you O' Allah and I bear witness that Mr. Elijah is your last, greatest Messenger and the true and only Muhammad RasulAllah. Allah U Akbar there is none worthy to be serve besides you.

CHAPTER 16

THE HIDDEN TRUTH

This chapter we will be examining the mind set of these foolish so-called African Americans and the supremely foolishness, of these so-called said followers of the Holy Messenger of Allah and what they believe and how delusional they all are in their perception and understanding. Many of our people believe that a suit, fancy shoes, and car make them something special as they walk around and throughout the poor part, of our planet and especially America. The ridicules colors that they wear as they parade through the poor part of America trying to project to the people their people, that they are more successful than their people. These fools even wear these ridiculous colors at so-called business meetings and these ignorant fools, with their narcissist demeanor and behavior, our enemies know for an absolute fact, that these fools can be use against their own people. Our enemies also know that they are not sincere in that which they claim, to believe in and follow.

Every intelligent human being on our planet know they are fools, and they are ignorant because of their lack of understanding of the English language and their extremely limited word comprehension. These fools want to be recognized by the enemies of themselves and their people and the enemies just string them along, knowing that they could and will be use as a destructive, against themselves, their people and their so-called belief in Allah and Allah's Holy Messenger. Our enemies also know if fools like these unlearned fools continue to project themselves, as the superior amongst their people; our enemies with supreme certainty that neither them nor their people will ever be a threat to our enemies' rulership. Our enemies also know that these narcissist ignorant fools will be extremely helpful in making sure, that their people will forever remain in a state of absolute confusion and ignorant As I have said before these ignorant narcissist disgraceful fools cannot keep their mouths and want to feel important, so, justifying to their own delusionary perception and weak understanding, make useless clowns of themselves, all their people and kind, and what they claimed to believe in.

These fools as I said before walk around and throughout the poor parts of America wearing their, not so expensive suits, shirts, ties, and shoes, even their cars; believing they have supreme wisdom and are special also blessed. When in truth the enemies laugh at them office personnel as well, how utterly ridiculous they look and are. There is a reason why these so-called now referred to as African Americans and this includes every single one of them. The so-called African Americans ex-slaves of and for America were presented with two gifts, from Allah. Now what I am about to reveal is going to send shock waves throughout this said Nation of Islam, here in America and amongst these so-called said followers of the Messenger of Allah, in my lifetime. The Names of these two gifts are the Holy Messenger of Allah Mr. Elijah Muhammad and his top Minister Al- Malik Shabazz more commonly known as Minister Mr. Malcolm X. These so-called followers are so blinded by self-hatred, until they cannot be led to the truth, of nearly all things and the sciences it will take and are most essentially needed, to build a civilization for themselves, wives, and children, for all eternity.

This intel or information is not commonly known amongst the new converts nevertheless, the truth is that many of the so-called Ministers at that time, hatred for Minister Malcolm was not a secret. The envy amongst the Ministers and high-ranking officials of the Holy Messenger of Allah Mr. Elijah Muhammad, conspired with this Illuminati and worked in conjunction with the FBI, CIA, and NYPD, to murder Minister Malcolm and these un-grateful, envious and selfish Ministers and high-ranking officials, murdered Brother Minister Malcolm X, in the Audubon Ballroom in Harlem, in front of Brother Minister Malcolm X, wife Betty Shabazz and their children. This forced the Holy Messenger of Allah Mr. Elijah Muhammad to rise from out of his sick bed and take back full control, of the Operations of the members belonging to Islam here in America and the government he the Holy Messenger of Allah spent his life building, since he began his mission back in nineteen-thirty-four.

Had not the Holy Messenger taken back control over the government and Daily Operations of the Nation of Islam here in the Wilderness of North America, everything the Holy Messenger had accomplished, would had been wipe away back in nineteen sixty-five. These so-called Ministers, Captains, Lieutenants and High-Ranking Administrators, began to spread hatred for Brother Minister Malcolm X to the newly converts and the less learned amongst them. Everyone must understand that these environs Ministers, Captains, Lieutenants and administrators, not all but very close to all, of these members were consorting and conspiring, with this Illuminati, their American government, their Arab partners and all the European governments throughout Europe, to murder our Brother Minister Malcolm X and the enemies got their wish and was rewarded, by these traitors, who at that time were nothing less than Ministers, Captains, Lieutenants and top administrators who claimed, to be members of the Nation of Islam in the Wilderness of North America.

This is the hidden truth my people and then these traitors were in bed with the Illuminati as this Illuminati tried to convince the so-called Negroes and the world, that Holy Messenger of Allah Mr. Elijah Muhammad gave the order, to murder the Top Minister belonging to Islam here in the Wilderness of North America. These traitors at the highest and supposedly most trustworthy level are the ones that participated, in the slaying of our Joshua out of envy, hatred and jealousy and absolutely none of the other Ministers of the Holy Apostle were capable of doing what Brother Minister had accomplished nor more sincere, than Brother Minister Malcolm. The proof is that the Holy Savior Allah in person visited Malcolm Himself, while Malcolm was in prison and gave Malcolm, his mission as well. This is all hidden facts of that time period my people, that sealed the fate of the ex-slaves of America. The Burden of Command and Leadership of such a backwards un-educated and rebellious people, as the ex-slaves of America was nothing short of tremendous and impossible, for one man to do by himself and for so long.

Here is something else that is an absolute historical fact it was Brother Minister Malcolm who presented the case against America, before the world leaders; of the ex-slave of America and this has not been done, since Brother Minister Malcolm X whose proper name is Brother Minister Al-Malik Al-Shabazz. Hate me for the telling the truth about this time period and not having hatred, envy, and jealousy for Brother Minister Malcolm X. In fact, I was captivated by his presence, his sincerity, dedication, his knowledge, his use of the dictionary and no fear of our enemies, I was twelve-years old when I first saw him in person at a rally in Harlem New York back in the summer of nineteen-sixty-three. If not for this encounter seeing Brother Minister Malcolm X {Brother Minister Al-Malik Al- Shabazz} led me to the Holy Messenger of Allah Mr. Elijah Muhammad and this is when my Journey began, and this is where my journey has taken me to and this is what I will continue to do, until I am called back to the womb of darkness where all life in the universe, is created. This includes the that great ball of fire called the Sun and all the planets as well as every life form in the universe.

The actions of these ignorant envious fools' hearts overwhelm with hatred and jealously for their brother, their people and yes for Allah and Allah's Holy Messenger; along with these cowards in the South led by this cowardly traitor Martin Luther King who incidentally was also conspiring with this Illuminati to destroy the rise of the ex-slave of America, to Freedom, Justice, Equality, and independence, from their former slave masters and the role of a second-class citizen. Martin Luther King, Jesse Jackson, Reverend Ralph Abernathy, the Big Six and all those Christian churches filled with Negro cowards, were lovers of the devil and are still lovers of the devil, in the times we are now living in. Martin Luther King and his crew of lying frighten cowards made up of little both boys and girls, frighten beyond any sane intelligent human being comprehension; were complicit they also conspired and aided this Illuminati, to murder the Joshua of their people and then accused the Holy Messenger of Allah, of giving the order to murder Joshua and this is an absolute falsehood. {Brother Minister Malcolm X whose proper name is Al-Malik Al-Shabazz}

So, rather these ignorant supremely foolish Ministers, Captains, Lieutenants and top Administrators, within the temples of Islam here in the Wilderness of North America were being played and manipulated by this Illuminati who controls the American government and all political activities of the American government, were also at the same time playing and manipulating Martin Luther King along with his frighten Christian little boys and girls and these traitors received a few pieces of silver, for their treachery all of them my people and all humanity I am revealing the Hidden Truth of this time period, that has caused Allah to resend his Blessings and promises, for the ex-slaves of America. These fools who dare believing they are going raise the dead and truth be told these Treasonous overwhelm by unadulterated hatred, envy, jealousy, and fear of Joshua; along with these Frighten Christian Southerners led by Martin Luther King, have disappointed and Angier Allah Almighty Himself and have also disappointed Allah's last and greatest Messenger, Mr. Elijah Muhammad, who gave everything of himself to help his people, change their animalistic conditions and mind set. So, having and independent government of their own for the ex-slave of America, is now off the table, this is a Devine Chastisement from Allah Almighty. There will be no unity amongst these un-grateful and un-appreciative fools. They will know only misery, misery, and more misery, until they change what lies deep in their hearts, minds, and spirit.

Remember my people Allah Chose us the ex-Chattel Slave of and for This Multi- Headed Corporation, {The Hydra} call America, to be his people and receive His Supreme Wisdom from the mouth of His Holy Messenger {MuhammadRasulAllah} chosen from the Ex-Chattel Slaves of America, Mr. Elijah Muhammad. Then Allah all merciful, beneficent, all wise, the best knower and is true and living, gave us Joshua and you fools conspired, calibrated, and even help physically carry out Joshua's execution, the members of the Ex-Chattel Slave of America, will forever be the Mental Slave, for America. Remember my people a real devil is any live grafted gene from the Original Man and Any Man Made Weak and Wicked. Now explain this to yourself, can you be any weaker and more wicked outside of murdering Allah's chosen Messenger; Can you be any weaker and more wicked when you yourself helped planned and assist physically, in the execution, of your brother, who was chosen by Allah Himself, to be the Joshua to lead his people, to being recognize, respected, and excepted, by all civilized people and governments on our planet? This what the Mission of the Holy Messenger Of Allah was about. With the weight of the entire black and red population on his shoulders, at the same time one of world's most powerful countries and the most powerful countries, government, and Military Presence, in the Western Hemisphere; pursuing the Holy Messenger of Allah, threating to murder him or have him murdered, by one of his own and close to him.

This the Hidden Truth my people and all of humanity this is what I am revealing to all humanity, till this very day is not spoke of because they were all partakers in this un-holy and most vile actions, of the twentieth- century, THE EXCUTION OF JOSHAUA and these fools were saying the vilest things and statements, against their brother. In fact, the un-gratefulness lack of appreciation, self-hatred, envy, lies, deceit and jealously so-called brothers and so-called sisters as well, had less to say about the Mob- Up Presidents John F Kennedy and Lydon B. Johnson and all the rest, of the cronies, of this Illuminati, in that day and time. This was a great deal upon the shoulders of the Messenger of Allah and surrounded by treachery day and night, seeking to murder Allah's Messenger. Here is something else that must be understood as well, the former Chattel Slave Of America approximately ninety-eight percent of the so-called followers of the Holy Messenger and the same goes for Martin Luther King and his supporter's ninety-eight percent could not read, write and many, many, cases, could not even count and that made matters even more difficult. So, Allah our Holy Savior and benefactor raised up from amongst us the Ex-Chattel Slaves of America Joshua to be a help to His Allah's Holy Messenger Mr. Elijah Muhammad. Rather you except it or not Brother Minister Al-Malik Al-Shabazz aka. Brother Minister Malcolm X was the Joshua chosen by Allah Almighty Himself. Remember Mussa only brother the chosen people of Allah to the River Jordan, it was Joshua brother Allah's people across the River Jordan into the promise land and this what Brother Al-Malik Al-Shabazz aka Brother Minister Malcolm X, was being prepared for, by Allah Himself.

So, now the once proud economic advancement and educational advancements are all gone and re-placed by African Tribalism, Now instead of temples of true learning about all the physical sciences, the once mighty and proud have been reduce, building lodges and conducting themselves like the so-called Freed Masons and Eastern Stars they all truly are. I hate to say this, but it is true all one must do is study and observe, it is right before your very eyes, if one seeks the truth. I absolutely know for a fact these so-called brothers or so-called followers are going to even more upset with because of my writings and will rally against me, even talk of silencing me permanently; nevertheless, I must reveal the truth so that one day if they read my writings, it should help all to understand what truth is truly about and how single out the frauds and hypocrites young and old, that could possibly be your circumference and quite possible, in your very mist.

I have heard some and many of these so-called followers say and I quote "I 'm about Nation Building" and since the Holy Messenger returned back the womb of life in nineteen-seventy-five absolutely nothing, has ever been or even started, .because of the lack of unity and trust. Narcissism, egotism, self-indulgent envy, and hatred are still buried deep into the hearts, minds, and spirit, of those who claim to be a so-called follower or followers of the Messenger of Allah. I am not attacking the so-called followers of the Message I am just pointing out to all, that you must responsibility for your actions and deeds. Study very closely and follow the trail of evidence all of it and then you draw your conclusion, study the parts that are and have been hidden, from the mass of people.

These other grafted groups came into existence in the beginning they were called the five percenters and the leader of this un-disciplined group had served under Brother Minister Malcolm. His X while in the Temples of Islam here in the Wilderness of North America, was Clarence Thirteen X who later would be known as the father/Allah/Pudding. He smuggles out from Temple number seven Minister classes, the Examination Of Kareem and became known as the one hundred-twenty degrees or the one twenty. Once again, this group of young black men and young black women were given the Examination Of Kareem and we ran the cities and throughout the country, quoting the Examination of Kareem {the one-twenty} on the corners, in the parks, in the educational system everywhere. So, the officials in the temples of Islam here the Wilderness of North America; became enraged and a bloody battle amongst us and against ourselves, began and the brothers began attacking these young members who had joined up, with the so-called nation of five percenters, this was back in nineteen sixty-four. The academy was shot up as they tried to assonate, the father of this said nation. In fact, he the father was hit in his chest with a shotgun and survived a brother named Bishmi Allah was also shot on another attack, separate from the first attack, I just mention.

Brother Minister Malcolm was no-longer apart of Temple number seven and the Minister that re-placed him, had absolutely no control of what the Captain and the Lieutenant were doing. This Minister that took over was none other than Lewis Farrakhan now holding the rank of Minister of Temple number seven. Minister Farrakhan was and still is extremely dynamic spokesman and extremely diverse, with the English language as well. It was not until after the execution of Joshua {Minister Malcolm} our enemies flooded New York with the purest Heroin, the streets of New York have ever known. Everywhere throughout New York city and especially black communities, this Heroin could be found, as it left behind body counts, misery, destruction of black communities throughout America. Diseases sights you could not believe. The Horrors that were plainly seen every day was and is more terrifying, than any horror movie Hollywood could ever produce. Crimes amongst we committed by ourselves had sky rocked to one hundred percent. Since the execution of Joshua there was no so-called black leader anywhere, who would do anything about this Pandemic, only the Holy Messenger of Allah Mr. Elijah Muhammad had the courage to address this issue head on.

Those that follow Martin Luther King, and his regime became the dope peddlers in black communities, throughout America.

Murdering millions of their own people, destroying black families with impunity for this Illuminati and this Illuminati American government. Martin Luther King and his regime are the ones, that helped and aided the open gay population, to secretly begin inserting their evil and wicket propaganda and themselves, amongst the children of these devastated families. This is so-called supremely ignorant foolish Negroes filled with self-hatred began calling themselves "the Black Mafia". This so-called Black Mafia carved out the trade routes for the Illuminati, American Government, CIA, FBI, NYPD, and every so-called Law Enforcement, in every black community throughout America; and this so-called Black Mafia was working for our enemies. Even when these ignorant fools thought, believed, and convinced themselves that they were doing this for themselves, they later learned from a representee of the Illuminati. With all their members; all their religions; all their politics; Law Enforcement at every and all levels, locally, nationally, and internationally; against all who have invested, in corruption and being a gangster, it is still the Illuminati and their American government is who you will always, be in-slaved to this Illuminati, its government, society, world, people, religions and corrupt politics, for investing in corruption and the execution of Joshua.

Any so-called Minister, Captain, Lieutenant, and so-called follower that is teaching that the Holy Messenger of Allah Mr. Elijah Muhammad, did not expire in nineteen-seventy-five, are teaching false teachings other than Islam. Any so-called Minister, Captain, Lieutenant, or so-called follower that are teaching that the Holy Messenger, is coming back, to give them a name, are teaching false teachings, other than Islam. Any so-called said Minister, Captain, Lieutenant, or so-called said follower that are teaching that Our

Savior and His Messenger are aboard the Mother Plain, are all teaching false teachings, other than Islam. All who is teaching this kind of false indoctrination, are teaching the same teachings as Christianity and all the other false religions, that have been plaguing us for nearly five-hundred-years.

The so-called five percenters were never taught any form of discipline or even self-discipline or about building a physical world, for themselves. So, the same corruption, evil, self-hatred, envy, jealousy, lies, deceit, stealing from each other and other types of evil such as murdering each other and more, is what their said nation is built on. Mayor Lindsay gave them a ninety-nine year least for that store front in Harlem, over fifty years ago and absolutely no progress, has been made in over fifty years. Remember these members were only quoting the Examination of Kareem yet had very weak and confusing so-called understanding.

There is absolutely no one who can or will guide them across the River Jordan, reason being is that they are all guilty, of execution Joshua and in the meantime these Martin Luther king and his conspirators, were setting the stage of introducing this homosexuality amongst their people; knowing that this filthy disease would morally bankrupt our people thus turning the Ex-Chattel Slaves of America, further away from the mercy of Allah and pleasures, of Allah our Holy Savior. The Hidden Truth must be revealed no matter who this truth may offend, this Hidden Truth must be known to our people and all humanity.

It was these so-called followers, these so-called Ministers, so called Captains, Lieutenants, and top so-called officials, who was supremely derelict in their duties and to their oath, are responsible for the conditions our people and all humanity are still suffering from being under control and at the mercy of our open enemies. It is since these members of the so-called father {Clarence 13x} never being taught discipline, unity, self-reliance, independence and total freedom, justice, and equality, could not understand the many errors, poor judgement, weak and confusing understanding and were very easily led into the wrong direction and still to this very day, are extremely hard to be led into the right direction. They also share a responsibility in the execution of Joshua. The Black Panthers and every other so-called revolutionary organization also share the blame, for the Execution of Joshua. These so-called Christians had absolutely no love for Joshua and rejoiced in the execution, of Joshua. The truth hurts and make angry the ones who are guilty of these crimes against Allah and Allah's Last and greatest Messenger, as they use His name to shield in truth, their filthy religion Christianity, as these hypocrites try to pass it off for Islam. Therefore, Jerusalem must and will be taken back from the devil and this is not speaking about the grafted devil.

I am not upset with anyone I am just speaking the truth that others want this truth, to remain hidden from everyone. Here is a question that should be asked by everyone; why is so impossible for us to unite or have any unity amongst ourselves, as other people on our planet have for themselves? Has Allah forsaken us, or have we forsaken Allah not through words, but by what is your minds and what truly lies in your hearts? The Execution of Joshua seems like a great sin, to me that Allah was not please, by this act of treachery. Then at least ninety percent of these so-called followers denounce Allah and Allah's last and greatest Messenger, who raised up from you to restore the love in you, for you.

If we my people and all humanity do not investigate ourselves and begin correcting the many flaws in our own character, there will never be any chance for redemption and mercy. The teachings of Allah our Holy Savior who visited us in the person of Master Fard Muhammad, to whom praises are due forever; and taught to His Holy Messenger Mr. Elijah Muhammad and Allah taught us all through the mouth, of His Holy Messenger; have been tampered with, distorted, violated, and even abandon by those who claims to a so-called follower of the Messenger of Allah. Pyramid schemes and scams are embrace by these so-c called followers and then these fools bring these scams, back to their people for the purpose of robbing their own people and they can feel important. How can you feel or be important scamming your own people? What kind of so-called Islam a practicing and teaching others? This is not Islam at all this is nothing more than Christianity my people and all humanity as well. When one has delved into the truth about everything that has happened in the last hundred years, you will see the hypocrisy that is being called Islam by these hypocrites calling themselves, so-called believers, and so-called followers of the Messenger of Allah.

Only the guilty live-in fear of the truth being revealed because the truth with all certainty revealed these frauds as being exactly what they are, the enemies of truth, freedom, justice, and equality, for all their so-called people and all humanity included, as well. These narcissism ignorant fools calling themselves the righteous, are disgraceful. They are not about building a nation they are only interested in building a lodge and then the heads of these lodges, dare believe they are doing the work of the Messenger of Allah. Do things the way say or want you to them, if not you are no-longer wanted around them. Some of these lodges are perhaps in better condition than others, but none of these lodges can prepare their members, for a future of total independence and freedom in Home and Nation with land and water, they can call their own. They do not believe in the Rise Of The Original Asiatic Black Patriot Rule and The Enforcement Of Our Will. I find it extremely hard to collaborate with anyone who is afraid or do not know any better, to tell the world Mr. Elijah Muhammad is the Messenger of Allah because it is an insult to referred to him as the Honorable Elijah Muhammad, Mr. Elijah Muhammad is Muhammad RasulAllah.

I consider it an honor for me to have blessed with this understanding that I am able to see the flaw in referring to the Holy Messenger as the honorable, when I know, and history supports what I am saying is the absolute truth. If this truth is not being taught and encouraged, by the ones who claim to be in charge; then there is not any truth really being taught. If you are wrong in the beginning everything will be wrong to the end only the pretense of being right. Yet mathematics refutes that what is being said is in complete error therefore what is being said, is supported by absolutely nothing tangible.

This is the Hidden Truth my people and all humanity that everyone should examine extremely closely and stop running to your enemies, to help you understand this truth because this Hidden Truth, will reveal these traitors, as being the enemies of all humanity. There are many things of the times we are now living in that must be understood, by all humanity. Due to the conditions and time period when our enemies {the American government} put this Heroin into every black community throughout every black community, throughout America was more devastating than what is being reported.

The job marks were now beginning to open all these jobs and business opportunities but because of these traitors amongst us and especially this despicable, so -called Black Mafia and the dereliction of duty by others, almost destroyed ninety to ninety-five percent of all Ex-Chattel Slaves of America, chances of learning any of the skills that every interloper, who have come to America are still coming to America, have taken full advantage of and to hell whit the struggle of the Ex-Chattel Slave of America. The irony of this is that these same people from South, Central America, and the Caribbean, were and still are peddling Crack Cocaine and other drugs, in the black communities throughout America and these are your friends and brothers. This how you know that there is a Dereliction of Duties of these said so-called followers of the Holy Messenger of Allah.

Now you ignorant fools have even now allowed these interlopers, disguising themselves as Ministers, Captains, Lieutenants, and top officials, to teach us the Ex-Chattel Slave of America, about Allah and Allah's Holy Messenger Mr. Elijah Muhammad; this is a disgrace and I cannot thank Allah enough for revealing to me, all our enemies. This also re-enforce in me that the Ex-Chattel Slave of America is now the Mental and Spirit Slave of America and all our open and secret enemies, are taking advantage of your stupidity and ignorance my people. I thank Allah our Holy Savior for visiting us in the person of Master W.F. Muhammad, to whom praises are due forever. If you believe these interlopers are your brothers and sisters, I am happy because I know that you cannot be my brother or sister and our enemies' brother and sister, at the same time or ever as it stands. The Teachings that Allah gave to His Holy Messenger have been perverted, by the ones who claimed to believe and in truth they believed not. Perverted by the ones who claimed to a so-called follower of the Holy Messenger. Perverted by the ones who executed Joshua and the hypocrites who laugh, scorned, praised these murderers that re-juiced in the cold-blooded murder, of Joshua {Brother Minister}. Perverted by these lying hypocrites dare calling themselves, the righteous, the gods, the freedom fighters and everyone else, with their nonproductive religions or beliefs, standing on a corner screaming about in truth absolutely nothing. This is nothing but non-productivism and non-productivism comes into play when you have done absolutely nothing, when it comes to doing something, for self and kind.

Now here it is January two thousand and twenty-one and perhaps the greatest traitor from amongst us, our enemies expect us to praise and follow this traitor and this despicable and disgraceful traitor name is, Martin Luther King. His disgraceful Christian organization and all its disgraceful members have willfully, betrayed all his and their people; while these cowards were laying in motels and hotels, with these cheap Caucasian prostitutes. Then our enemies prompt these cowards up and make and made these cowards, our leaders. If these despicable and disgraceful were members of any other people on our planet, they all would have been executed for being cowardly traitors. All this evil sick homosexuality and perverts living amongst and in the education system, is due to these cowardly traitors led by cowardly Martin Luther King.

All these cowardly Christian organizations are still eating the slop that their Slave masters, taught them to eat and this disgusting slop is called, Soul Food. Martin Luther King, Jesse Jackson Reverend Ralph Abernathy, James Farmer, Percy Sutton, and there are plenty, plenty more hated their own people and consider being beholding to Caucasian People, back then and till this very day an honor. Being invited or allowed to visit the white house these disgraceful coward's male and female, believe they are better than their people and then allowed these enemies, to join their filthy and disgusting so-called churches.

All of this was able to take place due to the Dereliction of Duty these so-called followers of the Messenger, are guilty of. With these narcissistic ignorant fools participating with assignation of Joshua, gave Marin Luther King and his Bands of Traitors to join up with their enemies and the enemies of their people. Everyone involved in and with this atrocity new their would-be minimal resistance, from these said so-called followers and so-called believers of the Messenger of Allah. Not a one of any of these cowardly Christian churches or organizations, cared about their then and they do not now. This disgraceful slogan black lives matter is nothing but a filthy mockery, of the Ex-Chattel Slave of America.

Go inside of any so-called Negro church and from my own experience this is one of the most disgusting places to visit on our planet. Filth, evil and abominations are all you will encounter in these places of absolute evil and supported by dumb, backwards, ignorant worthless people. How could believe that you have intelligence when you allowed our nearly five-hundred-year-old enemy since landing in the Western Hemisphere, make your woman the planet Concubine and your cowardly worthless self, stand back approvingly with your disgraceful looking smiles on your faces. Then to see how many Ex-Chattel Women Slaves which is perhaps ninety-nine percent, were and agree with our enemies. What did these disgraceful cowards overcome? I will happily tell you absolutely nothing because their so-called people are nothing more than twenty-first century Mental and Spiritual Slaves.

Our enemies knew who Brother Minister Malcolm was and therefore they went after him, so vigorously and enlisted the help from you said so-called followers, of Mr. Elijah Muhammad the Holy Messenger of Allah. Our enemies also knew that these so-called Ministers, Captains, Lieutenants, and so-called Top Officials, did not know who Brother Minister Malcolm was. It was not Musa who guided Allah's Chosen People across the River Jordan, it was Joshua who led them across the River Jordan, to land they could call their own. The worst of this atrocity is that you narcissistic ignorant fools walking around twice maybe three times a year, with your FOI uniforms on and pins, just like every other Masonic Organization does and believing that they are special. This the Hidden Truth my people and all humanity, must be aware of as well as the false religions humanity maybe caught up into.

How can you say black lives matter when black lives have absolutely any meaning, to these so-called African Americans? Africa and the people living in the Jungles of East Asia never cared about you and I and they still do not care about us today. If not for the Arabs storming throughout West Africa, there would not be any Sunnah Islam in West Africa at all. So, Allah nor did Allah's Prophets, introduce this so-called brand of Sunnah Islam amongst these servants, of this devil name Alexandria; it was Alexandria that named the Jungles of East Asia Africa, after his Homosexual lover. So, I see absolutely no honor, no glory, no black pride, no self-respect, no since of value or anything else of positivity, from calling myself an African. No, Allah Himself said we are Original Black Asiatic Black man and Black woman Allah the best knower, never said we are Africans. Also, it is these narcissistic ignorant silly fools who marry them, dress like them, and act them because in truth, they are nothing but lazy cowards. These same cowards did nothing for their women and children that made this four-hundred year sojourned with us. These are the ones my people and all humanity that betrayed and denounced Allah, Allah's Holy Messenger, and the Islam that Allah brought, gave, and taught us through the mouth of His Holy Messenger, Mr. Elijah Muhammad.

When I was around these ignorant narcissistic fools, they all enjoyed putting on a show of so-called self-importance and at the same time lying, stealing, deceiving and betrayal, was always and still are, being carried out daily amongst their selves and everyone else. These narcissistic ignorant foolish cowards, calling themselves so-called followers and so-called believers, dare call Brother Minister Malcolm a hypocrite. In truth these are the hypocrites and the decedents, of these murdering cowardly hypocrites. Therefore, the Caucasian Race has absolutely no respect and having been reduced, in world matters to being insufficient for your lying deceitful backwards narcissistic ignorant hypocrites. Now like the obedience slave that you all are start preparing your ignorant selves, for your so-called Savior's Day, in which in truth none of you cowards believe in; you are just using this trying to convince the whole of humanity, you are righteous. Yet our enemies know that all of you or ninety-nine percent of you are the real and true hypocrites. This is the Hidden Truth my people and all humanity do not be deceived by these cowardly murderers that murdered Joshua, in front of his wife children. Here is a question that we all should ask ourselves; Who or which one is worst the Grafted Devil or the Made Devil? This is what I do know the grafted and the made devil conspired together, plotted together, and executed Joshua together as they patted each other on the back, saying good job. Then the grafted and made devil operating together, braced themselves for the fallout, of their evil diabolical plan's, actions, and wicket deeds.

I will elaborate further about and on this subject but not now I believe I have disseminated enough information on this subject, that anyone can clearly see and understand that there was more going on than what has been told, to the world and us, by the people who are the conspirators and the actual murderers, of Joshua. Then these so-called followers and so-called believers, dare tried to implicate the Holy Messenger as the one who gave the order, to murder Joshua. There was just as much evil flowing throughout the ranks Brother Minister Malcolm began recognizing the evil and even where the evil, was and is omitting from. Do not my people feel proud because this evil and supremely diabolical American government and people, call you a so-called African American. In fact, this is extremely disgraceful being named, after a homosexual. I say to the world I Saladin Shabazz-Allah am not an African; never had been one and never will be one of them. Also remember if the Arabs had not come through the Western region of the Jungles of East Asia and super-imposed their will and religion upon What is now called West Africa and the people living in that region, these so-called West Africans will be living like the total savages, they were and still are. These are not our people, and these so-called West Africans have no love for us. You have some fools amongst us that love and mate with these enemies believing these West Africans, are our people. These narcissistic ignorant fools are the traitors that murdered Joshua or was incredibly happy that Joshua was murder. Allah Himself Told us all that we are the Original Asiatic Black man and woman. Allah never said that we were and are Africans and I refuse to allow anyone to call or referred to me, as being an African or and African American and you should not either.

CHAPTER 17

THE BROKEN SPRIT OF THE EX-CHATTEL SLAVE

As I sit at my desk and ponder over the things I have been involved in and have seen, I understand the value, of the ability to record and remember the history that I lived through. At least ninety eight percent of my generation has been wipe out and my children's generation wiped out or imprisoned, by the greatest evil and most diabolical minds, our planet has ever known. This Illuminati has camouflage and woven itself so deeply into the American way of life, until this diabolical secret society, cannot be recognized, by the so-called average and the so-called above average American citizen. These Ex-Chattel Slaves of America {So-called African Americans} have not a clue on what is really happening, to and around them. Due to the so-called un-impressive leaders and the un-impressive so-called followers, who have failed miserably, at their sworn duty. This is a great spiritual disappointed because of the unilateral negative affect, this dereliction of duty has produced not only for their own people but all humanity as well.

There are no other people on our planet that is more improperly informed, than the Ex-Chattel Slave of this Illuminati and its

American government, the so-called home of the free and the brave. False religions, diabolical politics and false friendships are being and have been embraced, by the narcissistic ignorant fools and then these fools bring these evils, to and amongst their people. These are the fools who believe because they may have a lodge or belong to a lodge, they call them temples; are still using antiquated twentieth-century methods, here in the twenty-first century, You will find out once closely examine that this cannot be the Nation of Islam, this is the said Nation of Islam. It does not matter what they call themselves the Nation of Gods an Earths, Black Conscious minded and a bunch of other useless names and said organizations; none of these above mention is capable of teaching anyone the truth because none of these said organizations are about the truth due to the fact they do not believe, in the truth. These fools only believe and submit to the illusion of truth and knowing the truth, to stroke their own narcissistic ignorant inflated worthless egos.

As you may travel throughout America everywhere one may look in and amongst black communities, none of these black communities have any more sprit to fight any longer. The communities throughout America feel and believe, that our enemies are too strong and too powerful, to be stopped and this is in-correct. The disappointment, the hurt, the betrayal, the deceit, the lies, the drugs, alcohol and the hidden self-hatred, are more than enough to break anyone and any people. The smiling faces that always tell lies to us my people from amongst our people who claim to be righteous, is an extremely hard pill to swallow by any people. To have your hopes and dreams completely shattered by the people who you have placed your trust in, is absolutely devastating; so, devastating the possibility of recovering is virtually impossible and we see these results everyday amongst ourselves. Then to hear these silly narcissistic ignorant fools one step above a sharecropper, boast they have Supreme Wisdom, does not give our people or any one from the human family on our planet, any hope or relief at all. Forever the Chattel Slavery of and for the dreadful home of the free and the brave, called America is something our great-grand-children will never see, or experience, if they believe and trust some other people, to help guide them on the path of success and prosperity, is never going to happen for the Ex-Chattel Slave of America and forever the Mental Slave of America.

I cannot understand why our people call themselves Africans when they are not African. It is not true that life began in this so-called Africa. There are un-doubly great civilizations that did exist in the Jungles of East Asia, but they did not call themselves Africans. It is a historical fact that Alexandria the not so great named this continent Africa, after his homosexual Caucasian boyfriend. So, with this historical facts and proof, why are the people living on this continent still calling themselves? This tells me that these dark people are still beholding to the Caucasian Race. It is totally ignorant of us to continue to allow some other people to call us whatever they choose and worst part of this travesty, is that black people except this nonsense with a silly smile, on their faces. Only when dealing with other black people they become hostile and aggressive, but when it comes to dealing with Caucasian people every one of them is totally submissive, flashing their menstrual smiles. This behavior is disgraceful, and I will not have any part of it.

I would rather be looked upon as an Apache Indian rather than be looked upon as some worthless, so-called African or African American. I had this fool from Ghana say to me "come to Africa and I will make you a King". I answered him by telling him "I am a king and how are you going to make me a king, without a kingdom"? If you believe that this so-called Africa is so beautiful, filled with riches, resources, land, diamonds, gold, pearls, and an assortment of other resources, then why are you so-called Africans here in America? Allah our Holy, most merciful Savior warned us through the mouth of His Holy Messenger, for us the Ex-Chattel Slave of America; not to marry them or dress like them. Allah the best knower through the mouth of His Holy Messenger also warned us the Ex-Chattel Slave of America, to worry about yourself first and let this so-called Africa, take care of themselves. You will find many of the so-called followers and so-called believers of Allah and Allah's Holy Messenger, have violated the warnings by Allah to us all, through the mouth of His Holy Messenger, Mr. Elijah Muhammad.

Black people in America and throughout the world spirit have been broken by these deceitful religious and political liars and disbelievers from amongst our own ranks. To violate the warnings from Allah our Holy, most merciful Savior and the best knower, for a few pieces of silver are not true believers in Allah and were ever true followers of Allah's last and greatest Messenger. If I had not been in the present of Joshua, I would have never known who the Savior is and who is the true Muhammad RasulAllah because Joshua {Brother Minister Al Malik Shabazz Malcolm X} is the one and only one, who led me Allah and Allah's Holy Messenger; which has led me to being the man I am today; All Praises Are Due To Allah The Holy Savior, Most Merciful and Best Knower Of Allah Things not just for us the Ex-Chattel Of America, but the entire planet and all life, in the university.

Absolutely no other person or said organizations including the said so-called nation of now called the gods and the earth, the

Black Panthers, So-called black Israelites every so-called Christian organizations and every other organization, religious and political organizations, has done or will never be able, to do. These are all frauds started up by envious, narcissistic, and jealous people calling themselves, our leaders, and teachers, who hated Joshua and Joshua teacher Allah and Allah's Last and Greatest Messenger, Mr. Elijah Muhammad. I Stand Accused Of Loving The Holy Savior, Allah's Holy Messenger, and Joshua the one to take us all, across the River Jordan.

Zionism and Christianity are the evilest religions on our planet, for all dark people and humanity period. Both god forsaken so-called religions are riddle with this filthy homosexuality, that has been a part of these evil filthy religions since their conception from hell. This is not hatred everyone this is an absolute fact and truth; so, I ask this question, why would this so-called Sunnah Islam and all the rest, join up with evil that Allah Himself, speaks against through all His prophets" Before Allah visited all humanity in the Supreme Holiness Presence of the Master of all Master W.F.Muhammad, to whom all praises are due forever there was absolutely nothing to live for? If not for this Supremely Mighty One Master Fard Muhammad, this society and world, would have been destroyed in Nineteen-fourteen and all humanity would not had any chance, of Redemption and a reprieve back into the bosom, of Allah the universal creator and sustainer, for all life and life forms, in His Universe. What is perplexing is why and how could these Arabs and their so-called ram dictions of their version of Islam, join up with the enemies of Allah and all of Allah's prophets and this includes Prophet Muhammad {may the peace and blessings be upon all, of Allah's prophets}.

My people all humanity please lend an ear in less than two

hundred years this so-called American government, is headed for Civil War once again. You have on this side a child molester Joe Bidden a known pervert is the president elect, he represents old Abraham Lincoln a hater of dark people. Then you have Donald Trump on the side the dethrone president who represents Jefferson Davis another hater of dark people and the reincarnation, of Adolf Hitler. Do not be surprise when everyone sees the Confederate Flag once again, flying high over America. As it was back in eighteen-fifties and early eighteen sixty-one. Here now America has two Caucasian Mad Men a child molester and power-hungry dictator once again fighting over the resources and control, over the military forces that is protecting this corporation called America. Supreme Evil in all directions and from both parties and then these disgusting so-called African Americans Christian preachers and people, still teaching that these devils are Jesus that going to save us and the world. Perverted Homosexual Children Molesters and the re-incarnation of their ancestor Adolf Hitler, is what these Christian Cowards, want us to believe in. Martin Luther King was such a coward him and his band of thieves look at what they led you, to believe in. Homosexuals and Mad Men here is your Jesus you so-called African American cowardly, ignorant, and disgraceful fool.

You cowardly so-called African American worthless fools cannot and will not protect yourselves, you will not protect wives and women folk and you cowards will not protect your children, but you had better protect your Jesus and you cowards will do, just that with those silly smiles on your faces. How can any so-called African American Political or Religious fix your mouths, to spread the lies of Satan The Accursed Devil to and amongst your people and all humanity? Every so-called religion has failed the Ex-Chattel Slave of America as well as all humanity and these so-called political and these so-called religious leaders with their false concepts of the Universal Creator and so-called false politics, continue to lead all humanity, to absolute destruction and not a one of these false political and false religious so-called leaders' care; about the millions and billions of lives they are about to destroy, and this is democracy.

This is not the Fall Of America everyone this is the destruction of Mr. Yakub's world, society, and his makings, all of them. You can see the destruction of this society political structure and their religious structure, right before our eyes. I had this old silly fool telling my wife he will sell her the MGT training manual. I took care of this foolishness my wife does not need any training manual because she is, civilize woman and knows how to conduct herself at home and abroad, also take care of her husband and our children. Sell this to these African women but this one coward is too afraid, to introduce this to his African so-called wife. This woman does not take care of her children she allows others to take care of her children, while her and husband rob and under pay, his so-called FOI Brothers, while her husband at night and on weekends, believes he is the Karaoke King of New York or more correctly the Karaoke King Of The Poor Part Of New York, known as the Ghettos; and her and family scheme to bring in more of her kind, with her silly narcissistic ignorant foolish so-called husband help and he gladly helps people, that have absolutely no love for the Ex-Chattel Slave of America. No wonder the spirit of the Ex-Chattel Slave of America has been broken. These all these imposters are responsible for the execution and assignation of Joshua, tell me why did these cowards did and supported the execution of Joshua? I will tell you why these cowards love the devil grafted and made devil because they give them absolutely nothing.

These undercover spies for our enemies with the peace and As Salaam Alaikum and all the other ghetto slang, will sell everyone out for a few pieces of silver from their masters. Then at least three times a year just like any other Mason, wear their uniforms, proclaiming they are the righteous and followers of the Messenger of Allah. Then you have these so-called gods and earths who un-like Yakub's followers or makings, believing in a misconceptions given to them, by a rebellious so-called follower. Name Clarence 13X whom these mis-guided and mis-led Ex=Chattel Slaves of America, believe to be Allah. Many were able to get their hands on the Examination of Kareem, by this time these ignorant fools, began changing Kareem's Examination and the Examination of Kareem became corrupted and had no more power. Thus, they are only producing and teaching Christianity and aiding the enemies of Allah, Allah's last and greatest Messenger, their people to help destroy all humanity. This is the truth that is being kept hidden by these hypocrites and disbelievers, disguising themselves as so-called Muslims, Christians, Gods, Black Conscious Minded and Revolutionaries.

Therefore, this is one of the many methods how our enemies the so-called American government and this not-so-secret society called the Illuminati, were able to break the spirit of the Ex-Chattel Slave of America now so-called, African American. Now during this un-holy vacuum after the execution of Joshua and death of the Holy Messenger Mr. Elijah Muhammad, the most insane thoughts, ideas, and beliefs came into existence by cowards who never did anything in life, to support the Holy Messenger believe they constitute the truth. I say to all humanity beware of these foolish ignorant people, they as I told everyone they are narcissist and care nothing about you, Allah or Allah's Prophets and Allah's last and greatest Messenger, at all these disgrace fools care only about the insane thoughts in their own minds, I have a so-called biological brother like this and if it were not for me, this self-indulgent fool would had never known anything about our Holy Savior, His Holy Messenger Islam nor anything else. He is not the only one I brought the truth to and then was betrayed by these ingrates they will not buy my books they will tell you because I Have Joshua picture on my first publication; this is a lie the real reason is due to the fact, they are not able to do this work because Allah knows, they are nothing but disbelieving cowards all and every one of them.

These silly non-productive Facebook Groups these ignorant fools and their weak useless websites, are only re-enforcing the destruction of the Ex-Chattel Slave of America and all humanity as well. Arguing, bickering, name calling, and threats is all you see on these disgraceful groups and sites. Doing nothing more than breaking down the spirit of all humanity and none of these frauds care, about how destructive and counter-productive, their actions are to the Ex-Chattel Slave Of America and all humanity as well. Social Media is the easiest for every government agency and Law Enforcement Agency, to monitor everyone who is currently active, on these medias. The President of the American government is guilty of Insurrection and holding the American Senate as hostages, hiding under their desks in fear while the Insurrectionaries were on a search and destroy mission. The tranny that this American government and people have super-imposed upon all humanity, is now being super-imposed on the American government, people, this secret society called the Illuminati, all its members and associates.

The Broken Spirit of any people is the worst possible condition for all humanity because you are left without any hope, inspiration, aspirations this is another form of Chattel Slavery without the physical chains because the physical chains have replaced by Mental and Spiritual Chains. Which gives your enemies the power to control and manipulate you in any direction, your enemies desire. There is not any forgiveness for this society and world all forgiveness has been totally exhausted, there is only destruction. I do not walked around with hatred in my heart for anyone or people, this includes the Caucasian Race; but there is no sympathy or empathy or forgiveness for the Caucasian Race for the most horrible, supreme diabolically conceived evil, that myself, my ancestors, our women, and children had to endure, for nearly five-hundred-years to this present day and time. This Supreme Evil has affected all humanity, corrupted all said religions, corrupted all politics, until only a sterilization can solve the cancers, that invaded and completely overwhelm this society, world, and ninety-eight percent of all humanity.

I think sometime about being an Original Asiatic Blackman growing up in America stripped of all knowledge of kind and others. Stripped of my Original language and the sciences that allows all humanity to conduct themselves, in a civilized and respectful manner. The poison foods physical, mental, and spiritual that were forced upon us. With no protection from the government which allowed their kind, to commit murder and rape and other diabolical atrocities against my people for over four-hundred-years now close to five-hundred-years, with absolute impunity. Deprived of education and despised for not being of the Caucasian Race and being of the Original Asiatic Black People, of our planet. The physical abuse by cowardly Zionist teachers grown men and women and how they took pride, in beating up young Asiatic Black men even being double teamed by these Zionist Cowards as the female Zionist Cowards, shouting out kill that little Nigger and even took cheap shots with their hands and sometimes rulers, with impunity.

The lies these Zionist Demons will tell our parents with straight faces, falsifying documents and even getting their Zionist Demon children, to support and make up lies on us and always with impunity. The elder Zionist Demons even encourage our fathers and mothers to physically beat and sometimes these beatings by our parents were carried out, in front of these Zionist Cowardly Demons. What choice was I or we were left with either be broken by our open deranged Zionist and Christian enemies or fight these deranged Zionist Cowardly Demons to the death if need be and put an end to their abuse and this impunity, these Zionist and Christian Demons, have been enjoying for over four-hundred-years. This false and insane Homosexual so-called Jesus has never answered any of our prayers and will never answer any of our prayers, if you are still dumb enough and cowardly enough to continue, to believe in these lies perpetrated upon us and all humanity as well, by our Zionist and Christian Enemies. This was before the Arabs were incorporated into the Illuminati and the American society, to stop the spread of Islam, throughout America by the Holy Messenger of Allah Mr. Elijah Muhammad.

They our enemies knew who Brother Minister Malcolm was for black people in America and he began sharing this knowledge to black people throughout the world; then he began teaching and spreading this truth, to all humanity as his leader and the Holy Messenger of Allah Mr. Elijah Muhammad, had done before him. I do not care who does not like what I am saying or does not share my observation of things that happened, but the true history will support what I am saying, and writing is the absolute truth.

How is it possible to forgive lying murderers, their deceitful government, and hypocritical laws? When you examine below the surface of this society one can see nothing has changed at all. Yes, I would agree that the illusion of change is plaster all over social media, television, and radio even advertisement has involved themselves, into keeping these illusions going and alive. In the meantime, the moral compass of this country, people, and every aspect of this American government, is zilch.

We are living in a society and government are completely bankrupt and murder, rape drugs, degradation are ruling the country, government, people, and so-called laws that are supposed to uphold the human rights of everyone, of their so-called citizens; and with such clear proof, facts and evidence staring everyone in the face, the American government, people, religions, and politics are all lies. After nearly five-hundred-years of living under these Pandemic conditions since fifteen -fifty-five, how can human being or people continue to believe and trust such lying, selfish and ruthless government and people, when the President himself is guilty of Insurrection for ordering the armed storming and seizure of the state capital building in Washington DC, by Confederate Armed Desperadoes Insurrectionaries and loss of life as well as the destruction of property, owned by the Federal Government of America?

This country and so-called American government have not used this term Insurrection, since the American Civil War which ended, in eighteen-sixty-five. More than a hundred and fifty years ago. Now today January of two thousand and twenty-one, the President Donald Trump is guilty of provoking a Second Civil War and through symbolic gestures making his last stance in Texas, at the Alamo in Dixieland. Not only President Donald Trump is committing another act of Insurrection, by sabotaging the America's Foreign Policies that is leading pervert President Elect Joe Bidden, into a war with Taiwan and other countries as well. The American government, people and supporters' spirits are also broken and everyone who believes in this corporation called America, spirits are broken as well.

The self-hatred that this so-called American government and people have placed and put in us the Ex-Chattel Slave of America and our Indian Brothers and Sisters, nearly five-hundred-years ago has now visited America and the American people. The evils and fears that had been installed in us by the American so-called government and people, through the most diabolical methods ever conceived by any life form on our planet; have come back to haunt the perpetrators of this evil, this so-called American government and people. We are witnessing humanity the destruction of Mr. Yakub's world, society. His makings and all who believe, support, and follow his false religions as well as his politics.

The Rise of the Original Asiatic Black Rulership and the Enforcement of Our Will is a must and should no longer be ignored by us and all humanity. Everything has failed us and all humanity as well. All these false religions have failed us and all humanity as well. All these false religious and political so-called leaders have failed us and all humanity as well. There is no hope in American or European the Mid-or Far East as well, political, or religious structure; there is only death, destruction, sickness, diseases, un-merciful pain and suffering and then a horrifying death, that's even more horrifying, then Stephen King, Alfred Hitchcock or a Rod Sterling Movie all put together. To the Ex-Chattel of America and our Indian brothers and sisters, We Must Have Our Own we owe this corporation called America absolutely nothing at all.

As I am no African American you my Indian brothers and sisters are no native American because neither one of us, are Americans; Never have been and never will be. We the Ex-Chattel Slave of America and our Indian brothers and sisters from the Western Hemisphere, are the remnants of the most diabolical and evil genocidal plan out planet history, has ever recorded. In fact, the most Diabolical, Evil and Devastating Plan that has ever been un-leashed by every Caucasian so-called country and people, upon us the Ex-Chattel Slave and you my Indian brothers and sisters in the Western Hemisphere with impunity. Make what Hitler, the Nazi Party and German people, nothing but child's play and we have nothing at all to do with it. The only thing we did wrong was coming to the aid of our enemies to help destroy the Axis Powers and received nothing but our enemies un-dying hatred for us. This is the history my Indian brothers and sisters because I am one of you and not some so-called African American.

These so-called African Americans and other believing people in American government have an extremely diabolical and more evil time on the way from their newly elected President Joe Bidden a known pervert and children molester, than the soon to be ex-President Donald Trump. The less of the two evils which one is eviler ex-President Trump or newly elected President Bidden? Evil is evil diabolical is diabolical and both these, are the American way; always have been and always will be. Your newly elected Homosexual Jesus cannot save anyone because he cannot save himself nor can he save his maker's, world, and society. Reason being is that their maker Mr. Yakub was only given six-thousand-years to rule, is now up. Remember this also Mr. Yakub's making/people lost two-thousand-years living in the cave sides of West Asia, now called Europe.

The hypocrisy of these false religions the hypocrisy of the world's politics and the hypocrisy of all the people that claim to believe in these so-called biblical and qur'anic prophecies are trying to avoid, what must happen and is happening. What is happening is due to humanity believing in these false religious and political leaders; if you honestly believed in what you say is from the Universal Creator, then explain why you are here in America the land of the ultimate doom? This is the land of the un-brave, the land of the evil spirits, the land of murder, rape liars and a government that supports this evil behavior, always has and always will.

The Indians did not come here on any Trans-Atlantic Slave Ship. The Indians did not sail here with Cristofer Columbus, Ponce De Leon, Ferdinand Magellan, or the Mayflower and none of Europe's so-called ships of exploration. When all these European explorers arrived here the Indians were here and have been here for close to six-teen-thousand-years and the Indians did not call themselves Americans. The Indians did not come here to Ellis Island our enemies came to Ellis Island where they were processed or better yet received by their criminal brothers and sisters and this is the history. The Indians were exile from the Eastern Hemisphere and they walked to the Western Hemisphere. During this time both Hemisphere were connected by passages leading to certain parts, of the Western Hemisphere. This was ten-thousand-years before the birth of Mr. Yakub and Mr. Yakub's experimentations and the birth of Mr. Yakub's makings, the Caucasian Race. This history is closely guarded amongst this secret society called the Illuminati and their high-ranking Masons {33-degree masons}.

This is where and how this Mystery God Myth came into existence approximately two-thousand-four- hundred and fifty, years later. The Original Mr. Yakub never physically lived to see his experimentation come, into reality but Mr. Yakub knew it would if his followers or subordinate's follower his plans of making, a people other than the Original People, who were already here on our planet. This information and history are not known amongst the above average Caucasian person and most surely amongst the Ex-Chattel Slave of America and our Indian brothers and sisters. This is not hate teachings this is the hidden history that the enemies of the Universal Creator, never want us and our Indian brothers and sister to ever learn.

The Scientist Mr. Yakub was extremely wise and understood better than the scholars that question him, when he was in the prisons, Arabia under the name Israel and this includes his uncle Isaiah.

Hollywood uses their power of producing movies and distorting the truth project this poison into the minds of these so-called African Americans, that as long as you fight and defend the lies and false promises of this Caucasian Homosexual they call Jesus; and as long as these ignorant so-called African Americans fight and defend the most diabolical government and people America and the American people; they will be saved by this Homosexual Jesus and his diabolical and evil American government. These are all lies my people and all humanity as well America is doomed and there is no saving her America.

If you believe in these lies perpetrated upon all humanity your spirit will be broken, until you die, and the enemies know this is the truth. Yet, in this society and this American government the truth means nothing lies, and deceit mean everything. The people that control the court system be it Federal, State or Local, have more to do with breaking the law than most of the prisoners, being held in prison. Falling for this obvious lie leads every one of us in a most precarious position and we have been in this position, since we crossed the Atlantic Ocean in fifteen-fifty-five, nearly five-hundred years ago. To surrender your true heritage which has no recorded beginning and no ending, to be called some ridiculous African American is insane. To surrender our Indian heritage, which is older than our enemies time being, birth on our planet, is also insane. By the very nature of us allowing our enemies to re-name us has separated us all, from our ancestors and our Universal Creator.

I was blind, deaf and dumb to the truth believing and loving this devil way of life, although the devil gave us nothing but despair, self-hatred, ignorance, the raping of our mothers wives, daughters and sons, being robbed by our enemies, hopelessness, fear, food not made for human consumption, poor medical and dental, reduced to being a savage in the pursuit of happiness, deprived of Freedom, Justice and any kind of Equality, homosexuality and the worst of everything, this American government and people had to offer. We my people the Ex-Chattel Slave of America our Indian brothers and sisters included had been suffer four nearly five-hundred-long tortuous years and no relief came to us until the coming of the Son Of Man, the Great Mahdi Allah In Person of Master Fard Muhammad, to whom all praise is due forever.

This is the only truth and course of actions we the Ex-Chattel Slave of America our Indian brothers and sisters included, should submit to, and put into real action. Nothing else will save us; nothing else will bring us justice; nothing else will ever bring us comfort; nothing else can reverse the poisons placed in us by our enemies. Nothing else will drive these homosexual demons from amongst us;

nothing else will bring us closer to our Universal Creator; nothing else will put an end to us being mis-led by liars religious and political; nothing else will teach and show us how to love our second self {women} and or children; nothing else will lead us back to the peaceful, loving, happy and prosperous lives, we once enjoyed until the coming of these demons, from Europe to the Jungles Of East Asia and the shores of the Western Hemisphere; I could go on and on about this but we all should know the rest; nothing else will lead us away from the false religions and politics as well as those who bring us this destruction, of self and kind; nothing else will re-move this broken spirit in us and re-place it with the courage, the will, the sincerity to stand up like the Original Asiatic Black Men and Women, we all once were and defend ourselves against all enemies.

Here is something else you should consider to all humanity say, Musa did not bring the so-called Ten Commandments to any of the Original Asiatic Black People or any people belonging to the Original Family. The Ten so-called Commandments were given to the Children of Israel and the children of Israel are Mr. Yakub making or experimentation. The Children are these Zionist who try to steal their brothers and sisters, birth right because the Children of Israel is the entire Caucasian Race Mr. Yakub's experimentation/ grafted people/Satan the Accused Devil in the flesh. Musa brought Mr. Yakub's/Israel out of the cave sides of West Asia now called Europe. The ones who heard Musa first and ventured out of the caves of Europe, took, and understood the best of Musa what taught them from Jehovah and kept these teachings amongst themselves and cared not to share them, with their brothers and sisters. Thus, setting themselves up as Jehovah chosen people and taught their other brothers and sisters that came out of the caves later, this made-up religion they the Zionist named Christianity. In the meantime, the Zionist were took the sciences and hid them, from their brothers and sisters, especially the medical field and engineering fields, also astrometric field, educational fields, manufacturing and production fields, economical fields and the financial/banking and the printing of currency.

This is the history of all humanity enemies that have been kept hidden for the past sis-thousand-six-hundred-years. Also remember that there were some black people that were exile into the caves of West Asia now called Europe and these were the ones who brought these strange looking people, back to the Holy Land in Arabia, where they began causing mischief, stealing, telling lies and deceit amongst our ancestors. No different than what they have been doing and are doing to this very day. All humanity must know the truth regardless, if they reject it or not, this is the truth. Mr. Yakub's making/experimentation have murdered over six-hundred- million Original Black people and counting all the rest of the Original family, they Mr. Yakub's makings are guilty of murdering billions of Original People. So, anyone can see who are the people that violated the laws given to Musa by Jehovah and it was not us. How can any good come to us by believing, trusting, and wanting to be a part of such murdering, lying, evil and supremely diabolical demons that are still, murdering us today?

The Broken Spirit of humanity is what's happening now and the many distraction that take president over the survival of humanity, is shameful. What is more dis-hearting is how these who claim to know the truth making these as well as a priority, get that paper. These fools love taking pictures and posting them on social media, casting a false image that they are righteous which is a lie; that they are successful which is a lie; that they believe in Allah and Allah's last and greatest Messenger which is greatest of these hypocrites lies. These selfish fools are doing and have done more harm to their own people and humanity, then all the drugs that the American government has sanctioned to be distributed amongst our people. Stealing and lying to their people is their way of life as they wear crowns and fez's. ornaments that are to create the illusion, that they are this when in truth they are the same share cropping Negroes, they always have been and always will be. This attitude, mentality and spirit is keeping the Broken Spirit flourishing amongst our people alive which is clearer than ever before, overwhelming all humanity as well.

All the despair in the world today; all the self-hatred in the world today; all the suffering in the world today; all the misery in the world today; all the raping and murdering in the world today; all the diseases in the world today; all the envy and jealously in the world today; all the hunger and starvation in the world today; all the ignorance in the world today; all the wars and talk of wars in the world today; all the lying and deceit in the world today; all the broken families like Humphry Dumpty, all the king horses and men can never put it back together again, in this world today; all the narcissism, arrogance and self-importance in the world today; all the governments under attack in the world today; all the false religions and wicked politics in the world today; all the evil and diabolically conceived plans in the world today; all the false religious and political so-called leaders, in the world today; all the prayers that go un-answered in the world today; all the cries for mercy, freedom, justice, equality, salvation and redemption in the world today; all the love and desire for materialism at the expense of humanity and all life forms, in the world today; all this sick homosexuality and trans-gendering in the world today; all the drugs and alcoholism in the world; all the false and broken promises in the world today; has been and still are caused and made up by Zionism, the author of this said Jesus Christ your lord and savior Christianity and the rest of the false religions, and politics, that humanity has been swallowing; since Mr. Yakub's/Israel/ John the Revelator; journey to the Island of Pelan also called Patmos, with his fifty-nine-thousand nine-hundred and ninety-nine, followers that completed the journey.

We my people this includes my Indian brothers and sisters I am more of them than I am of these so-called Africans and I am proud of my heritage, here in this Wilderness of Sin, Iniquity and Transgressions because we have fulfilled, the prophecies of Allah to his Holy Prophet Ibrahim. So, if other so-called cultures, religions, and people worship the Universal Creator as they choose to do then I will be damned if I will not stand up and tell the world and every so-called religion in the world; that Allah the Universal Creator Himself visited us the Ex-Chattel Slave of America and our Indian brothers and sisters in the persons of Master W.F. Muhammad to whom all praises are due forever. I will be damned if I will not stand up an announce to the world that Mr. Elijah Muhammad is Allah's last and greatest Messenger and the true Muhammad RasulAllah and this I Saladin Shabazz-Allah stand on the Square Of Life for, even if this cost me my life, MY SACRIFICE MY LIFE AND MY DEATH ARE ALL FOR ALLAH, MY MOST MERCIFUL SAVIOR, REDEEEMER, PROTECTOR AND GUIDE, WHO HAS NO ASSOIATES NOR ANY EQUAL AND THERE IS NONE LIKEN TO HIM. ALLAH U AKBAR ELIJAH MUHAMMADRASULALLAH.

Before the American and European Medical also Pharmaceutical Laboratories which controls all the production, research and manufacturing of all drugs and medicines and apparatus, murdered our brother Dr. Sebe, Dr. Sebe had proven that proper vegetables medicinal herbs could cure diseases, that the medical field said there were no cure for these diseases like cancer, aids, syphilis and other diseases deemed incurable, by this so-called Medical Board of professional Medical Doctors who are making tons of money, by keeping their patients sick with very little chance of survival or recovering from. Now if the government feels that you are needed to aid their plans of implementation, then you may have a chance of recovery or if you can afford to pay an un-imaginable fee, then you may also have a chance of recovery. If you do not fall into one of these categories then goodbye and you become nothing more than a lab rat, for the rich and famous. Ask yourself why are there two serpents coiling around the medical staff? Here ais the answer to this symbol; one-to lie to Medical Doctors Patients and two- to use poisons through chemical manufactured medicines, which are extremely addictive drugs. In ninety-nine percent of the medical profession cases and case studies, once hooked on these chemically made drugs there is no getting off them. This medical field substance is to control population by shorting life under the illusion that one is getting better, but you must continue to ingest their chemical manufactured drugs.

Since Dr. Sebe proved the medical field and profession are not concerned about elimination of the problem, but so-called arresting of diseases therefore making sure one is always depended upon their chemical manufactured drugs called medicine. Dr. Sebe also sat at dinner table of the Holy Messenger of Allah Mr. Elijah Muhammad;

where he Dr. Sebe studied How To Eat To Live Part One and Part Two, also the many lectures on this subject by the Holy Messenger of Allah.

Diet is extremely important in persevering of life eating of any flesh is not all that healthy for anyone's health, be it physically, mentally, or spiritually. The belief in three meals a day and snacks in between are extremely unhealthy. The consuming of pig meat and the scavengers of the sea are serious and most deadly poisons that should always be avoided at all cost. Even nuts are not good for human consumption as well because nuts do not break down by the Hydrochloric Acids in human digestive system and cause colon or pancreas cancers, due to an over whelming build up in these areas. Study How To Eat To Live By Mr. Elijah Muhammad and you will learn what the medical profession does not want you, to know about preserving and extending your life expectancy. Therefore Dr. Sebe was murdered by the medical industry because what he was performing on the physically dying and restoring them with life. His actions were beginning to eat into the profits of the medical and pharmaceutical fields.

Dr. Sebe went to the so-called high-ranking brothers in the so-called Nation of Islam and Christianity and had an idea of opening clinics, in every black community throughout America and was turned down by these so-called high-ranking officials, in the so-called Nation of Islam and Christianity. Here are my questions: How can black lives matter when these so-called African Americans, religious and political leaders, do not care about them and you judge them by their actions? How can you dare say you are a follower of the Holy Messenger of Allah and refused to work with your brother, who has proven to be right, in his workings? How can any of you expect me or anyone who is truly aware of things, be a part of such imbecilic decision making? How can you stand by and give our enemies control over our brother works and deeds and you walking around with your pompous attitude, like you are important, as you claim to have supreme wisdom?

It is these type of actions by so-called leaders that make us all appear as foolish sharecroppers, wrapped up in their own make-believe importance. These imbecilic decision making and actions, Re-Enforce the Broken Spirit amongst our people, while all humanity shake their heads at all of us, in total discuss. Then these idiots dare say they are god with their suits some wear bowties and some wear string tie, nevertheless the results are the same, absolutely no Nation Building at all, only talk and more talk and no production. It is so pathetic to see how ignorant these so-called enlighten people think they are and in truth, they still have the mind set of sharecropping Chattel Slaves. Now they have better looking clothes, shoes, and a few measly dollars, in their pocket. I have even had a so-called brother trying to involve me in some idiotic pyramid scheme. In fact, this same brother borrows three-hundred dollars from me and when it came back to paying me back, just like John Hawkins the trader disappeared. If this is the brotherhood, I want no part of this said so-called Nation of Islam and I can tell you about more under handed deals, involving these so-called brothers.

These so-called brothers are also involved in helping to keep the Broken Spirit in our people, to continue because there is no sincerity at all, in ninety-eight percent of them. In the nineteen-seventy-four Savior's Day Address which was the Holy Messenger Farewell Address, the Holy Messenger said because a white dress but what is under the dress is filthy and unclean, it amounts to nothing at all.

The brothers thought the Holy Messenger was talking about the women, in truth the Holy Messenger was talking about the brothers. I have seen my share of the under handedness from many of these so-called brothers and narcissistic inflated worthless egos. If you agree with their foolishness then you are cool, with them but once you disagree with them and refuse to let anyone of them to use you, they will throw you under the bus quick and fast.

How can this Broken Spirit amongst the Ex-Chattel Slave of America be reversed when the ones who claim to have supreme wisdom, are the ones mis-leading their own people? These fools are not capable of leadership because they simply are not qualify and never will be qualify to anything more than what they are because they have freed themselves of the selfishness and ignorance, of plantation living. The Rise of the Original Asiatic Black Patriarch Rule and the Enforcement of Our Will is impossible to achieve because in truth they are disbelievers; and these fools call Joshua {Brother Minister Malcolm X/Al-Malik Shabazz}, a hypocrite. None of these arrogant fools have the power, the will, the sincerity, or the conviction, to dare attempt to bring their people across the River Jordan because they fear for their lives. They were strong in belief when the Holy Messenger of Allah Mr. Elijah Muhammad was physically alive and amongst them, taking all the heat and responsibilities upon himself. Now that the Holy Messenger is gone and been gone since nineteen-seventy-five, all we have been experiencing is deceit, lies, conniving money hungry sharecroppers and nothing else with their worthless so-called websites and foolish social media groups.

The Broken Spirit amongst the Ex-Chattel Slave of America is more broken now, than they were when they were nothing more than Chattel Slaves, less than hogs, pigs, and their master's dogs.

These so-called self-appointed so-called ministers only know how to conduct themselves in church like fashion and they love this. Even though many have visited the Sunnah Faith self-included, I was never comfortable with the whole church structure and false brotherhood it cultivates. I am a student of the Holy Messenger of Allah Mr. Elijah Muhammad. I understand what he meant when he said Allah visited us in the person of Master Fard Muhammad to whom all praises are due forever and this statement has been overlooked, by these so-called said followers of the Holy Messenger.

The desire to be recognized and feel important is a disease amongst black people here in America, until they leave the back and front doors un-secured and wide open for everyone - other than themselves, to walk right in and take whatever they want including their women. Those who claim to be followers of the Holy Messenger and have so-called Supreme Wisdom, are the worst of the lot. Do not pay attention to what they are saying, pay attention to their actions and deeds and you will see that they have not changed their evil deceitful ways. I had this one older fool say to me that when he calls, I should end whatever call I am on, for him. I told him he is not that important you do not rule me, and you certainly do not tell me what to do. His wisdom is not that great to me and there is extraordinarily little he can tell me. I had this other fool a much younger fool whom I brought Islam to and we were awfully close, until he married this West African woman. Then his behavior towards me and the brotherhood he claimed to love changed. Him and his West African wife who incidentally hates black people who are the Ex-Chattel Slave of America. So, this so-called brother and his West African wife while driving in the truck together, dare think they can make decision and plans, for me. Even after I told this idiot I would not be available the next day and that I did not want to this, these two arrogant fools without any regard for me, dare make plans for me and the following day. Then this imbecile said to me bring your car so you can drive her mother home. Well since he would not respect what I told him I then had to show him and his West African wife they do not rule or tell me what to do, so I did not show up nor did I answered any of their calls; and since Allah revealed to me the real weakness in him, we do not speak with each other today and this suits me fine.

This same egotistical fool allowed this West African dog to rob us of twenty-thousand dollars and this silly fool said to me, "he can be trusted because he is a Muslim from Africa". This fool learned from this other old fool I just mention and they both claimed to be followers of the Messenger of Allah. This mentality is the way of life for these fools and flourishes throughout, this said nation calling themselves Islamic, Muslims or gods. When in truth they still nothing more than the Ex-Chattel Slave of America with a weak understanding of Allah and Allah's last and greatest Messenger. It is pitiful to see them group together acting like they are important, wise, and knowledgeable, when in truth the majority like ninety-eight percent of them are just as blind, deaf, and dumb when they came to Muhammad and this ninety-eight percent are using the teachings of Allah, to shield their dirty religion.

There is not any wonder why the spirit of Ex-Chattel Slave of America is Broken because ninety-eight percent of the ones who claimed to be righteous, are no different than the Christians. In fact, if not for the obvious difference in the ornaments they both love to wear, their ways and actions are the same and this ninety-eight percent dare call Brother Minister Malcolm a hypocrite; it is obvious these fools do not look in the mirror because the real hypocrites are looking back at them. How can the Broken Spirit of any people be reversed and revived with silly, narcissistic ignorant and arrogant fools, believing they are calling the shots? None of these arrogant disbelievers in Allah come anywhere close to filling Brother Malcolm's shoes and are the ones that are happy they murdered Brother Malcolm in front of his wife and children; therefore, executing the Joshua that could think and lead us all, across the River Jordan. None of these fools can do it; none of these fools have been chosen by Allah to do anything, except be the absolute fools they all are well at least ninety-eight percent of them are and always will be. The Holy Messenger of Allah realized this before he physically died and he also knew that nothing but complete non-productive cowardly fools when it comes to building a nation for themselves, wife and children will come after he was gone, and this suits our enemies fine.

CHAPTER 18

THE SIGNS OF LIARS AND
THE DECEITFUL

In my lifetime growing from a child to adulthood I have only seen two men worthy of my attention, due to their impact on myself, society, and humanity. What I learned from them is the importance of being sincere and truthful. Even the ones who claim to be righteous are the ones to keep your eyes wide open for and upon. Setting up churches and temples and claiming to be doing the work of Allah/God are in fact doing absolutely nothing. If you have a church or temple and make yourself a so-called minister you are not doing the work, of Allah or Allah's last and greatest Messenger because you are being deceitful and being deceitful make you liar. You are lying and deceiving yourself therefore lying and deceiving everyone, you encounter. When you hear certain things that come out of their mouths you must pay close attention due to these charlatans, being able to gain your trust. Once you relinquish your trust to them, they will always betray your ninety-eight percent of the time. These charlatans will then begin to see how they can relieve you of your hard earn funds, many ways.

Self-importance is what they believe in and are trying to achieve and now with the help of social media, these charlatans can reach masses of people. Their egos are so inflated they cannot be reached by common since and rationality because this does not exist in them. These fools always want to talk about themselves to anyone that is foolish enough to listen to them. If you do not buy into their hype you can see how phony and mis-leading they truly are and what their true intentions are, as well. Their mannerism is all an act to convince whoever will listen to them, when in truth there is no sincerity in them, this included women as well. They use the teachings of Allah as a weapon against the downtrodden and the ones that maybe seeking, to learn the teachings of Allah.

There is no true honesty in them but like any good actor these frauds put on a performance, in public, over the phone and social media. I visited a temple in Virginia the setting and treatment were spectacular, and I was truly overwhelm and grateful, for the attention that was bestow upon me. Then as time went on, I began receiving hints that they wanted to recruit me into their fold. Once I made it clear to everyone that I had something else to do in life, things began to change. If you refuse to allow another man to choose what is best for you, your life will be filled with misery because if you and your spouse maybe having some difficulties you should not need anyone else to solve your problem or problems. I am one that does not need anyone else to help me solve any problem my wife and I, maybe experiencing.

I am a student of the Messenger of Allah and I learned a great deal from listening to him while he was physically amongst us. Others believe he is not physically dead or that he is aboard the Mother Plain is absurd and I do not need a structure to gain any confidence from. I understand the greatness and pleasure of being blessed with the rewards of my research and I am forever grateful to the Holy Messenger, for guiding me in the right direction and away from these dis-believing people.

Narcissism, self-importance, false belief will lead you away from Allah and Allah's last and greatest Messenger, as well as other things and people. I put my faith and hope in Allah and absolutely no one else. I strive extremely hard to implement the Islam and teachings that He Allah taught to His Holy Messenger Mr. Elijah Muhammad, in my daily living and activities and especially to my wife and children. If any of my children want to be an infidel or live the life of an infidel, then stay away from me and they are nothing to me. This is what I think about these hypocrites that so-called self-proclaimed ministers and their lodges, as we as their worthless websites. These fools are secretly working for the enemies of all humanity and these idiots dare call this, having friendship in all walks of life.

I do not hatred in my heart for anyone, but I will not let anyone disrespect me or my faith, my wife, and our children. My wife does not need any foolish person be male or female to sell her the MGT GCC handbook because my wife is not, some Muslim Girl In Training and my wife Knows how to conduct herself at home and abroad. The Holy Messenger taught us in his Farewell Address if one listen very closely, the clothing means absolutely nothing if what is under the clothing is filthy and un-cleaned. I can tell you from firsthand experience ninety-eight percent of those who claim to be righteous are just as un-righteous as they were, before the Holy Savior Allah in the persons of Master Fard Muhammad, to whom all praises are due forever, visited us in early nineteen-fourteen, nineteen-twenties and nineteen thirties. Ninety-eight percent of them are still liars, thieves, deceitful, conniving un-grateful fools, who are using the Savior's name to shield, their dirty religion which in truth is Christianity.

Pay attention my people and humanity they use their lodges designed after the temples of Islam, to confuse, mislead and rob you of your hard-earned funds. I would not give the lot of them two cents for what they are doing and call themselves teachings. Islam is Universal and you do not need anyone to sanction you or approve you as being a Muslim. Once you submit to Allah, keep up prayer and follow the example of Allah's Holy Messenger and turn your daily practices and thoughts around, you are a Muslim. These frauds take power and pleasure in approving you to be a member, of their lodges and if you disagree with them then the so-called minister will exile you. In fact, you are born a Muslim just by being physically birth, by and from your mother. In fact, every life form in the universe is born submitting to the Universal Creator and that makes every life form Muslim. Regardless of if one knows it or not this is an absolute mathematical universal fact.

If you choose to study the Quran-an, Bible, history, the sciences of all types are an extremely great thing and experience but never believe in being a servant or beholding to any man because if you do, then you are committing a great sin. Do not ever make the misstate of thinking that being supportive, devoted, and respectful to your wife or husband is wrong in fact this is the natural order of creation and a universal mathematical principles and practices; therefore, this is Islamic and the true Islam. If you are in violation of these universal mathematical principles and practices, you are not serving or worshipping Allah the Universal Creator, Lord and Master.

To bring comfort, love and security to your wife and children is being nearer to the Universal Creator, than walking around saying the black man is god and the black man cannot demonstrate that he is god. In fact, before the eyes of civilize humanity these fools calling themselves god, or minister, supreme or something else they are not able to manifest; is telling civilize humanity that the Ex-Chattel Slave of America, is now the Mental and Physical Chattel Slave of America and are not welcome amongst civilize humanity and I cannot blame civilize humanity for not wanting you, amongst them, their wives, and children.

The Ex-Chattel Slave of America is now the Mental and Physical Chattel Slave of America due to the fact, they refuse to get up, unite themselves as a civilize productive people with their own government and laws to govern themselves and begin to build a Nation, a society and world, for themselves, wives' children, and people. How can you dare claim to be a civilize people when you have no culture of your own? How can you claim to be civilize people and you have no language, of your own? How can you claim to be an independent civilize people when you completely depend on the enemies of yourself and ancestors, for your subsistence? This is the biggest and most pathetic comedy show on earth and ever witness before; the Mental and Physical Chattel Slave of America, calling themselves god, claiming to having supreme wisdom and yet always dependent on their enemies, to do something for them because they refuse to stand up be men and take responsibility for themselves, wives' children, and people.

These lodges and churches are producing absolutely nothing that civilize humanity can and will respect, with their narcissistic, egotistic, self-proclamation of importance, worthless, arrogant paper ship so-called leaders; while their so-called audience shout and scream that is right brother minister. These narcissistic, ignorant, most arrogant fools, are no different from any other Christian preacher, leading our people back on to the plantations of America; now into being the Chattel, Mental and Physical Slaves, of America, this Homosexual Illuminati, their Members and Associates. As these narcissistic, arrogant, and ignorant fools are doing nothing and none of them care. This is the reason why civilize society and their religious beliefs do not except whatever these fools have to say because in truth, by their actions and deeds cannot show and prove that Allah visited the Ex-Physical Chattel Slave of America in the person of Master Fard Muhammad, to whom all praises are due forever. Through their actions and deeds civilize society and their religious beliefs do not except Mr. Elijah Muhammad as Allah's last and greatest Messenger as well as the true and only MuhammadRasulAllah. Although civilize society knows this to be true but the inadequacy of these false so-called representatives, are causing more harm than good because of imbecilic and insane desire for recognition and none of these frauds are Joshua and are not capable of leading our people across the River Jordan, only capable of leading our people back onto the plantations of America, as Mental and Spiritual Chattel Slaves, for eternality.

The truth I am revealing believe me my death is being talked about if not even being planned and then just like Brother Minister Malcolm, I will be label a hypocrite, the real and true hypocrites, that want this truth kept hidden, from their people. This does not bother me at all because this truth must be revealed not only to our people, but to all civilize humanity. These are the signs of the Liars And the Deceitful my people and all civilize humanity, everyone must be alert to and for because these Liars and Deceitful false leaders, are popping up everywhere, amongst our people and now you have other than our own people, dare think and believe they can lead our people. This is excepted by the ignorant amongst our people because they have no understanding of the teachings of Allah or Allah's last and greatest Messenger. These arrogant ignorant fools are only out for the few pieces of silver, that their masters promised them, if these arrogant, ignorant fools can deliver, you and I back into Mental and Spiritual Chattel Slavery.

My people and all of humanity pay heed to what I am saying there is not one amongst them, who has the power to lead anyone to a better more productive and prosperous way of life. It does not matter whom they claim to be or who they claim to be a so-called follower of none, of them are able to help you. Anyone that uses this Allah Shabazz is a fool and has no clue about the truth because Allah is the first and Allah is the last. You find these frauds are not one of us so, who authorized these frauds to be your teacher? Why these frauds will not go amongst their own people and teach them and relieve their people, of their hard-earned money? The reason being is that these frauds have the Mental and Spiritual Chattel Slave of America, mark as an easy target and very gullible. With the help of these traitors amongst the Mental and Spiritual American Chattel Slave, these interlopers come amongst you with their lies and deceit. These are not your friends in fact they are your enemies and the fools amongst that are capitalizing from these frauds, are happy because they are taking your hard earn money as well.

This is not the Islam that the Holy Savior Allah in person taught His last and greatest Messenger. Do not be fooled by the pictures and décor these lodges love show off and false behavior, they love to demonstrate because in fact they are in truth nothing, but Masons and these frauds are using the Savior's name, to shield their dirty religion. Money is the name of their game and the methods of obtaining your hard earn money, is still the same. Beware of these websites and groups on social media these are traps to mis-lead you into believing, things and people everyone should avoid. We are not the Nation of Islam we are the lost and now found members, belonging to Islam here in the Wilderness of North America. The Temples of Islam were riddle with thieves, liars and deceivers and these lodges are filled with thieves, liars, and deceivers, no different than any other church in America. There was plenty of progress when the Holy Messenger was here physically amongst us and all humanity and since his death, there has not been any progress made on any level, and most definitely not on any National Level.

As I said before this is the greatest and most dis-graceful comedy show ever produced and witness on our planet and therefore the now Mental and Spiritual Chattel Slave of America, will never be respected or excepted by civilized humanity and especially our enemies. Your ranks are riddle with liars, deceivers, petty thieves, egotistical, narcissistic, arrogant fools, starving for recognition, from a society that has no respect for the so-called backward false leadership, claiming to be followers of Allah and Allah's Holy Messenger. It makes me wonder who is the true enemy of the now Mental and Spiritual Chattel Slave of America, now called African American?

If you know and understand the truth that Allah revealed to his Holy Messenger and Allah taught us all, through the mouth of His Holy Messenger, then you must see what is surely before your eyes. How much longer are the black women in America who been suffering for nearly five-hundred-years, are going to be Muslim Girl in Training when Allah himself has visited us nearly one hundred=years ago? After nearly one-hundred-years she is still a girl in training, this is a shame and it shows absolutely no growth and surely no development because after nearly one-hundred-years since the coming of Allah, she still needs General Civilization Classes.

You are not recognized in the United Nations at all and if for Brother Minister Malcolm having the courage to take our case before the United Nations in nineteen- sixty-four or nineteen- sixty-five, this would had never happened, and it has not happen since Brother Minister Malcolm. Absolutely no other so-called minister or reverend has even come close to doing anything near this, during the nineteen-sixties to this present day and time. Examine all the evidence the now Mental and Spiritual Chattel Slave of America, now called African American and do not listen to the haters of Brother Minister Malcolm X because the ones calling Brother Minister Malcolm X a hypocrite, are greater hypocrites than what they claim Brother Minister Malcolm X was or can ever be. Yes, Brother Minister Malcolm X said some things he should not have said, and I do disagree with, nevertheless if there was not this interference by these other haters amongst the ranks of top officials and so-called ministers, father and son could and would have worked things out and the father would had forgiven his son.

Examine what took place in nineteen-seventy-five these same so-called brothers, Ministers, Captains, and lieutenants, either jumped ship and ran to the Arabs and the Arab's so-called Sunnah Islam. or they went into hiding and did nothing because they were afraid. Examine this humanity who fed Brother Minister Malcolm X these lies and staged that entire event, about the Messenger of Allah? It was the Messenger of Allah biological son Wallace D. Mohammad and his family, who committed this evil. Now, I ask everyone this question why did not these so-called Ministers, Captains, Lieutenants and top-ranking officials in the Temples of Islam, Murder Wallace D. Mohammad? Why did ninety-eight percent of those who claimed to be followers of the Messenger of Allah, excepted Wallace D. Muhammad back amongst them? Wallace D. Mohammad was already conspiring with the Arabs, the Arabs were conspiring with the Illuminati and the American government planning a coup, against Wallace D. Mohammad father. Brother Minister Malcolm X was the only person standing in the way. Most of the Ministers, Captains, Lieutenants, and so-called top officials, were with Wallace D. Muhammad. Why was not Wallace D. Muhammad taken out In accordance with what Constitute Treason and Treasonous Acts against Islam, here in the Wilderness of North America?

Why Didn't any of the said elders had a counter plan against this coup, that they had to know was taking place? How could the said elders and so-called followers of the Messenger of Allah so they claimed to be, stand by and did absolutely nothing to put this rebellion down? These are questions that must be answered everyone due to the lack of intervention by the said elders and said followers, the second coup became a reality which led to Wallace D. Mohammad taking over as the new leader, of Islam here in the Wilderness of North America. Then the massive migration of Arabs and their so-called Sunnah Islam, which has been welcome by this Illuminati, their American government, and the American people, into every black community throughout America and American culture and society? The lies, the deceit, the stealing, the fornication erupted even before the death of the Messenger of Allah; Why was not something done by the said elders, the said so-called believers and followers of the Messenger of Allah?

The liars, the deceivers, the cowards, the thieves, and murderers of self, were able to walk in take control, without any resistance; Then explain this to me and the world how dare these cowards call Brother Minister Malcolm X, a hypocrite, when in fact they are the hypocrites and are guilty of Treason, against Islam here in North America. The ones who claim to be this and that are guilty of committing Treason against Allah the Holy Savior of all humanity and who personally set up Temple Number One in Detroit Michigan in the Bottom, Islam here in the Wilderness of North America? How could these said elders with these said so-called followers sit back and let this travesty happen and did nothing but call Brother Minister Malcolm X a hypocrite. It was in Detroit Michigan in the Bottom where Allah would and did find MuhammadRasulAllah, in the personage of Elijah Muhammad and these said elders and said believers, allowed the enemies to just walk in and take over, without any resistance? Took over Temple Number One and handed it to the Arabs and nothing was done, about this insult except they turned the other cheek. Then these Insurrectionists went to Chicago and took over Temple Number Two which was built by the Holy Messenger Mr. Elijah Muhammad and those who claimed to be his followers; and handed it over to the Arabs and their so-called Sunnah Islam. Why should I believe or trust anyone who supposedly received their teachings, from out of the Mid-West? These Insurrectionist marched throughout America destroying everything Allah and Allah's Holy Messenger built, for Allah's chosen people and handed it all to the Arabs and their version of Sunnah Islam, without any resistance? Why should Allah bless such cowards and the descendants of these cowards, when they denounce Allah and Allah's Holy Messenger?

These frauds in your mist today are not lovers of Allah or Allah's last and greatest Messenger these frauds are lovers and believers in

Mr. Yakub disguising themselves to act like Shabazz, when in truth they are the children of Israel. There is nothing any of them can do to turn this travesty around because of the treachery, that has been directed at Allah Himself and Allah's last and greatest Messenger. How could these un-grateful people be deserving of Allah's blessing. I am extremely grateful to Allah for removing me from amongst them and blessing me to be able, to write and reveal the truth about these lying, deceitful, thieving hypocrites. Examine the history everyone and do not listen to these children and worshipers of Mr. Yakub, they are very skillful at deceiving, lying, and stealing from their own people. Do not listen to these frauds that are not of the Shabazz People and have absolutely no history, of being a Chattel Slave for America. Do not listen anyone claiming to be one of us when in truth, their ancestors were and are the Conquistadors. It is impossible for any of them to be a part or one of the lost and now found members of the Nation/Tribe of Shabazz. Why don't these religious pimps go and raise their own people? This would be the right and proper thing to do in which others have done when the Messenger of Allah was amongst us.

These are not the teachings of Allah who visited us the Ex-Physical Chattel Slave of America and this homosexual riddle Illuminati; in the person of Master Fard Muhammad to whom all praises are due forever. I am not writing about hatred my people which includes my Indian brothers and sisters, I am writing about Truth, Freedom, Justice and Equality as taught and given to us through the mouth of His Holy Messenger Mr. Elijah Muhammad. The truth only hurts the guilty and it is only the guilty who does not want this truth exposed, to their people and all humanity. These are not the teachings of Mr. Muhammad these are the teachings of Allah taught and given to Mr. Muhammad including the name Muhammad. The Holy Messenger was to open his mouth so that Allah Himself, could make Himself know to us all and the world. I do not hate the Caucasian Race I do not trust the Caucasian Race because of the Supreme Evil, they have done to me and my people as they continue to do their evil to me and my people. Now the Caucasian Race are getting help from the hypocrites from amongst my people disguising themselves as sheep's when in truth they are blood thirsty wolves and vampires.

These liars, deceivers' arrogant thieves are not building Temples of Islam these frauds are building lodges, because they failed at their duties and abandon their post, while under fire by the Insurgents who and are the insurrectionists, led by Wallace D. Mohammad, to destroy the work of Allah and Allah's Holy Messenger Mr. Elijah Muhammad; therefore casting the Ex-Physical Chattel Slave of America into what they are today the now Mental and Spiritual Chattel Slave of America, called African Americans and Native Americans. These are the reasons why I say to all humanity pay attention to the signs of the Liars and the Deceitful because they are amongst you.

Now these mis-guided fools are revving up for Savior's Day out comes the uniforms, out comes the crowns and fez's, out comes the flags, jewelry and ornament's and the many pictures, out comes the feast, just like all masons do once or twice a year, may be three times a year and one of the greatest acts you ever want to see, will be performed on that day and you will see the separation amongst them. On this Holiest of days there will still be no unity amongst them, and therefore in the Examination of Kareem, he referred to their religion as being dirty and nothing more than Christianity.

Therefore, Jerusalem must and will be taken back from these devils, in disguise as righteous people.

There is so much self-hatred, lies, deceit, thievery amongst the now Mental and Spiritual Chattel Slaves of America now called African American, all because some elders fell asleep, at their post. The Holy Messenger said to us all every wolf taking a bite out of us and now these so-called Africans have joined the orgy and taking their bites out of us as well. The Conquistadors are guilty of slaughtering our Indian brothers and sisters from Cuba to Florida all through South and Central America Mexico included. Raped the women and then super-imposed their filthy Christianity upon them, with impunity. The Brutality of the Spanish Conquistadors is second only to their European brothers and sisters, in North America and the Caribbean Island. Let us not forget the brutality of these Conquistadors on the Island now called Porta Rico, as well. You present yourselves as complete fools in the eyes of civilize humanity because only ignorant fools would give to his enemy/enemies, the power to rule him, his wife, children, and his way of life.

In every black community throughout America, you have hateful, envious jealous people that has never done anything to prove themselves, yet these fools have convince themselves they are leaders. They sit in their homes doing nothing except hating anyone who does something, these people will never do anything because in their hearts, they are cowards. Hatred always comes out of their mouths for self they have no humility or humbleness in them only the desire to be a leader yet does nothing to demonstrate leadership potential or qualities. Beware of the ones who believe the delusions they make up in their own heads and once given the chance to prove themselves, they will always fail themselves and everyone else. These envious in capable fools always blame others for their failures and never take responsibility, for their actions or lack of. If you believe you are what you convince yourself to be, then prove it and you cannot prove it by staying home doing absolutely nothing but fanaticizing.

Imagine this I am hated because I do not hate Brother Minister Malcolm X/Al-Malik Shabazz and there were others whom these fools love, respect and admire, that deserted their post during the time of Insurrection, ran and hid themselves from the Insurrectionists amongst us who were also the Insurgents. Yes, they had all the teachings from Allah many of them were in the presence of Allah and still they deserted their post. How or why should I have any confidence in any of them? I do not care what their names may be or where they are from or whom they were with, when It came down to showing and proving they did nothing at all. These younger fools are to mesmerize they cannot see the truth and they only want whatever material they can get their hands on, to try and validate themselves and so that they can sell the teachings of Allah our Holy Savior to whom praises are due forever.

We took an Oath to Allah that my sacrifice, my life, and my death are for Allah and no associates has he and this I am command, I am of those who are first to submit. So, what happened this should be explained? The Holy Messenger Mr. Elijah Muhammad fulfilled his Solemn Oath to Allah, why did not you? How can you claim to be the Nation Of Islam and you have absolutely no resources, to approach any civilize human being? If narcissism, envy, lying, deceiving, thievery, arrogance, ignorant, self-inflated egos, and importance are the resources of Mr. Yakub's making and these are the resources that these hypocrites bring to the table, of all humanity and all civilize humanity rejects these resources because these are the resources of the enemies of Allah, Allah's last and greatest Messenger and all of Allah's Prophets.

I really do not care if these frauds hate me for what I am writing because I am only telling the truth, about the real hypocrites and disbelievers in Allah and Allah's Holy Messenger. This truth must be made known and what these frauds are demonstrating to all humanity, is nothing short of disgraceful. There is no sincerity there is only self-gain and this written in the Examination of Kareem, in which another defector called it the one-hundred and twenty degrees. Which was stolen from Temple Number Seven in New York by a defector, in Allah Allah's Holy Messenger and Islam here in the Wilderness of North America. Saying the black man is god, has absolutely no validly at all. When you have absolutely no clear demonstration, that the black man is god, then you cannot prove that you are god, of righteousness. My people and this once again include my Indian brothers and sisters, in this day and time you must be hyper vigilant and guard yourself against these liars and deceitful people, pretending to be something that clearly can be seen, they are not.

So, I conclude this chapter with a warning be on your guard against these frauds that are in your mist, seeking to mis-lead you in order that they may steal from you your money and trust, with their lies and deceit. It is absolutely impossible to have a nation or consider yourself to be a nation when you do not believe in laws to govern the nation by and the people belonging to said nation. It is absolutely impossible to have a nation or even consider yourself a nation when said nation has no rules or regulations, to guide the people of said nation. It is absolutely impossible to have a nation and no government to guide the nation and the people who may belong, to said nation. These are absolutely impossibilities that every civilize people understand and abide by. All humanity submits to these mathematical certainties in fact every life form in the universe submits to these mathematical certainties. The only so-called said nation believes in this insanity is the said nation, that this defector made up. This said so-called nation mixed, fixed, diluted, tampered with, and changed the Examination of Kareem, as their so-called defector leader did.

The only cowardly people believe this was and is a good thing for are the ones who were and are afraid, to stand up for Truth, Freedom, Justice and Equality, which is the Islam that Allah Himself taught His Holy Messenger Mr. Elijah Muhammad. This is the Islam that Allah brought, gave, and taught us all, through the mouth of His Holy Messenger Mr. Elijah Muhammad; and Allah's Holy Messenger gave to us all. The only other Asiatic Original Black man I saw that was so, hated, despised, envied by his so-called brothers Outside of the Holy Messenger himself who was hated, despised, envied and even worst by his own family and those he was trying to help, is Brother Minister Malcolm X/A[-Malik Shabazz and no one else. I take great pride in what I am doing, I cannot thank Allah for allowing me to do this work. If what I am revealing offends anyone then to bad, the truth on hurts the guilty and the guilty has plenty to be guilty of.

This poison, this cancer of narcissism, arrogance, self-importance, lying, deceiving, stealing, ignorance and self-indulgence, have eaten into the brains and hearts of these fools trying to pretend to be your minister, trying to pretend to be your leader, claiming to be your brother and sister; are more deadly than a Rattle Snake, a Cobra and Python together, to everyone that truly believes in Allah our

Supremely Merciful and All Knowing Savior, who visited us in the person of Master W.F. Muhammad to whom all praises are due forever; and His Allah last and greatest Holy Messenger raised up from amongst us, Mr. Elijah Muhammad. Allah U Akbar Mr. Elijah Muhammad is the true and only Muhammad RasulAllah. This I say to the world; this I say to the Sunnah Community or world; this I say to the Sufi Community world; this I say to the Zionist Community or world and this I say to the Christianity World.

CHAPTER 19

THE AMERICA'S MEDICAL DEATH LIST
IS THE BURDEN OF IN SINCERITY

This chapter is about the burdens of a people that have trusted the wrong people, religions, politics, and beliefs. There is so much confusion in the world today more than it has ever been on our planet and the now Mental and Spiritual Chattel Slave of America, is catching the blunt of it. No matter what direction they turn in hell is always the end product and no relief in sight. Religion and politics have failed them and always have failed them and yet the now Mental and Spiritual Chattel Slaves of America referred to as African American, always gravitate to everything that is wrong for them. The so-called religious and political leaders of these Mental and Spiritual Chattel Slaves have failed them and always will fail them. It is a crying shame that they cannot see how blessed they had been and how much the Universal Creator loved them, until He took on a form, to find and retore them back to prominence and glory. Instead,they chose and still choose the opposers that lead them back to the mercy of their enemies.

To watch your young daughters cozying up to these strangers' men and women, selling themselves to these strangers for the sole purpose, of satisfying these strangers, warp sexual fantasies. These are your young girls and, in some cases, your young boys with no concern for themselves catching some deadly disease or virous, from these filthy strangers. There is no god coming to save you from your crimes of rejecting truth for falsehood and this has been going on, for nearly five-hundred-years. In fact, since the murder of Joshua and this is when the Genocidal Plan was Engineered and Orchestrated by the American government of flooding all black communities throughout America with the Heroin Pandemic; and the American government and people went into full nonstop over drive production and operation, around the clock seven day a week. Still, you refuse to except the truth about the government and people, that these Negro traitors were actually working for and that you brought this Heroin Pandemic upon yourself because you rejected the truth for falsehood and gave honor and praise, to the culprits who actually were behind this entire Heroin Pandemic.

The same thing with the Cocaine and Crack Pandemic this genocidal plan was also engineered and orchestrated by the same people and government, all directed at murdering you, your wives, and children now Mental and Spiritual Chattel Slave called African Americans. In both of these Pandemics designed by the American government every so-called Civil Rights organization and their leaders, were receiving contributions from the American government paid by you, to assist the American government to murder their own people. This is what happened examine the history and anyone can see this to be true, the religious and political so-called leaders, were very instrumental in murdering their own people including women and children and wiping out generations, of their own people. For what I ask this so-called Jesus who have hated black and Indian people, since crossing the Atlantic and even before then. It was and still is this so-called Jesus who was and still is pulling the strings, on keeping your population under control and in a subservient position, which is nothing more than twenty-first-century Mental and Spiritual Chattel Slave of the American government, people and all who believe in this mystery god. This Burden of Rejecting the Truth for falsehood is and has been plaguing us and all humanity, for thousands of years.

The more you my people which always includes my Indian Brothers and Sisters, try to evade this truth of Mr. Yakub, is the stronger this medical monster becomes and right now in this present day and time, this monster is conducting their business of genocide with impunity. The medical field and this medical board that over sees every hospital, clinic, and office, are the Frankenstein, that their own people called monsters. Yet as long as we my people became and used as Lab Rats, these same monsters became men and women of great prominence, and are revered, worship and extremely wealthy. These doctors, nurses, and all practitioners in the medical field, are liars and deceivers. Smiling faces my people are always telling you lies, and we have the proof. Also, my people and all humanity must these so-called righteous African Americans, have sold their services to Mr. Yakub's scientist, what hypocrites they all are.

They these so-called followers of the Holy Messenger of Allah are also under the secrecy laws of Mr. Yakub. I am telling everyone what I personally have witness from these frauds and you will see them come February 26, in their FOI uniforms, suits and crowns, beautiful white dresses saying As-Salaam Alaikum and Peace, lots of embracing, while many of them so-called brothers and sisters, are down with Mr. Yakub's Birth Control Program, against their own people. These are ones calling Brother Minister Malcolm X/ Al- Malik Shabazz a hypocrite.

This American society and government make sure and work hard on preventing positive black thing people male and female, from entering into these sciences. All those that are in this field are just as guilty of genocidal murders, as everyone in this field because they will lie to you at the drop of a penny and then smile at you and this is part of the deceit that haunts them all. This American Medical field and society treats us so-called Ex-Chattel Slaves of America, as nothing more than Lab rats and our so-called own kind know this is true. All of these immigrants coming into America and have come into America and they all say with nothing, live in better housing than you my lost and confused people. Yet they are given scholarships and grants into the best medical schools, this society of Mr. Yakub the Mystery God, has to offer. The East Indians, the Chinese, the Philippines, the Russians, the Polish, the so-called Africans, and others, while we my people are their Lab Rats. These people the above mention are promised to have a great life, wealth, recognition, fine homes, cars, and jewelry, as long as they do the master bidding and we all should know this. Lying is the language that they all use to their human Lab Rats and the ultimate murders called Law Enforcement stands at the ready, to enforce every law, policy and regulation of their god, Mr. Yakub.

America during world Two after Einstein stole the mathematical formular from a young Black man, and then America was able to make what is known as the Atomic Bomb, which at that President Harry S. Truman, gave the order to dropped on two cities in Japan Hiroshima and Nagasaki, killing millions of Japanese citizens and people. This was in nineteen- forty- five. Nine years later nineteen- fifty-four

Hollywood and Japan film industries began making movies and pictures, of Godzilla, King Kong, and other so-called pre-historic creatures; due to the radiation fall out, of these Atomic Bombs, supposedly creating mutations of other life forms in Japan and the South Pacific, hostile to human existence and must as well as had to be killed, to preserved humanity.

So, as I was saying the American government brought these scientist of Nazi Germany to America, gave them new in many cases American names to hide them from the Russians and compete in the outer space program and Population Control programs, of the Ex- Chattel Of America. This is the history my people that can be examine by anyone if one dares to search, for the truth. The American government told the Holy Messenger of Allah as they were imprisoning the Holy Messenger, that they were imprisoning him to remove him off the Sean because they the American government needed the help, of his people, to guarantee America, will have ample bodies that could be sacrifice, during the wars in Europe and the South Pacific.

It was after the fall of Nazi Germany Russia and America were kidnapping these Nazi German Scientist, to further develop their own societies and preparation of White Supremacy and White Nationalism. During this time America help to set up Zionism in Palestine and Jerusalem in the Mid-East or Asia Minor. America could offer to these German Devils complete autonomy, security wealth and false admiration, that can and will be reclined and rescinded once you defy your masters. So, you live in fear and participate in planetary mass murders, in the name of this demon called Jesus Christ, your lord and savior. I am so happy no matter what I must endure that this demon called Jesus Christ is not my lord and savior.

So, America has me and others no doubt on their Medical Death List greater than the so-called Mafia hit list, ever was or ever could be because the Mafia Dons, Capos and Lieutenants, are on the same death list. The so-called Mafia does not realize is that they agree with us being on the death list, they are also on the death list, by this Zionist Control American so-called government. The home of the free and the brave what a disgrace these words are and always have been. We have close to five-hundred years of living experience of hypocrisy from a government, that makes Adolf Hitler and the Nazi Party appear as one of their saints and my people and all humanity had better see, understand and except because this is the real truth.

Being on this American Medical Death List is an honor to me because I realize that the American government is afraid of me and so they placed me on their Medical Death list. Why is the American government and people are afraid you Mr. Saladin Shabazz-Allah? The reason is simple everyone I am not afraid to revealed, the truth about America and America's Medical System and how America uses their Medical System, to make and treat my people, as nothing more than lab rats; when others are trembling in their boots and I am speaking about these so-called said followers, of the Holy Messenger of Allah Mr. Elijah Muhammad {Muhammad RasulAllah} and even the so-called Sunnah believers as well as these so-called Sufi believers, in Prophet Ibn Abdullah Muhammad.

This Medical Death List my people and all humanity had better realize is death to every life form, on our planet. Every life form on our planet and in the sea have a purpose for being here, but now there are other grafted and mutated life forms on our planet, that came into existence from Mr. Yakub's experimentations hundreds of millions years ago and these are the beast of pray and poisonous insects like roaches, snakes, flies, in the sea shellfish, and certain fish that are bottom feeders scallops, lobsters, crabs, shrimps and fish that are more than one hundred and more pounds could be mammals or not fit, for human consumption. Which are poisonous to human life and the beast of the fields and certain birds as well. The beast of the fields have no claws or fangs and does not emit any poisons, that is detrimental to humans, the beast of the field's certain birds and planet life as well, So Saith Allah the Best Knower Of All Things.

I cannot thank the Holy Savior enough for the knowledge and information He brought to us and to all humanity, through the mouth of His Holy Messenger, Mr. Elijah Muhammad. When you examine the history of America closely you will every people that came to America in the last fifty years or so, brought with them some kind of drug and dropped these drugs, into black communities throughout America. While we were being betrayed by these false religious and political leaders, open this Pandora's Box and un-least the demons that will destroy their own people and these false leaders did not care, as long as they could have some cheap Caucasian woman or some little boy; this goes for the Negro women as well. The truth must be known everyone and the wicked must be expose no matter who get hurts, nor does it matter who does not like it; the truth remains the truth. The many cowards that were amongst are still amongst us believe they can lead their people, in truth a coward can do nothing but be a coward and a coward will run, hide, and wait until the smoke clear, before they surface. Marijuana, Hashes, Opium, Morphine, Heroin and Cocaine are from the countries of these immigrants, America imported from Central America, South America, the Caribbean Island, the Orient and Turkey. The Poppies which Opium, Morphine and Heroin comes from the Orient and Turkey; Hashes comes from Turkey as well; Marijuana comes from South America and the Caribbean Island and Cocaine comes from South and Central America. All of these later to be known as recreational drugs did not come from North America, they were all imported to America and then saturated throughout all black communities, in America. Why was this done Saladin and who were the ring leaders? The reason why it was done is make sure that the Ex-Chattel Physical Slave never be able to produce, a Black Messiah. To also make sure our oppressors will never give us our just and well-earned due. So, our brothers and as I always say our Indian brothers and sisters included, we are in the final battel of life and death, liberty, or death but we refused to live under these deplorable conditions, of America and the American people any longer.

We the Chattel Slave and my Indian brothers and sisters stand before the world as a people who have suffered the un-merciful and un-godly physical slaughters and mental and physical brutality, than any human being has ever suffered before on our planet and we survived. When America brought these Nazi German scientist here to America to enhance America's gene experimentation program, by using us my people as their lab rats; the Jewish people and community did not care; the Jewish people and the Jewish community joined up with these Nazi German Scientist, who were nothing more than sadistic war criminals, the Jewish people and community participated in their experimentation side by side with these sadistic German war criminals, on Black and Indian people in America, with impunity. Thus, setting the stage of birth control and extermination of black and red people, in America with impunity.

Since we crossed the Atlantic Ocean in fifteen-fifty- five and since Columbus sailed into the new so-called world, Hell erupted on all Asiatic Original People and this is the history, I tell all humanity. The Holy Messenger of Allah told us all to make America know of her sins and I stand proudly bringing America the truth of themselves and the cowards, that supported and helped America then and are helping America now, an in America approximately five-hundred-tears ago. A coward is a liar who is afraid to answer his phone and have his wife lie for him, saying he is sleep. Such a person could never be anyone leader because he is a sniveling coward and always be a sniveling coward and not worth mentioning or even consider. We my people and all humanity had better keep our eyes wide open because Satan The Accused Devil, is on the move against us all. America is still operating with impunity because of these cowards who believe in their delusional cowardly minds, they are important; and at least ninety=eight percent of them, are scared and frighten cowards. These cowards with their crowns of cowardice on their heads because they are afraid to represent, the uniforms in which they have disgraced, America knows these cowards are not going to do anything but run and hide. America knows these are cowards and all these cowards genuinely want is to crawl back on the plantation and be in the grace of America The Accused Devil and have crawled back on America's plantations, in some shape, form or fashion.

To all of my people that have suffered from and under the brutality of this so-called American Government, for nearly five-hundred years in the Northern Region, of our planet, especially the so-called Ex-Chattel Slave of America, our chance for redemption and restoration have been forfeited, these so-called Civil Rights Activists Martin Luther King, the so-called High Ranking Officials with in the Temples of Islam here in North America, the American Government, the Zionist and the Arab community or world, Conspired together on how prevent any more progress, from the Ex-Chattel Slave Of America. By these scientist studying their dilemma they then discover the avenue to penetrate, every black movement, organization and program including Islam here in the Wilderness of North America; that avenue my people and all humanity is ENVY, SELF HATRED, JEALOUSLY, NARCISSIM AND SELF-IMPORTANCE.

During this time period I was at war with death and this war was and is intense beyond the above average person, comprehension' the only people that reached out to me, were my youngest son Ibn-Saladin Shabazz-Allah, my Eldest Brother Julius, my younger brother Mahdi, and this beautiful young sister, my wife Shakara Zenobia Perez now Shakara Zenobia Shabazz-Allah, reached out to me and no one else has reached out to me, on this level. I love her and this is the woman, I need. This is the woman I want. I owe her so much that I must always be right and exact because she was there for me, during my war with death. Her soothing and smoothing voice, her belief in me. Her confidence in me and her love for me, is un- reachable, by any woman, on our planet, I owe this to her to make it crystal.

I sit here filled with confidence of the work I am doing is pleasurable and extremely important, for myself, for my people and for humanity, if I am hated because of my writing, this shows me how shallow minded they all are. We are on the America's Medical Death list and these simple-minded fools, are upset with me, as though what they have to say, has any credence. As long as the fools stay in their cage they are fine even when the cage door is opened, their masters know they will not come out, out of fear. These lodges that are beginning to open throughout black communities in America, has no healing power because the ones opening these lodges, are not sincere to total diagram of raising a people. They all might have heard the Holy Messenger of Allah but till this very day, do not except who he is and anyone with intelligence, know that what I a am saying is true. If you believe then why are you calling the last and greatest Messenger of Allah, The Honorable Elijah Muhammad, when he actually a head of state, as Mr. Elijah Muhammad or Mr. Muhammad, in every spiritual gathering place or show, He should addressed as the Holy Messenger of Allah or Muhammad RasulAllah? The many fools who are doing this is due to their weak understanding and wanting to stay on the plantations of America, believing they are free and have friendship, in all walks of life.

This American Medical Death List my people is supremely diabolical and operates twenty- four seven, nonstop and we are at the top of the list. Our very existence is at jeopardy and we have fools, dare believing they control or represent us, on the world level. It has been proven through time none of them have the ability, to take us across the River Jordan. The suffering never ends the false promises and lies, never stop, the pain mental, physical, and spiritual, never ends. All of these false religions have failed us including this so-called Sunnah Islam, which in truth is nothing more than Christianity with their version of Mr. Yakub the mystery god. The pure hatred that this so-called Sunnah Islam is just as poisonous, as Zionism and Christianity.

This supremely evil and supremely diabolical American government has committed genocidal Extermination upon us and then imported these immigrants into America each set of people, brought a drug with them, for our destruction. The results were and are they were given the employment, homes, and greater chance, at enjoying this American way of life and you my people were dumped into the sewers, of America. Martin Luther King was and is a great enemy to and for his people because he, his organization, and people, cared more about other people, than any of them cared about their own people. The cowardice from Martin Luther King, his organization and people are a disgrace and deplorable, they all betrayed the Physical Ex-Chattel Slave of America, for others than their own kind. This is the American Medical Death List all of these so- religious, so-called righteous people, surrendered their people and these are greatest hypocrite the twentieth- century and the twentieth-first century, have ever produce.

You worship this holiday call Christmas and you have known understanding what it means, the bulbs represent the different shades of black people, they lynched and murdered, the lights represent the murdering of the many black children he and his crusade had murder and capture, to satisfy their animalistic and perverted sexual appetites and the missal toll, represent the raping and kidnapping, of the young black girls. The evergreen tree is the belief of that the spirit of Nimrod, lives in these tress and the evergreen tree holds it greenness in the coldest of weather. It is not Silent Night Holy Night It is Hell Night and the is Un-Holiest night, of the year.

I clearly understand why Allah told His Holy Messenger to build a hospital for ourselves, in order for us to avoid this American Medical Death List, all who ancestry goes back thousands of years here in the Western Hemisphere and the last approximately five-hundred-years, in the Western Hemisphere. This an extremely hard truth to face but it is a must and absolute necessity will then be looking at real freedom, everything else is an illusion.

CHAPTER 20

SELF REBELLION AND SELF HATRED

What is self-rebellion Mr. Saladin Shabazz-Allah? Why must such a thing happen amongst us Mr. Saladin Shabazz-Allah? These are great questions my people and humanity at large. Self-Rebellion comes from us believing we can escape our destination. Self-Rebellion is due to us as a people not doing what we all know is right. Walking around pretending that you are is not being free. Our people walk around believing and pretending they are free when in truth they are still wild savage animals, locked in a cage. The reason why tragedy, sorrow, pain, and suffering is a way of life for the so-called African Americans because you just lay down and take what-ever sewage this American government and people give you and you will not do anything to stop it or prevent it. There is nothing more disgraceful than seeing these So-Called Ex-Physical Chattel Slaves in their Sunday best and uniforms, believing they are making an impact. Truth be told you are nothing but a bunch worthless clown to afraid to do anything for yourself.

This is self-rebellion my people you have known love for yourself and all these strange women {all Caucasian} it does not matter where they come from, only when you make a great deal of money and never before. These so-called African American women through themselves at any man, if they believe they may get some monetary reward. These so-called African American women do not even have any love, for the children they have birth because if they did, they would do a better job at raising them. I am not saying all of them but the majority of them producing plantation cowards and have produced plantation cowards. These so-called African fathers are not doing anything to stop this travesty, they are all waiting on some mystery god, to come and help them. They will kill each and have killing each other not for hundreds of years, but for the pass six-thousand-years and our enemies know this to be true.

The many black sport legends that have made great sums of money, which is a great accomplishment for every black man, that has achieved this; but this society and government make sure these individuals never come home and help to up lift their own people. They concentrate their energies on helping other than their own kind and this is by designed, while their people and children are suffering without any hope or someone to even look up to. This is Self-Rebellion and Self Hatred. I thank Allah enough for guiding me to Brother Minister Malcolm X when I was twelve years old because this is when learning for me began and I will never denounce Brother Minister Malcolm X/Al-Malik Shabazz, for anyone.

Self-Rebellion and Self-Hatred are the diseases that are destroying and have destroyed us, as a people. In my lifetime there were only two men that cared about us and both of these men, where chosen by Allah and you ignorant supremely foolish people, rejected one and murdered the other. You have no love for yourself why should anyone have love for you? You so-called original black man have no love for your wives, children, and our ancestors, what right have you to believe that others, should have love for you? Your behavior to each other and your cowardice, are below human standards and this why humanity treat African Americans, as they do which is nothing.

You have absolutely no love for your link to tomorrow and you treat your link to tomorrow as a whore and you make hideous, and disgraceful remarks and statements, and do not forget veil of her to and before strange men about her and your daughters included In the Problem Book always remember, you, black man are Problem Number One, She is Problem Number Two. You cannot solve her problem until you solve the problem with in yourself and this idiotic philosophy that has been adopted, is nothing but gasoline on a raging fire.

Here is something everyone seems to be forgetting the distribution of the Examine of Kareem, should had never been given to the public because it caused irreparable damage, than it did good. The person who stole and smuggle the Examine of Kareem out of the Temples of Islam her in North America, was and is a traitor to all, Ex-Chattel Slaves of America now referred to as African Americans. Only those who prospered off of this treason and are still prospering of this particular traitor acts and deeds, are the ones robbing you of your money . This is not Islam this is Christianity through and through their flag will never fly down at the United Nations because their flag represent absolutely nothing, except death and destruction and this so-called flag is not recognized or wanted, by humanity and I do not blame humanity, for not wanting this amongst them.

I am not running to some so-called African who does not who she is over the Asiatic Black Woman that brought me or us back under conditions, that angered Allah Himself, for nearly five-hundred-years under conditions these so-called African women, could never deal with. So, you so-called brothers believe you found or think she is better than our Asiatic Original Black Woman, show and proof that you are a liar, hypocrite, disbeliever, and a coward. This my people and all humanity is Self-Rebellion and Self Hatred at the maximum level. These clowns walking around in black communities throughout America calling themselves this and that are in truth, detrimental to rise of the Ex-Chattel Physical Slave of America. In fact, all of this insanity from these supremely ignorant fools calling themselves this and that, has cast you into being the Mental and Spiritual Chattel Slave of America.

The truth is supremely powerful, and the truth will always show falsehood no matter how falsehood try to disguise it-self, the truth will always reveal the falsehood. I am only telling everyone the truth of themselves, religions, and politics. A great accomplishment for me is to sit with my wife and not be afraid to tell or reveal to her, the truth of myself. The only woman to this very day that reached out to me, when I was in mortal combat with death and her soothing voice and belief in me, is second to none because she helped me to overcome, that most trying period in my life and she loves till this very day. Also remember I have not heard from these make-believe brothers or their make believe said nation. This self-Rebellion and self-hatred I have to conform to your warp coward way of thinking get out on a corner and sell newspapers, to prove I am a believer, in Allah and Allah's Holy Messenger. I should sit and allowed another man, to tell me what I should do is totally insane I do not care what kind of lodge they have put together and how successful, they believe they are or maybe.

A coward is a coward no matter how or how they may try and cover it up, you will find more cowards saying and calling themselves believers and so-called themselves followers of the Holy Messenger, are the so-called cowards I am speaking about. Why are they cowards Mr. Saladin Shabazz-Allah? They are cowards for the simple they have all sold out Allah, Allah's Holy Messenger, and you my people. These are the cowards calling Brother Minister Malcolm X/Al-Malik Shabazz a hypocrite and these cowards are the true hypocrites, hiding under a façade. These cowards will kill you and me and walk around proudly, but they will not kill the enemies, of their people. In fact, the enemies of their people, the enemies of Allah, the enemies of the Holy Messenger, are their friends. These idiots are so stupid they call the enemies of Allah, the enemies of the Holy Messenger, the enemies of Islam and the enemies of us, Friendship in All Walks Of Life.

You have disgraced the lost and found members belonging to Islam in this Wilderness of Sin, Iniquity and Transgressions, you are telling our enemies, they are safe as long as I, can be your friend. Our enemy is the enemy of Allah; our enemy has been negotiation deals, since Jacob wrestle with the angel six-thousand and six-hundred years ago and it was then, he was recognized as Israel. So, saying you follow or believe in Israel, is saying I am an opposer of the Universal Creator. These are your friends I am happy they are your friends because the opposers of the Universal Creator, are not my friends and they cannot be my brothers, if truth be told.

Mackerelled whole primes was and is about divide and conquer and this method has been exploited, amongst us my people. This concept of divide and conquer has been a way of life, in America amongst black and Indian people, until it is accepted amongst our people and our Indian brothers and sisters as well and has been continuing without any intervention, for nearly five-hundred-years. These so-called righteous brothers have abandon their post, many years ago and are not up-holding Allah the Holy Savior of all humanity and Allah's Holy Messenger Mr. Elijah Muhammad. Talk is cheap because these cowards have no action, they have no motion, with everything they do. To take money from a struggling mother is nothing but a sorry parasite and should be treated as such. They brazen, loud, flamboyant, narcissistic, ignorant, and totally arrogant, this is Self-Rebellion, and this is Self-Hatred.

While Martin Luther King was missioned by the enemies of Black and Indian people here in this Wilderness of Sin, iniquity, and transgression, to deliver us all back into Mental and Spiritual Slavery and Slaves, for America; Brother Minister Malcolm X/Al-Malik Shabazz was presenting our case for Human Rights in the United Nations, before the world leaders and this has not been done since him. This was an extremely powerful brother and man and to be equated with his murder, is disgraceful for us as a people. The Mackerelled concept of divide and conquer of was began operating on all cylinders twenty-four-hours a day. The reason why was told to us by Law Enforcement, "THERE WILL BE NO BLACK MASSIAH", this statement was made by a NYPD Irish Police Captain.

I am not angry I want everyone to know the truth and learn how to search and find this truth. The only way we can stop and prevent these religious pimps from exploiting the mass of people, here in America, is to know and understand who these religious pimps are and the methods they all use, to keep you a Mental and Spiritual Chattel Slave while they relieve you, of your hard-earned money. I am telling you my people these cowardly traitors laugh and joke about, how they just rob you. A so-called follower of who I do not know nut he claims to be a follower of the Holy Messenger, as it was reported to me, I am using the Messenger teachings to make money and these are the cowards selling the teachings of Allah that the Holy Messenger, revealed to us.

The truth must be told about everyone the falsehood must be revealed because these frauds are using the Holy Saviors name to shield their dirty religion, while they claim to be god and the original man. The ill dealings within this said so-called nation of Islam has no substance because they surrender it, in nineteen-sixty-five, when they conspired with our enemies and murder Joshua Brother Minister Malcolm X/Al-Malik Shabazz in front of his wife and children. This is even more barbaric these conspirators did everything they could, to put the blame on the Holy Messenger of Allah and Islam in North America. More damage has been done by these foolish idiots in the sixty years for our people, then you can see or imagine. Self-hatred for our women and children and to parents have gone off the charts, of civilize humanity and all life forms on our planet.

Therefore, such personnel could not possibly be representing Allah and Allah' last and greatest Messenger due to their mentality, their spiritual essence are not for Allah, nor for Allah's Holy Messenger, nor for Islam or their people. Therefore, they are in capable of Enforcing Their Will due to the fact, they have no will, to enforce. The ones claiming to be all wise and took on names they have not represented and cannot represent, are running the show, here in America. Then to hear one of these clowns trying to sell my wife some MGT and GCC handbook this now Mental and Spiritual Chattel Slaves who is completely and totally insane, thought he could approach my wife, with his insanity.

We are living in very terrible times and there are many people out there like the scavengers they are, waiting to take advantage of you by any means necessarily. Blaming the Caucasian Race for what you are suffering through is an in Justice, to the Caucasian Race, you should be blaming yourself, for not doing anything for yourself. This is a very disturbing situation that we are all living in and under. The evil that we have done to ourselves and continue to do to ourselves, is a mockery to and before the eyes of Allah Himself. The Law Enforcement System and this includes the Department of Corrections, are filled with many this includes women as well, who hate their own people and cannot wait to demonstrate their self-hatred to their Caucasian, Spanish and whatever other person, that is there or present.

I am amazingly comfortable with my wife and I do not need my wife going to any other man, if we have a disagreement about anything, it does not matter who this person claims, to be. We love each other, we trust each other, and we depend on each other; then why do we need some third-party intervention in our personal business. I and she have enough confidence in ourselves, to handle whatever may come at us, we stand together. All of our children safe, growth and development, is our primary concern and our love for each other, falls in this realm as well. As the man of the family. I accept my responsibilities without question or reservations. My duty as a man is to love, respect and honor my wife and in return she honors, respect and love me and she teach our children to do the same. What can some third party do for us? The answer everyone is nothing.

Allah came for the purpose of redeeming and restoring the lost and found members, of the Nation of Islam and this is the Nation/ Tribe of Shabazz. Who was hidden because of the rapes and race mixing of the Caucasian Race, this includes every member of this Race of People? After these demon's planet their seeds into our women, they sent them back home, pregnant with their child and this the Method that was used, to hide us from our people. You can hate me all one may want but this truth came from Allah in person, Our Holy Savior, Our Deliverer, Our Redeemer, and Our Great Restorer. No mercy, kindness, compassion, empathy, no sympathy, no nothing from this American government and people, at all. This absolute insanity of forgive and forget my people, I say to all humanity, the American government, and people, is just that insanity that only a terrify coward would, could and did, bring to his people; and we get to say THANK YOU JESUS MY LORD AND SAVIOR. I ask you my people and all humanity what do I or any of my brothers and sisters, have to be thankful of from this make believe, Jesus Crist insanity.

If being Demonic is based upon nearly five-hundred-years of evil, diabolical, hatred, rape murders, homosexuality, the annihilation of two original people to the point of in-significancy; this is the Jesus Christ we and our Indian brothers and sisters have known and experience, for nearly five-hundred-years; we must be insane and cowards, to believe in this demon, called Jesus Christ. This is not complicated my people and all humanity to see the historical history of the devastation and genocide performed, under the name of Jesus Christ our lord and savior, on and upon the Ex-Chattel Slave of America, Our Indian Brothers and Sister as well, whose populations now have been reduced to being in-significant, amongst humanity and the Ex-Physical Chattel Slaves of America are now the twenty-first century, Mental and Spiritual Chattel Slave of America, called African American.

When Brother Minister Malcolm X fell out of grace with his leader and teacher and started paying attention to Wallace D.

Mohammad and Wallace introduce him to his Arabs conspirators, Brother Minister Malcolm X became confused and during this time period, he embraced the enemy of his people, as Wallace sat back in the shadows, with the Arabs. Brother Minister Malcolm did not know the Arabs, with the aid of the American government and do not forget, the entire Sunnah so-called Islam belief, were against him, the Ex-Physical Chattel Slave of America, the Holy Messenger of Allah, and the Islam that Allah brought and to us, trapped in this Wilderness of Sin, Transgression, and Iniquity. These are the some of the mistakes Brother Minister Malcolm X made, and they were extremely dangerous mistakes and these mistakes cost our beautiful brother Minister, his life. This still does not take away from who the brother was one bit, this was part of the journey, he did not understand. By the time he did the real hypocrites were entrenched around a now physically sick Messenger.

I would love to be able to enjoy my Asiatic Original Black Women in totality and our children as well, this would be a blessing from Allah to me, But there is so much confusion and obstacles always waiting around the corner or right outside the door and this means I must always be alert, for the protection of my wife and children. For the past approximately five-hundred-years, the Asiatic Original Black man, woman, children, and family period, had and still have, a communication and trust problem. From my own experiences and close observation, I can see why, this exist, and it is not our fault but nevertheless, we must solve this problem amongst ourselves. Why must we solve this problem when I do not care, or it is not relevant to me, Mr. Saladin Shabazz-Allah? The very first thing this problem should matter to you and the relevancy is off the scale and the only chance to save ourselves, wives, children, and people.

It is our duty as men to want to protect and provide for your family with the insurgent and the emergent of this so-called American Gangster Wrapped music, the debasement of our Original Asiatic Black Women and yourselves, went ballistic and this poison carries over today. You have no will of your own now the Mental and Spiritual Chattel Slave of America, called African American; are and have been enforcing the evil and diabolical will of our enemies, amongst and upon your people. If this is friendship in all walks of life, then this should be barred from amongst our people. How is it possible for any man to be so selfish and uncaring, that he could, would and have done, sacrifice black children and mothers on an altar of a life of misery, pain, suffering, ignorance and then an un-merciful and cruel death; because he can convince himself, they are nothing to him.

The past approximately five-hundred-years has been and on-going nightmare for all original people, in the Western Hemisphere that is un-imaginable. When the heavy migration to Elis Island in the early twentieth century by every European in Europe, running from Hitler and El-Douche, were complete haters of the Ex-Chattel Slave of America and our Indian Brothers and Sisters and were in complete agreement, with the Jim Crow Laws and the Willie Lynch methods and application the most horrible, evil, and diabolical methods ever experience by humanity. These scares immigrants performed these evils upon us with impunity. Zionism was and has been the ring leaders these un-imaginable evils ever witness before on our planet.

These immigrants that came to America from all over Europe including Italy in which El=Douche ran the Mafia, out of Italy and those who stayed, were servants to El-Douche. This continue until the Allied Invasion of Italy led by three-star general George Patten, the Supreme Commander and five-star Dwight D. Eisenhower, over the European War theater. Our forebears had to endure the absolute hatred from these European, landing on Ellis Island and got away with the raping of black women, young black-girls, and black-young boys. Robbing black people left and right and Law Enforcement was apart, of these horrific and diabolical crimes and none were eviler, than Zionism, back up by their Christian brothers and sisters. What dreadful time these were and still are, the different is this instead of Caucasian Men and women, prowling black communities for the purpose of committing some evil act, have been replaced by ignorant, silly, and foolish African American so-called men and women.

Only by Enforcing Our Will can we put an end to such in human treatment of ourselves, wives, children, family, and people. I conclude this manuscript and book with these words, stay strong, wise, committed, and determine, to save, provide and protect your wives, children, parents, family, and people; in other words, stand up and be an intelligent, wise, and caring Original, Asiatic Blackman, and Woman; so that we may end this Self-Rebellion and Self- Hatred.

BIBLIOGRAPHY

AFRO USA Reference Work on the Black Experience And Slavery in the Western Hemisphere
Brown, John E., Brown, Donald, Buckstein, Barbara, Carbone, Joseph, Fontinel, F.J., Harris, Middelton, A. "Spike", Rev. Hoggard, Clinton J. Marr, Warren ll, Rosenthal, Richard, Utterbach, Clinton

The Atlanta Compromise Speech by Washington, Booker T. 1895

The Black Book

Harris, Middleton A., Levitt, Morris, Furman, Roger, Smith, Ernest Publish by
Random House 1974

The Destruction of the Black Civilization by Dr. Professror Williams, Chancellor
Published by Third World Press 1987

They Came Before Columbus The African Presence In Ancient America by
Dr. Professor Sertima, Van Ivan Published by Random House 1976

Before The Mayflower, A History of Black America by Bennett, Lerone Jr. first Published
by Johnson Publishing Co. Inc. 1962

World's Greatmen Of Color Vol. 1 by Rogers, J.A. Originally Published by Macmillan
Publishing Company 1972

World's Greatmen Of Color Vol.2 by Rogers, J. A. Published by Macmillan Publishing Co.
1972. First Touchstone Edition 1996

Christopher Columbus and the AfriKan Holocaust Slavery and the Rise of European
Capitalism by Dr. Professor Clarke, Henrik John Published by Eworld Inc 1994

The Myth Of Genesis And EXODUS and the exclusion of their African origins by
Dr. Professor Jochannan, Yosef ben A. A. Published by Alkebu-Ian Book Associates 1974

Cultural Genocide In The Black And African Studies Curriculum By Dr. Professor
Jochanna, Yosef ben Published by Alkebu-Ian Book Associates 1972.
Published by Black.
Classis 2004

NEW DIMENSIONS IN AFRICAN HISTORY by DR. Professor JOCHANNAN, YOSEF BEN AND

DR. Professor CLARKE, HENRIK JOHN Published by Brawner Press St. John 1991 The
London Lectures of Dr. Professor Jochannan, Yosef ben and Dr. Professor Clarke, John Henrik

BLACK MAN OF THE NILE AND HIS FAMILY By Dr. Professor Jochannan, Yosef A. A. ben
Published by BLACK CLASSIC PRESS 1989

Sex and Races Negro-Caucasian Mixing in All Ages and All Lands Volume 1 The Old World
By Rogers, A.J. Published by Wesleyan University Press First Published in the 1940s

Sex and Races Volume 2 by Rogers, A. J. Published by Wesleyan University Press in the 1940s.

Sex and Races Volume 3 by Rogers, A. J. Published by Wesleyan University Press in the 1940s. Reprinted Edition by African Tree Press 2012

Black Justice in a White World by Judge Bruce, Wright Published by Barricade Books Inc. 1996

None Dare Call It Conspiracy by Allen, Garry and Abraham, Larry Published by Buccaneer Books 1971

The Creature from Jekyll Island by Griffin, Edward G. Published by American Media 1994
First Edition

The Arms Of Krupp 1587-1968 the Rise and Fall of the Industrial Dynasty That Armed
Germany At War by Manchester, William Originally Published In Hard cover by Little.
Brown And Company 1968

Alexander Hamilton by Chernow, Ron Published by the Penguin Group 2005

The Secrets of The Federal Reserves by Mullins, Eustace 1993

The International Jew The World's Foremost Problem by Ford, Henry Sr. Published 1951

The Secret Relationship Between Blacks and Jews Volume One by The Nation Of Islam,
Published by The Nation of Islam 1991

The Holy Bible Old and New Testaments In The Kings James Version Publish by WORD,
AFLAME PRESS

THE HOLY QUR'AN with English Translation and Commentary by Maulana, Muhammad
Ali Published by Ahmadiyya Ajuman Isha' at islam Lahore Inc. First Edition 1917

THE MEANINGS OF THE HOLY QUR'AN BY MAULANA, ABDULLAH YUSUF ALI Published By Kutub Khana Ishayatul Islam

The Message To The Black Man In America by Muhammad, Elijah {Messenger of Allah},
Published by Muhammad's Temple Of Islam 1965
The Fall Of America by Muhammad, Elijah {Messenger of Allah}, Published by
Muhammad's Temple Of Islam 1973

How To Eat To Live Book One by Muhammad, Elijah {Messenger of Allah}, Published by
Muhammad's Temple Of Islam 1967

How To Eat To Live Book Two by Muhammad, Elijah {Messenger of Allah}, Published
By Muhammad's Temple of Islam 1972

Our Savior Has Arrived by Muhammad, Elijah {Messenger of Allah}, Published by
Muhammad's Temple of Islam 1974

The Genesis Years Unpublished & Rare Writings Of Muhammad, Elijah {Messenger
Of Allah}, {1959-!962} Published by Secretarius MEMPS Publications Co. 2003

Theology Of Time {Secret of The Time} by Muhammad, Elijah {Messenger of Allah},

Published by Secretarius MEMPS Publications Co. 1997

Christianity VS Islam By Muhammad, Elijah {Messenger of Allah},
Published by
Secretarius Publications 1993

The Time & The Judgement The Day When Self Tells The Truth
On Self by Muhammad,
Elijah {Messenger of Allah}, Published by Secretarius Publications
1994

The Supreme Wisdom Solution to the so-called NEGROES Problem
Volume One by
Muhammad, Elijah {Messenger of Allah}, First Edition February
26, 1957

The Supreme Wisdom What Every American So-Called Negro
Should Know About
Volume Two by Muhammad, Elijah {Messenger of Allah}, Published
by U.B.&U.S.
Communications Systems

Salaam by Muhammad, Elijah {Messenger of Allah}, Trip To Mecca
Published by Salaam
Publishing Company July 1960
100 Answers To The Most Uncommon 100 Questions by
Muhammad, Elijah {Messenger of
Allah}, Published by Secretarius MEMPS Publications 1992

The Secrets of Freemasonry by Muhammad, Elijah {Messenger of Allah}, Published by
Secretarius MEMPS Publications 1994

YAKUB {Ja-cob} The Father of Mankind by Muhammad, Elijah {Messenger of Allah}, Published.
By Secretarius MEMPS Publications 2002

THE GOD TRIBE OF SHABAZZ THE TRUE HISTORY BY Muhammad, Elijah {Messenger of Allah},
Published by Secretarius MEMPS Publications 2012
TAPES AND SPEACHES By Muhammad, Elijah {Messenger of Allah},

Savior's Day by Muhammad, Elijah {Messenger of Allah}, February 26, 1954

Uline Arena Address Washington D.C. by Muhammad, Elijah {Messenger of Allah}, 1959

At The Mosque Theatre Newark New Jersey By Muhammad, Elijah {Messenger of Allah},
October 5, 1959

At The Pittsburg Syria Mosque by Muhammad, Elijah {Messenger of Allah}, 1959

At The 369th Amory by Muhammad, Elijah {Messenger of Allah}, August 27, 1961

Savior's Day by Muhammad, Elijah [Messenger of Allah}, February 26, 1964

Savior's Day by Muhammad, Elijah {Messenger of Allah}, February 26, 1967

Savior's Day The Assassination of Malcolm X by Muhammad, Elijah {Messenger of Allah},
February 26, 1965

Historic Buzz Anderson Interview with Muhammad, Elijah {Messenger of Allah}, 1964

The History Of The Nation Of Islam Documentary, 1930-1970

Black Muslims At The Crossroads A Vintage Documentary, 1964

At The 369th Armory By Muhammad, Elijah {Messenger of Allah}, 1964

Savior's Day by Muhammad, Elijah {Messenger of Allah}, February 26, 1971

Savior's Day The Birth of a Redeemer by Muhammad, Elijah {Messenger of Allah}, 1972

Savior's Day A Savior Is Born by Muhammad, Elijah {Messenger of Allah}, February 26, 1973.

Savior's Day When The Sun Rises In The West by Muhammad, Elijah {Messenger of Allah},
February 26, 1974

The Theology Of Time Complete Lecture Part One to Part Five By Muhammad, Elijah
{Messenger of Allah}, Beginning from June 4, 1972, To October 29, 1972

Six Disc CD Collection The Black Man's History, Harlem Rally, Message To The Grassroots,
The Ballot Or The Bullet by X, Malcolm {Malik Shabazz} 1962, 1963, 1964

Newspaper Articles Taken From Muhammad Speaks Newspaper
The Sure Truth by Muhammad, Elijah {Messenger of Allah}, Muhammad Speaks.
Newspaper July 21, 1972

Hell Erupts by Muhammad, Elijah [Messenger of Allah}, Muhammad Speaks Newspaper
June 14, 1974

The Shaking by Muhammad, Elijah {Messenger of Allah}, Muhammad Speaks Newspaper
August 13, 1971

The Devils Going Rampant by Muhammad, Elijah {Messenger of Allah}, Originally Published.
May 16, 1954

The Beast With EYES Before And Behind Revelation 4: 6-8 by Muhammad, Elijah {Messenger of
Allah}, Muhammad Speaks Newspaper December 22, 1967

The Hypocrites by Muhammad, Elijah {Messenger of Allah},
Muhammad Speaks Newspaper
June 7, 1968

The Greatest Story Ever Told by Muhammad, Elijah {Messenger of
Allah}, Muhammad's Mosque.
1971

The Gods At War The Following Article is Transcribe From a An
Audio Tape Copy Of The
National Radio Broadcast by Muhammad, Elijah {Messenger of
Allah},

While Europe was in Dark Ages The Story of Timbuctoo's
Astounding Civilization, Center of
Muslim Learning in Ancient Africa; Respected Throughout The
World by Dr. Professor Clarke,
Henrik John Muhammad Speaks Newspaper October 31, 1962

Plan Twenty Million Dallor Islamic Center for Chicago The Islamic
News July 6, 1959
Justice For My People by Muhammad, Elijah {Messenger of Allah},
Islamic News July 6, 1959

Capital Gives Muhammad Police Escort The Islamic News July 6,
1959

Persecution Follows by Muhammad, Elijah {Messenger of Allah},
Pittsburgh Courier.
April 16th, 1956

Who Is The Original Man? By Muhammad, Elijah {Messenger of Allah}, Pittsburgh Courier July 28th
1956

If the Civilized Man Fails To Perform His Duty What Must Be Done by Muhammad, Elijah
{Messenger Of Allah}, Pittsburgh Courier August 11th, 1956

Is There A Mystery God? By Muhammad, Elijah {Messenger of Allah}, Pittsburgh Courier Augus 18th,
1956

What Is Islam by Muhammad, Elijah {Messenger of Allah}, Pittsburgh Courier August 25th, 1956?

Magazines

Will Death Of Malcolm X Spur More Bloodshed Published By Jet Magazine
March 11, 1965 Edition

First Magazine Interview With Elijah Muhammad Black Muslim Leader By
Cavalier A Fawcett Publication 1964

Separation? Integration? Liberation? Which Way Black America By Ebony
Magazine A Johnson Publication August 1970

A Negro Photographer Shoots from Inside The Black Muslims By Life Magazine

May 31, 1963 Edition

Death of Malcolm X and the Resulting Vengeful Gang War A Monument To Negro
Upheaval by Life Magazine March 5, 1965 Edition

We Sailed The Columbus Ship: Dwight D. Eisenhower Danger From Within Black
Muslims Negro Hate Group Saturday Evening Post January 26, 1963 Edition

The Miss Education of the Negro by Woodson, G. Carter

What to the Slave Does the Fourth of July Means Freddrick, Douglass July 5, 1852?

For The Uplifting of Fallen Humanity by Prophet Ali, Drew Noble Published by
Seven Seals Publications
The Universal Negro Improvement Association Speech at Liberty Hall New York
By Garvey, Mosiah Marcus 1922

Atlanta Compromise Speech by Washington, T. Booker 1895

The Walker's Appeal by Walker, David September of 1829

The Jamestown Landing by William, Delaney April of 1619
Videos

The Synagogue of Satan Full Documentary by Hitchcock, A.C. From 1878-2006

The Money Masters Full Movie

Loose Change Third Edition 2014

Farewell Uncle Tom A Raw powerfull Documentary Never Seen on T.V. The Breaking
Of A Black Family, The MAKING of A Slave, Rape, Murder, Torture & Castration, Never
Seen Before Footage

Printed in the United States
by Baker & Taylor Publisher Services